A Guide to Tribal Employment

A Guide to Tribal Employment

An employment guide for tribal council, human resources, and enterprise officials

Richard G. McGee

Copyright © 2008 by Richard G. McGee.

Library of Congress Control Number: 2008908903
ISBN: Hardcover   978-1-4363-7528-3
              Softcover   978-1-4363-7527-6

All rights reserved. No part of this book may be reproduced or transmitted in any form or by any means, electronic or mechanical, including photocopying, recording, or by any information storage and retrieval system, without permission in writing from the copyright owner.

This publication is designed to provide accurate information regarding the subject covered, but is not an exhaustive statement of the law. It is sold with the understanding that the author and publisher are not engaged in rendering legal, accounting, or other professional services. If legal advice or other expert assistance is required, the services of a competent professional should be sought.

This book was printed in the United States of America.

To order additional copies of this book, contact:
Xlibris Corporation
1-888-795-4274
www.Xlibris.com
Orders@Xlibris.com
48811

CONTENTS

1. What are the Fundamentals of Tribal Employment? 15

   What are Indian tribes? 15
   What are tribal employers? 17
   What are tribal employees? 19
   What makes tribal employers different from
     nontribal employers? 28
   What is tribal self-determination? 30
   What is tribal sovereignty? 32
   What is tribal inherent sovereignty? 34
   Does inherent sovereignty preclude the federal government
     from diluting tribal sovereignty? 35
   Can tribal employers define the legal relationship
     with its employees? 35
   What is the legal relationship between tribes and other tribal
     governments? 36
   Are the tribes each unique? 37
   Does sovereignty have an impact on a tribal employer's ability
     to define the terms and conditions of the
     employment relationship? 37
   What impact does geography have on sovereignty? 44
   What is Indian Country? 45
   What is an Indian reservation? 47
   What is Indian title? 47

2. Do federal employment laws apply to tribal employers? 49

   What is the legal relationship between tribes and
     the federal government? 49
   Has the United States defined its relationship to tribes? 53

What is the federal government's trust responsibility to tribes, and
  how does the trust responsibility impact whether
  federal employment laws apply to tribes?...................55
What are the canons of construction?..............................57
Are the tribal-federal rules discussed in this chapter applicable
  to the tribal-state relationship?..................................58
Under what circumstances do federal employment laws apply
  or do not apply to tribal employers?...........................59
Which federal laws declare they are not applicable
  to tribal employers?..59
Under the exemption from Title VII,
  what is the definition of tribal employer?...................63
Do federal employment laws which do not declare application
  to tribal employers apply to tribal employers?...........64
What is the Tuscarora Donovan analysis?........................64
Can tribes rely on the Tuscarora-Donovan analysis?........74
Does the National Labor Relations Act (NLRA)
  apply to tribal employers?..77
Does the Fair Labor Standards Act (FLSA) apply
  to tribal employers?..81
Does the Family and Medical Leave Act (FMLA)
  apply to tribal employers?..84
Does the Age Discrimination Employment Act (ADEA)
  apply to tribal employers?..88
Do Sections 1981, 1983, and 1985 apply to tribal employers?......90
Does the Occupational Safety and Health Act (OSHA)
  apply to tribal employers?..90
Does the Employment Retirement Income Security Act (ERISA)
  apply to tribal employers?..91
Can a tribe consent to the application of federal
  employment laws?..93
Are there federal laws, which specifically apply
  to tribal employers?..100
Are tribal employers required to perform background
  investigations when employees interact with children?...........101
In this arena of uncertainty as to the application of federal
  employment laws, what options are presented to the tribes?....103
What does your vote mean?..105

3. Do state employment laws apply to tribal employers?.....................107

   What is the legal relationship between tribes
      and the state governments?..107
   Are there exceptions to the rule that state employment laws
      do not apply to tribal employers?..111
   Can state laws apply to tribal employers under
      tribal-state compacts?...112
   What is the influence of insurance on the application
      of state law?..113
   What impact do federal worker's compensation rules have
      on the application of state rules?..113
   Does Public Law 280 permit states to impose state employment
      laws to on-reservation tribally owned or operated entities?......114
   Can tribes voluntarily apply state law?...116
   Are the rules different for tribes in Oklahoma?............................116
   Are the rules different for tribes in Connecticut?.........................116
   Are the rules different for tribes in New York?.............................117
   Are the rules different for Pueblos in New Mexico?.....................117
   Are the rules different in Alaska?...118

4. Where are disputes between tribes and employees heard
   and what law applies?..119

   Do tribal employers use informal and formal internal dispute
      resolution mechanisms?..120
   Can tribal employers and employees agree to arbitrate
      employment-related disputes?..122
   What legal forums exist to hear and decide employment
      disputes between tribal employers and their employees?.........125
   Do tribal courts possess jurisdiction over
      employment-related disputes?..125
   When a tribe provides a judicial forum to hear employment
      disputes how does it work?..126
   If the tribe does not have a tribal court, does the tribe have
      jurisdiction over employment-related disputes?......................135
   Do state courts possess jurisdiction over tribal
      employment-related disputes?..136

Do federal courts possess jurisdiction over tribal
employment-related disputes?..139
Can a tribe be sued over an employment related dispute?..........143
Can a tribe assert the defense of sovereign immunity
in response to an employment related dispute?.......................144
Can an employee, official, or agent of the tribe assert
the defense of sovereign immunity if sued
in an employment related dispute?..150
Does a tribal employer waive its immunity relating
to off-reservation activity?...152
Can the federal government be responsible for the acts of
tribal employees when the employees work in programs
funded by the federal government?...153
What sovereign has the power to prosecute a crime committed
by a tribal employee?..154
When does the tribe possess criminal jurisdiction?....................154
When does the federal government possess
criminal jurisdiction?..154
When do states possess criminal jurisdiction?...........................155
What governments assert jurisdiction over
off-reservation crimes?..157
Are there civil remedies available to tribal employers for those
employees who violate the law but cannot be
prosecuted by the tribe?..157

5. How does gaming impact tribal employers?..............................159

What are the roles of the tribe as employer and as regulator
of the tribe's gaming enterprise?..162
Has the federal government promulgated law in
the tribal gaming arena?...164
Who is in charge of regulating tribal gaming?...........................166
Who is the employer in tribal gaming?......................................169
Does federal gaming law define the terms and conditions
of the employment relationship?..171
Does federal nongaming law define the terms and conditions
of the employment relationship?..171
Do tribal-state compacts define the terms and conditions
of the employment relationship?..174

What best practices do tribal employers follow because of
the unique regulatory and legal environment created by
tribal gaming?..174
What is an independent regulator and how does it impact
tribal gaming employers?..175
Is there a clear delegation of authority to the commission
in the gaming ordinance?..176
Do tribal members and tribal leadership understand
the gaming commission's limited role as a regulator?...............177
Is due process clearly defined for the issuance, denial,
suspension, and revocation of gaming licenses?........................178
What is the role of casino employer in performing due
diligence in evaluating prospective employees?........................179
Are there times when employer and regulator duties overlap?......180
Are there limits to the access demanded by the gaming
commission to employment-related documents?.....................181
If the gaming commission revokes a gaming license, which
disqualifies the licensee from employment in a regulated
position, can the employee seek unemployment benefits?......182
How are tribal casino employer best practices summarized?..........183

6. Can tribes promulgate their own employment laws and policies?.....184

Can tribes write and apply employment laws?...............................192
Can tribal employers prefer tribal members and nonmember
Indians in hiring and other employment-related decisions?.....193
What is a Tribal Employment Rights Ordinance (TERO)?..........205
Are there best practices in implementing a
tribal preference policy?..207
In addition to defining employment rules through tribal law, how
does policy address specific rules in the tribal workplace?........208
What is an employee handbook?..208
Are tribal employee handbooks different from those
handbooks used by nontribal employers?...................................210
If employee handbooks define the rules between employer and
employee, where do the rules come from?..................................211
What does the hierarchy show?...212
If employee handbooks define the rules, is it necessary
for employees to agree to those rules?..214

As compared to nontribal employers, is the explicit employee
  consent to the terms and conditions of the employment
  relationship imposed by tribal employers more important? 215
What are the limits to employee consent?.................................217
Do tribal employers include unique policies
  in employee handbooks?..220
What are the unique policies?..222

The Policies:

> Sovereignty..223
> Consent..223
> Tribal history and culture. 224
> Role of tradition and custom....................................225
> How the government works. 226
> The meaning of the tribe's logo. 227
> Working for a tribe is a fantastic opportunity........227
> Modification of the Handbook.................................227
> Employment at will..227
> Just cause..228
> Nepotism. 229
> Bereavement...230
> The tribe's language...231
> The tribe's elders 231
> Progressive discipline...231
> Equal Employment 232
> Collection proceedings 233
> Preference...233
> Personnel Files..235
> Solicitation...236
> Traditional dispute mechanisms. 237

To my wife Denise

PREFACE

This book is motivated by hundreds of conversations with tribal leaders, lawyers, human resources professionals, general managers, tribal administrators, judges, and regulators regarding a single basic and essential question:

Who defines the terms and conditions of the relationship between tribal employers and employees?

The answer or answers are moving targets, which are described by examining the impact of tribal sovereignty, the federal government's plenary power, the cases describing the relationship between the states and the tribes, and the choices made by tribes faced with difficult questions along the spectrum of sovereignty. Reading this book will not bring definitive answers to these important questions; however, it does grant access to the common issues, the important factors which impact those issues, and to helpful recommendations.

The book is focused on the question of who or what defines the terms and conditions of the employment relationship. As an overview of the laws and policies in the tribal employment arena, the book does not concentrate on the important question of what should be the law. This important question is worthy of an answer but is beyond the scope of this effort to describe the law and make practical recommendations. By offering opinion on numerous issues, the book is more than a dispassionate summary of tribal employment matters.

The book addresses unique relationships between tribes, states, and the federal government. For every general rule discussed, there are too many exceptions to count. For example, the declaration that as a general rule, state laws do not apply to tribal employers is a true statement. However, there are numerous exceptions to the general rule, and depending on the count, the exceptions could consume the rule. There are differences depending upon the state, the source of funds—whether the tribe is engaged in government or business—and myriad other circumstances. Accordingly, the general rules discussed in this book should not be applied to any specific circumstance unless the law and facts are evaluated with the assistance of competent legal and other professionals.

Thank you to the people whose support is instrumental to the completion of this book. This includes my wife, Denise, and our children and grandchildren; my parents, Richard and Mary Anne; and my brothers. I am grateful to the Prairie Island Indian Community and its members for a continuing education, which does not end. I am indebted to my clients for giving me the opportunity to serve the best profession. I am grateful for the time and wisdom of those who read the manuscript and provided valuable feedback to the final product. More specifically I must thank Andrew Small, Honorable B.J. Jones, Margaret Jackson and Richard Phelps.

CHAPTER 1

What are the Fundamentals of Tribal Employment?

The central question of who defines the terms and conditions of the tribal employment relationship demands preliminary analysis of employment fundamentals. Whether tribes define the terms and conditions, or they are defined for the tribes, or a combination of both, is dependent upon an understanding of tribal, state, and federal laws. The contours of tribal, state, and federal employment law are shaped by fundamental questions of what is a tribe, a tribal employer, a tribal employee, and the principles of self-determination, which includes a working definition of sovereignty.

One constant of law is change. A persistent constant of law impacting tribes is change and uncertainty. For most of the general rules set forth in this book, there are exceptions which, depending on the circumstances, could lead to the conclusion which is the opposite of the general rule. Simply stated, federal Indian law is full of contradictions. Layer that reality on the impact of ever-present change, and it reveals a complex answer with reminders that certain variables change the status quo.

1. What are Indian tribes?

Within the United States of America, there are over 600 sovereigns grouped into tribes, fifty states, and one federal government. Of these sovereigns, there are over 560 federally recognized Indian tribes, which count 2.47

million members or almost 1 percent of the country's population.[1] Tribes are bands, nations, rancherias, pueblos, colonies, communities, and Alaska Native groups.[2] Tribes are native nations, which preexisted the United States. Federally recognized tribes are those recognized by the federal government as eligible for services from the Bureau of Indian Affairs.[3] Congress is in charge of the federal recognition of tribes, and Congress has delegated the authority to the Executive Branch and more specifically to the secretary of interior.

The secretary of interior has promulgated regulations to assist in the analysis justifying federal recognition. Those regulations[4] impose seven criteria, which must be demonstrated before a group is recognized by the federal sovereign. The following seven questions describe the criteria:

1. Has the tribe been from historic times to the present on a continuous basis been recognized as American Indians?
2. Has a substantial portion of the tribe inhabited a specific area or live in a community viewed as American Indian?
3. Has the tribe maintained governmental authority over its members as an autonomous entity throughout history until present?
4. Does the tribe have governing documents and membership criteria?
5. Is the membership comprised primarily of persons who are not members of other tribes?
6. Does the tribe have a list of members?
7. Has the United States terminated the tribe?

There are more tribes located in the United States than those tribes which have received federal recognition. Since 1978, nearly 250 tribes have requested

---

[1] Stephen L. Pevar, *The Rights of Indians and Tribes* (hereinafter *Rights of Indians and Tribes*) (Southern Illinois Press, 2002) at 2. Some of the fundamentals discussed in this chapter like the definition of Indian Country, reservations, Indian Title, and other concepts are drawn from the excellent discussion found in Mr. Pevar's book.

[2] "Tribe" is used throughout this book to reference all categories of native nations.

[3] 25 C.F.R. § 20.1

[4] 25 C.F.R. § 83.

federal recognition,[5] and final decisions have been issued in less than thirty cases. Many tribes are ineligible for federal recognition because the federal government terminated them, and other tribes are denied because they have difficulties showing "continuous political or geographical existence," which is a hardship caused by the federal government's efforts to disrupt and displace the tribes.[6] The Federal Register publishes a list of federally recognized tribes.

The definition of tribe used by the federal government is the "legal" definition of tribe from the federal government's perspective. In addition to the federal government's perspective of what is a tribe, there is an ethnological definition of Indian tribe. The ethnological definition describes a group of people who may call themselves a tribe and be recognized by other tribes.

From the federal government's perspective, the above-enumerated seven elements are a prerequisite to the formation of a tribe recognized by the United States. All of the cases evaluated in this book address tribal employers which are federally recognized tribes. Therefore, the definition used is the legal and not the ethnological. Also, the book refers to tribes and not to nations or bands and that word "choice" is not intended to diminish other names used by tribes.

What are tribal employers?

Tribal employers are governments, regulators, enterprises, health clinics, schools, colleges, casinos, convenience stores, manufacturers, and many other entities. Tribal employer includes the tribal government, subdivisions of the government, chartered corporations owned by the government, or a consortium of tribal governments. For purposes of this book, the discussion of tribal employer is limited to a governmental entity or enterprise.

The necessity of strong tribal employers is impacted by the available workforce. The employment numbers relating to employment in Indian Country reveal a landscape much different than outside Indian Country. Federal government statistics show that half the 800,000 Indians available

---

[5] Stephen L. Pevar, *The Rights of Indians and Tribes* at 311.
[6] Id. See, *Miami Nation of Indians of Indiana v. United States Department of the Interior*, 255 F.3d 342 (7th Cir. 2001).

for work are unemployed, and one-third of those employed earn less than the poverty level.[7]

Tribal governments and enterprises employ 778,000 people.[8] Seventy-five percent of those employees work for gaming operations; and in those facilities, as a national average, twenty-five percent are Indians,[9] and the remaining balance of seventy-five percent are non-Indian casino employees.[10] Employees working for tribes frequently consider themselves as working either for a tribal

---

[7] *The 2003 American Indian Population and Labor Force Report*, United States Department of Interior, Bureau of Indian Affairs (the *Labor Force Report*). The *Labor Force Report* concluded that 49 percent of an Indian workforce, numbering 800,000 people, were unemployed. Moreover, the report concluded that 32 percent of the Indians employed earned less than the poverty guidelines established by the United States Department of Health and Human Services.

[8] The conclusion of 778,000 is a guess based upon the National Indian Gaming Association's assertion that 600,000 workers are employed at tribal casinos and adding the number of public employees referenced in the 2003 *Labor Force Report* (see footnote 7 above). The 778,000 does not account for overlap between NIGA estimates and the Labor Force Report. Importantly, the 178,000 is based upon the "public" category in the *Labor Force Report* and tied to the assumption that public employees equates to employees working for "public" tribes. Efforts through contact with federal agencies to determine a more definitive estimate of size of tribal employment did not yield an answer.

[9] The use of the terms "Indian" and "Native American" are used to describe members of Indian tribes. See *Dawavendewa v. Salt River Project Agr. Imp. and Power Dist.*, 154 F.3d 1117 (9th Cir. 1998). As Mr. Pevar asserts in *Rights of Indians and Tribes*, there are reasons to use the word "Indian" instead of "Native American" in books, which address the law. In discussions of federal law the language of the law references *Indian:* Indian Gaming Regulatory Act, Indian Civil Rights Act, Indian Reorganization Act. Secondly, most Indian organizations use "Indian" in their titles: National Congress of American Indians and National Indian Gaming Association. Finally, many Indians use the term to describe themselves. *Rights of Indians and Tribes* at 1.

[10] The National Indian Gaming Association estimates that 75 percent of employees working for tribal casinos are non-Indians. Anecdotally as a percentage, more Indians and less non-Indians are employed on the government side of tribal operations.

enterprise or for the tribal government. There may be a legal distinction between the tribal government and the tribal enterprise if, for instance, the enterprise is formed as a separate corporate entity. On the other hand, many tribes organize their gaming operation by promulgating a comprehensive gaming ordinance, which creates another box in the tribal government's organizational chart. In the latter instance, the employer is the tribal government; and in the former, the employer is a corporation owned and operated by the tribal government. This distinction between working for the government or working for a separate entity owned by the government applies to tribal casinos, schools, convenience stores, and tribal oil companies. These threshold questions are important in determining what is the "tribal employer."

Tribal governments, therefore, employ workers in government jobs, which focus on traditional governmental functions as well as government employees working in for profit enterprises. Tribal employers are also fictions (corporations for example) created by tribes under the law, which encompass profit and nonprofit entities. Generally speaking there are at least three categories of tribal workers.

The first category references a federally recognized tribe, which employs people in tribal administration, courts, natural resources, child welfare, a health clinic, or a business entity, which is not separately organized. The second category, business entities controlled by tribal governments, references incorporated gaming enterprises owned and operated by tribes. The third category, on-reservation entities owned by private entities, includes—but is not limited to—a sandwich shop located on the reservation and owned by a tribal member. The examples of entities in the three categories are not exhaustive.

This book focuses on tribal employers and therefore addresses categories one and two, but does not address the third category, which references private (nontribal government) ownership of on-reservation employers. The book references employment issues for tribal employers located outside tribal lands and beyond the reservation boundaries, but these issues are not the focus of the book.

What are tribal employees?

Tribal employees work for tribal governments and their enterprises. Tribal employees have job descriptions which include traditional governmental functions and duties, which focuses the employee's workday on the range of services provided by the tribal government on behalf of its members. Tribal employees are also those workers in enterprises separately organized to handle education, gaming, and housing to name a few.

A peek at a tribal government's chain of command helps define tribal employee. For example, a tribal administrator reports to the tribal council, and from that, the administrator is delegated the authority to supervise the government's various departments including land management, environmental protection, enrollment, legal, maintenance, child welfare, finance, economic development, and other subdivisions of the government. On the enterprise side of the ledger, the general manager of the tribal casino manages thousands of employees through directors administering food and beverage, slots, table games, marketing, human resources, and hotel. The chain of command within tribal government and enterprise is comprised of employees of both genders, all ages, resumes, and ethnicity.

(a) Employee defined

The book focuses on employees hired by tribal government and business enterprises. Tribal employees are in the service of the tribal government or its enterprises under a contract for hire, express or implied, oral or written, where the tribe or its enterprise has the power or right to control and direct the employee in the material details of how work is to be performed.[11] "Contract for hire" is a dated phrase but accurately reflects the commercial aspect of the employer-employee relationship. When employers trade dollars for control over employee time, talent, and skill, an employment relationship is a contract for hire. These contracts for hire are almost always not reduced to a written agreement. Note that most contracts in the employment arena are not evidenced by a written document, but nevertheless, the contract is comprised by the meeting of the minds between employer and employee.

---

[11] The definition is borrowed from a non-tribal case called *Riverbend Country Club v. Patterson*, 399 S.W.2d 382, 383 (Tex. App. 1966). *Riverbend* did not address a tribal employer so therefore the language used above to describe employee applies *Riverbend* to the tribal context.

Tribal employees frequently are viewed as either working for the tribal government or tribal enterprises even though there may not be a legal distinction between the two categories. In some tribes, employees are viewed organizationally as either a government employee working for the tribe's court, department of natural resources, or the governing body of the tribe; and on the other hand, employees will be categorized differently if they work for the tribal casino or separate housing authority or school. Even though there may be differences between these subsets of employees in the tribe's organizational chart, there is only one employer, which is the tribe.

In contrast to those tribes which engage employees directly as subdivisions of the tribal government, some tribes are creating entities (corporations) which are separate legal entities, and these separate legal entities are the employer. For example, the tribe could own a utility, incorporate the utility under tribal law; and the corporation will, through its articles and bylaws, delegate authority to a board, directors, officers, and employees of the corporation. That same entity could be formed under a federal statute, which creates a chartered corporation.[12]

Tribal employees are tribal members, Indians from other tribes, and non-Indians. When tribes evaluate the degree to which the tribal government can determine the terms and conditions of the employment relationship, the employee's status of member or nonmember of a federally recognized tribe is an important factor in several relevant United States Supreme Court decisions.

Tribal employees are officially characterized with descriptive adjectives like part-time, full-time, probationary, at-will, and exempt. To the extent that these employee qualifiers are unique to tribal employees, they are more fully explored later in chapter 6, which discusses tribal employee handbooks.

(b) Employee versus independent contractor

Determining which workers are employees from those who are independent contractors can impact employer liability for overtime compensation,

---

[12] Section 17 corporations are formed under 25 U.S.C. § 477.

tax, liability, workers' compensation coverage, and whether the federal government is responsible for an employee's negligence. Because the definition of employee and independent contractor describe different categories of workers and those categories can have an important impact on how the terms and conditions of the employment relationship are defined, defining what is an independent contractor is relevant to this discussion.

There is an abundance of nontribal law, which compares and contrasts the definitions of employees against independent contractor. Simply stated, an employee punches the time clock, reports to a desk owned by the employer, uses the employer's tools, and her task list is defined by her supervisor's directives. On the other hand, independent contractors show at a time designated by the contractor, carrying his tools and defining for himself how the job will be accomplished. Between a true employee and the true independent contractor is a spectrum of individuals working for tribes some of whom are closer to one end of the spectrum or the other. Courts and agencies have focused on a variety of variables in determining whether a worker is an employee or an independent contractor.

The Equal Employment Opportunity Commission,[13] through the interpretation of a decision from the United States Supreme Court, has provided a sixteen-part test[14] in determining when an individual is an employee.[15] Those factors are

1. Whether the employer has the right to control when, where, and how the worker performs the job;
2. Whether the work does not require a high level of skill or expertise;

---

[13] The Equal Employment Opportunity Commission's jurisdiction over tribal employers in the enforcement of Title VII of the Civil Rights Act is questionable and discussed in detail in chapter 2 and 4. The EEOC's test is mentioned here because it is used by courts to address this question of who is an employee and is similar to the tests used by most courts.

[14] EEOC Compliance Manual §2-III A.1 (2000).

[15] *Nationwide Mutual Insurance Co. v. Darden*, 503 U.S. 318 (1992). The Court was not enamored by ERISA's definition of employee as "any individual employed by an employer," 29 U.S.C. § 1002(6), describing the definition as "completely circular and explains nothing."

3. Whether the employer furnishes the tools, materials, and equipment;
4. Whether the work is performed on the employer's premises;
5. Whether there is a continuing relationship between the worker and the employer;
6. Whether the employer has the right to assign additional projects to the worker;
7. Whether the employer sets the hours of work and the duration of the job;
8. Whether the worker is paid by the hour, week, or month rather than the agreed cost of performing a particular job;
9. Whether the worker does not hire and pay assistants;
10. Whether the work performed by the worker is part of the regular business of the employer;
11. Whether the employer is in business;
12. Whether the worker is engaged in his own distinct occupation or business;
13. Whether the employer provides the worker with benefits such as insurance, leave, or workers' compensation;
14. Whether the worker is considered an employee of the employer for tax purposes (the employer withholds federal, state, and social security taxes);
15. Whether the employer can discharge the worker;
16. Whether the worker and the employer believe that they are creating an employee-employer relationship;

The first question posed on the list is the first question asked, and the most important factor evaluated since courts increasingly find an employer-employee relationship as control increases and conversely will discern an independent contractor relationship when control is at its lowest. Understand that the label an employer and worker place on the written agreement between them is not determinative of whether the worker is an independent contractor or employee. Courts will evaluate the relationship through a test, like the EEOC's, and decide where the relationship fits on the employee-contractor spectrum.

The question of where the worker fits on the employee-independent contractor spectrum raises numerous practical questions for employers. Those practical questions address the extent of employer liability to third parties because of worker conduct, the taxes due and owing, workers' compensation coverage, and applicability of insurance policies.

For a small segment of tribal employees, whether the worker is an employee or a contractor can have practical implications for attributing responsibility to the tribal employer or the federal government. When tribes administer governmental programs, which are funded by federal monies, the United States can be responsible for the acts of the employees.

The United States, like tribes, is immune from lawsuits unless the government waives immunity. When immunity is asserted by a sovereign, it is more difficult, and oftentimes impossible, to assert rights granted by the law. Under these limited circumstances, the United States' responsibility for those employees can be enforced under the federal government's limited waiver of immunity under a federal statute called the Federal Torts Claim Act (FTCA). Employees who are independent of federally funded employers are not the responsibility of the federal government, but employees who are controlled by employers, which are subjected to federal requirements may trigger federal government responsibility. The FTCA sets forth the relevant rules.

The FTCA is a limited waiver of sovereign immunity that only applies to federal employees.[16] The act defines "government employees" to include "officers and employees of any federal agency, but excludes any contractor with the United States."[17] The Supreme Court has emphasized the importance of the "federal employee" requirement as a gatekeeper. "It is inconceivable that Congress intended to have waiver of sovereign immunity follow congressional largess and cover countless unidentifiable classes of 'beneficiaries.'"[18] In other words, courts scrutinize the facts in support and against before workers are declared the responsibility of the federal government.

The Supreme Court has described the test for ascertaining whether a claimant is a federal employee covered by the act or an independent contractor not so immunized. "A critical element in distinguishing an agency from a contractor is the power of the Federal Government 'to control the detailed

---

[16] *United States v. Orleans*, 425 U.S. 807, 813, 96 S.Ct. 1971 (1976).
[17] *Id.* (quotation omitted); 28 U.S.C. § 2671.
[18] Orleans, 425 U.S. at 816, 96 S.Ct. 1971.

physical performance of the contractor.'"[19] The question here is not whether the community action agency receives federal money and must comply with federal standards and regulations but whether its day-to-day operations are supervised by the federal government. The courts devised seven factors to guide this determination:

1. the intent of the parties;
2. whether the United States controls only the end result or may also control the manner and method of reaching the result;
3. whether the person uses his own equipment or that of the United States;
4. who provides liability insurance;
5. who pays social security tax;
6. whether federal regulations prohibit federal employees from performing such contracts; and
7. whether the individual has authority to subcontract to others.[20]

Like the EEOC independent contractor test set forth above, application of these FTCA factors inevitably focuses on the extent of employer control over the employee. For example, in *Bird v. United States*,[21] the court held that a nurse at an Indian hospital was a federal employee because "he was not only subject to the rules and regulations and, indeed, a statute placing him under the control and supervision of physician employees of the hospital, but he was under their actual control to the extent they chose to exercise it." Additionally, the court relied on the following considerations:

> The nurse was required to work with patients designated by others. He maintained no separate office. He used hospital equipment exclusively. He could see patients in no other place nor under any other circumstance than as directed by government employees. He was under the control and supervision of the government surgeon at the hospital to the same extent that . . . a regular employee of the government.

---

[19] "Id. at 814, 96 S.Ct. 1971 (quoting *Logue v. United States*, 412 U.S. 521, 528, 93 S.Ct. 2215, 37 L.Ed.2d 121 (1973))._

[20] *Lilly v. Fieldstone*, 876 F.2d 857, 859 (10th Cir.1989); see also *Curry v. United States*, 97 F.3d 412, 414 (10th Cir.1996).

[21] 949 F.2d 1079, 1086 (10th Cir.1991).

When it comes to physicians, the "day-to-day control" test may be more difficult to apply. In *Lurch v. United States*,[22] the court suggested that a modified control test may be more appropriate because "a physician must exercise his own professional judgment, no one controls the detailed physical performance of his duties."

Accordingly, whether a worker is controlled by the tribe or by an outsider impacts the worker's status as an employee of the tribe. Moreover, control over the worker by the federal government guides the determination of whether the worker is the responsibility of the tribal sovereign or the federal sovereign.

(c) Employees and elected tribal officials

An interesting variation on this discussion is whether elected officials are also employees. Elected officials include members of tribal councils, which meet once a week to councils which meet every day. Elected tribal officials also include tribal governors, presidents, judges, and regulatory officials. Tribal officials are oftentimes paid either a wage or a stipend.

There are at least two categories of elected officials who may also be classified as employees. In the first, for example, the chairman of the tribe is also the director of finance for the tribal enterprise. In some tribes, serving as chairman does not generate a living wage, is described as a part-time position, and therefore seeking full-time employment may be a viable option. In this instance, the chairman is a tribal official; and in his capacity as director of finance, he is an employee. As the director of finance, the terms and conditions of his employment relationship with the tribe are the same as the terms and conditions for other employees. There may be some practical implications of his other role as tribal official, which separate him from the other employees, but the official relationship is the same.

In the second instance where an elected tribal chairman is full-time and the tribe compensates their chairman, elected official and employee merge. This

---

[22] 719 F.2d 333, 337 (10th Cir. 1983); *see also* Thomas K. Kruppstadt, *Determining Whether a Physician is a United States Employee or an Independent Contractor in a Medical Malpractice Action Under the Federal Tort Claims Act*, 47 Baylor L.Rev. 223 (1995). Also see, *Harjo v. U.S. Department of Health and Human Services*, 2008 WL 906156 (E.D. Okla. 2008).

merging of elected official and tribal employee creates interesting intended and unintended consequences. When tribal officials are classified as employees, there is an intended consequence of imposing rules in the workplace, which apply to the entire chain of command including tribal council. Furthermore, the chairman can receive employee health care insurance, participate in retirement programs, use the education assistance policy, and utilize the employee assistance program.

An unintended consequence of classifying a tribal official as an employee is the complicated question of discipline. While termination is an option for other employees, only the electorate can recall a tribal official; so therefore, there are limitations on separating an official from employment for misconduct.

In employment, if an elected official receives compensation from the tribe, the presumption of an employer-employee relationship exists. The presumption of an employer-employee relationship is supported by the receipt of wages and benefits, officials' supervisory role over staff, and final say on termination of employees. For these reasons, the conventional advice is elected officials need to follow the employer's rules since a failure to follow the rules could expose the tribe to liability. In the normal course, an employer may be subject to vicarious liability to a victimized employee for adverse employment circumstances created by a supervisor with authority over an employee.[23]

For tribal council members, the presumption may not be accurate. Tribal employees pay federal income taxes, and therefore, the Internal Revenue Service's view of the issue is relevant. Under the federal government's Internal Revenue Code, an employee includes "an officer, employee or elected official of a state, or any political subdivision thereof."[24] Tribes are not states or subdivisions of states; so therefore, the language does not apply directly but can be instructive on the point.

This issue was addressed in a case involving an application for state unemployment compensation benefits after three tribal council members were recalled by the voters and the state court dealt with whether these elected officials were also employees.[25] The case is not definitive on the issue

---

[23] *Faragher v. Boca Taton*, 524 U.S. 775, 807 (1998).
[24] IRC §3401.
[25] *Confederated Tribes of the Siletz Indians of Oregon v. Employment Dept.*, 995 P.2d 580 (Or. App. 2000)

since the precise legal issue turned on whether when the tribe opted into the state unemployment compensation system, the tribe included everyone, or a restricted pool of individuals. The state court concluded that the tribe did not restrict application of the unemployment benefits; so therefore, in this instance, the tribal council members were also employees.

The impact of whether an elected official is also an employee must be measured in determining the nature and extent of potential liability for the employee official's behavior. A tribal council member who sexually harasses another employee of the tribe may generate a claim as both official and employee.

The practical approach and the path which respects the tribal official's position does not equate remuneration for elected officials with employment. A better approach is an ethics ordinance reflecting the tribe's laws, traditions and customs reinforced by an oath of office where the elected official pledges adherence to those rules. For tribal officials a violation of the ethics ordinance generates a response which may include a range of penalties, but those penalties are not an aspect of the human resources function. Therefore, performance reviews for elected officials are not a component of the human resources function but rather an aspect of the ballot box.

There are legal principles which assist in determining whether the tribal employer is in charge of defining its relationship with tribal employees. The following discussion focuses on self-determination, sovereignty, and immunity in creating a firm foundation for determining whether tribes can define the rules, which apply to its employees.

What makes tribal employers different from nontribal employers?

The central theme of this book and the answer to this question focuses on who defines the terms and conditions of the relationship between the tribal employer and employee. Tribal employers are different from nontribal employers if tribes define the terms and conditions of the relationship with employees. If tribes do not define the relationship, from the law's perspective, there may be little difference between tribal and nontribal employers.

If the tribal employer adopts federal employment laws, voluntarily, through congressional imposition or judicial fiat, the federal government defines the terms and conditions of the employment relationship. Conversely, if the tribe does not adhere to the employment laws of the other sovereigns and instead promulgates tribal employment laws, which incorporate the tribe's traditions and customs, the employment relationship could be defined differently. Whether the tribe follows federal employment laws, tribal employees probably will see a difference in their workplace when compared to a nontribal setting. Some of the unique aspects of tribal employment are explained in the unique policies discussed in chapter 6.

Sovereigns exercise their sovereignty by defining the rules and applying those rules to people, places, and things. Tribes can exert their sovereignty in the employment arena by defining the terms and conditions of the employment relationship. Some tribes exert that sovereignty to a greater degree than other tribes. Therefore, one answer does not apply to all tribes. Instead, each tribe defines its rules and therefore exerts its sovereignty to the degree determined by its people, its leaders, and influences beyond the tribe.

When tribal employers exercise their sovereignty and define the rules in a way which reflects the tribe's circumstances,[26] traditions, customs, and values, the tribe, by defining its rules, is more self-determined. Employment is one of many categories where a tribe's self-determination can be measured.[27] For example, some tribes prefer tribal members over nonmembers in employment-related matters. Through tribe-specific preference, the tribe hires, promotes, and trains more of its members. By preferring its members over nonmembers, the tribe is exercising its rules and therefore, its sovereignty. Through this process, more members are given greater opportunity to succeed, which creates an environment where the tribe is more self-determined.

Self-determination is a broader concept, which is impacted by tribal sovereignty and other factors. Tribal sovereignty is impacted by a number of variables including geography, states, the federal government, agreements, and the tribe's exertion of sovereignty. Therefore, the answer to the question

---

[26] "Circumstances" refers to many factors including wealthy, poor, rural, urban, traditional, religious, secular, large, and small.

[27] Self-determination is measured by examining the extent to which a sovereign defines the rules in numerous arenas including employment, environment, commerce, justice, due process, and law enforcement.

of how are tribes different from other tribes is in part defined by how the specific tribe at issue defines its rules, and how those rules define the terms and conditions of the employment relationship.

What is tribal self-determination?

Tribal self-determination is autonomous rule, which aligns the tribe's culture (values, traditions, and customs) with its purpose. In the employment context, self-determination is exercised for example when the tribe's culture reinforces the employment of members, and the tribe acts on that value by promulgating laws and policy which require human resource directors to hire more members. When members have the opportunity to work for their tribe, membership is instrumental in the day-to-day operations of tribal government or enterprise. When members are the driving force behind governmental and enterprise decisions, the tribe is more self-determined than in those instances where nonmembers are the decision makers for government and enterprise.

The employment process of hiring more tribal members is a microcosm of the larger question of self-determination, which permits the tribal employer to make that choice. Beyond employment, tribes define qualifications for membership, the definition of due process—whether the executive and legislative processes are separate or joined—the nature of tribal enterprises, and myriad other questions.

When tribal governments define the rules of the workplace, self-determination is actualized. Self-determination is tribal control over its affairs by defining the rules of the workplace. And it is the creation of a workplace which presents an opportunity for young members of the tribe graduating from university to return and contribute; for elders returning to the workforce after years of unemployment; and for nonmembers to work for the tribe, respect the opportunity, and yield to the differences found in comparison to non-Indian culture.

Interaction between the tribal, state, and federal sovereigns has a significant impact on tribal self-determination. Exertion of authority over tribes by the federal government and states can undermine tribal self-determination. Many of these pages are used to measure to what extent the federal and state governments have and may exert their sovereignty by defining the rules of the tribal workplace. Importantly, the decisions made by tribal employers and how they treat their employees have and will have an impact on the degree to which other sovereigns attempt to exert their influence on tribal employees.

In the employment arena, the perception and reality of fairness between tribal employer and employee will reduce the incentive for federal and state governments to interfere in tribal operations. The perception and reality of fairness is not coincidentally a strong factor in differentiating between tribes, which develop economically and those which do not develop.

In their work on tribal self-determination, the team at the Harvard Project on American Indian Economic Development[28] points to factors, which lead to successful and sustainable economic development. Those factors[29] include

1. *Institutions.* Institutions which embrace the rule of law, separate politics from operations, and implement efficient systems;
2. *Culture.* Institutions which are legitimate in the eyes of tribal members and the institution's purpose is consistent with the tribe's culture.
3. *Sovereignty.* Self-rule and accountability provide two necessary sides of the currency of success.

According to this work, successful and sustainable economic development is dependent on implementation of these and other factors. Tribal institutions must apply the rule of law, be legitimate from the members' perspective, and enjoy both the benefits and responsibilities of self-rule. Application of these factors, for example, to tribal employers requires the gaming operation to implement a grievance policy, which treats every employee the same whether the tribal chairman's nephew or someone not related to a tribal official. The enterprise must generate benefits (dollars) for elder health care, and the enterprise must return a job to the slot technician who is fired over a political issue (accountability). The Harvard Project argues that when the ingredients of institution, culture, and sovereignty are utilized, the opportunity for success is enhanced.

---

[28] The Harvard Project on American Indian Economic Development, *The State of the Native Nations* (Oxford University Press, 2008)
[29] Id. at 121-128.

The project reinforces the purpose of self-determination by arguing for strong and objective institutions, which write their own rules based on the norms of its culture:

> Self-determination allows local desires, preferences, needs, and ways of doing things to be more accurately perceived and acted upon so that institutions and government can function in support of economic growth and community change.[30]

The exercise of self-determination is unique to each tribe—strong in some, weaker in others—dependent upon tribal resources, the integrity of leadership, the tribe's history, the voices of its members, and numerous other factors. For these reasons, there are many ways tribes define the terms and conditions of the employment relationship. Some tribes are very aggressive in hiring members over nonmembers. Other tribes favor zero-tolerance drug testing over a rehabilitation model. For tribes to be self-determined, they must be free from the mandatory compliance of federal and state employment laws and, moreover, free to develop their unique employment laws and policies without necessarily following the terms and conditions imposed by the tribe down the road or one thousand miles away. Self-determination permits the tribe to develop its unique rules free from the influence of federal, state, and other tribal sovereigns.

What is tribal sovereignty?

Sovereignty is writing the rules and applying those rules to people, places, and things. For a tribal employer, sovereignty is exercised by defining the terms and conditions of the employment relationship for all employees working for the tribal government and enterprise. This definition of sovereignty contemplates an active process where the sovereign not only has an opportunity to define the rules but more importantly exercises the right. By exercising that right, tribal leaders are in an excellent position to change the relationship between the tribe and its employees.

---

[30] Id. at 126-127.

The exercise of sovereignty must be guided by strong conviction, vision, and purpose since without conviction, vision, or purpose, change brings the illusion of progress. Said less elegantly, changing horses shows activity, but activity without purpose achieves little, or as Dr. George Sheehan said about having enough purpose to enter a race, "The difference between a runner and a jogger is an entry form." With clear purpose, self-determined sovereigns exercise their sovereignty by writing the rules and applying those rules to people, places, and things.

For tribal employers, there is a spectrum of sovereignty which is defined by an axis, which measures the exercise of a significant level of sovereignty on one end of the spectrum and, conversely, little use of sovereignty at the other end of the spectrum. A tribe's exercise of sovereignty may place the tribe at different places along the spectrum. At the end of the spectrum, which portrays the maximum exercise of sovereignty, the sovereign defines all the rules, and the rules apply to everyone within the sovereign's jurisdiction. The other end of the spectrum reveals a sovereign exercising less sovereignty by implementing rules written by other sovereigns. Those tribes following a mix of tribal and federal employment laws are located in the middle portion of the sovereignty spectrum.

Where a tribal employer is on the sovereignty spectrum is dependent on many variables including the tribe's assertion of its lawmaking authority, consent of the employees, the nature of the employer's purpose whether governmental or commercial, the location of the employer, the source of the funds, and the assertiveness of agents for other sovereigns. Tribal leaders have an opportunity to choose where the tribe will assert its sovereignty and where it will not. As will be discussed in chapter 2, the choice of exercising sovereignty is not made in a vacuum free of risk but rather in the real world. The exercise of sovereignty or the failure to exercise sovereignty brings an abundance of opportunity to attract expensive litigation, regulatory attention, and union activity. In this arena where tribal leaders choose a location on the sovereignty spectrum, there are no absolutes in right or wrong, but instead a range of options. Tribal administrators, consultants, lawyers, and human resource directors assist in evaluating the viable options available to tribes in selecting a location on the sovereignty spectrum; however, tribal leadership casts the votes necessary to address this complicated question of sovereignty and risk.

What is tribal inherent sovereignty?

Tribes derive their sovereignty from themselves and not from an external force or entity. Accordingly, tribes do not derive their lawmaking authority from the federal or state governments. Tribal inherent sovereignty is the recognition that tribes preexisted the United States, and the power of tribes over their own affairs is not dependent upon or derived from the other sovereigns including the United States.[31]

An illustration comparing tribal inherent sovereignty with the rule making authority of cities is useful in understanding the true (superior) sovereignty exercised by tribal nations. The city of Minneapolis is sovereign since it defines certain rules, which apply to people within the city's jurisdiction. Unlike tribes, before Minneapolis can create rules for its citizens and others, the city must consult state law to determine what authority the city possesses and just as importantly which authority the city does not possess. The city's ability to define the rules is derived from a specific delegation of authority from the state to cities of the state. Therefore, the city's authority is a derivative of state authority. Unlike Minneapolis, tribal sovereignty is not derivative of state or federal authority. Instead, tribal authority is intrinsic, defined by tribal law, custom, and tradition and more than likely exercised by officials through consent from the members of the tribe.

Inherent sovereignty is important in the tribal employment arena as it permits tribal employers to start from the premise that the tribe defines the terms and conditions of the employment relationship unless the federal government has imposed its authority through the exercise of the plenary power. Whether the federal government has exercised its plenary power and imposed federal employment laws on tribes is an open question, which is the subject of chapter 2. Inherent sovereignty leads to the conclusion that tribes retain the right to make their own laws regarding internal matters and to enforce the law in their own forums.[32]

---

[31] *National Labor Relations Board v. Pueblo of San Juan*, 276 F.3d 1186, 1192 (10th Cir. 2002).

[32] *Santa Clara Pueblo v. Martinez*, 436 U.S. 49, 55 (1978); Also see, *Oklahoma Tax Commission v. Citizen Band Potawatomi Indian Tribe*, 498 U.S. 505 (1991).

Does inherent sovereignty preclude the federal government from diluting tribal sovereignty?

No. Inherent sovereignty leads tribes to start from the premise that tribal rules apply, but inherent sovereignty does not supersede the federal government's plenary power. The federal government has not explicitly exercised its plenary power by declaring that federal employment laws apply to tribes. In two instances, Congress declared federal employment laws do not apply to tribes. As to other federal employment laws, Congress has not declared applicability to tribes. Even though Congress has not yet declared applicability of federal employment law to tribes, Congress can exercise that option. Congress has exercised its plenary power in numerous ways by legislating in the areas of gaming, crime, civil rights, and the sale of land. Congress could extend this exercise of authority to apply federal employment laws to tribal employers.

Can tribal employers define the legal relationship with its employees?

Yes. The extent of tribal sovereignty is at the root of this answer, and therefore, this single question is at the root of most of the discussion in this book. The question of tribal sovereignty seeps into most employment questions when a tribal employer is involved; and since tribal sovereignty is, in part, defined by the roles of the other sovereigns, there are relationship issues to understand. The relationships between the three groups of sovereigns—tribes, states, and federal government—certainly impact the tribe's opportunity to define the terms and conditions of the employment relationship. Many books[33] describe the relationship between the sovereigns, and therefore, this will be a brief discussion long enough to provide context for the application of the relevant employment principles.

In answering this question, it is necessary to start from the premise that the tribal employer is located within the tribe's reservation, the tribe is the employer, and the employee's duties limit the employee's activities to the reservation. Later, the book addresses off-reservation conduct and other variations of that theme and the impact on tribal employers.

---

[33] Stephen L. Pevar, *The Rights of Indians and Tribes* (Southern Illinois Press, 2002)

Accordingly, an element of whether tribes can define the terms and conditions of the employment relationship is dependent upon the relationship between the specific tribal employer and the state, or states, which share a common border with the tribal employer.[34]

The opportunity for tribal sovereigns to define the rules has changed with history and how the reins of power were gripped within the federal government. In 1832, the answer would have been the tribe defined the rules; and therefore, employees of tribes would have followed tribal rules. Today, the answer is less clear because tribal sovereignty has been diluted, and there are many factors which must be considered in sorting out a response. If there is one question which permeates every page of this book, it is to what extent a tribe may define the terms and conditions of the employment relationship. The fascinating answer or answers require a tool, which can capture a moving target with innumerable forces, pushing it in a variety of dimensions.

What is the legal relationship between tribes and other tribal governments?

In a word, "voluntary." There are many tribes which are independent on other sovereigns while others engage in formal and informal relationships with other sovereigns. Four hundred years ago, vast areas of the United States and Canada were controlled by a voluntary confederacy of tribes called the Haudenosaunee or Six Nations of the Iroquois Confederacy.[35] Today, tribes create joint ventures and engage in nation-to-nation relationships to enhance tribal governments, pool resources; create cooperative appellate courts; operate schools and utilities. These entities are employers, and these relationships present the numerous interesting questions about sovereignty, immunity, preference, and control.

---

[34] Some tribes are located within a state and therefore the state surrounds the tribe. For example, the Shakopee Mdewakanton Dakota Community is located within the state of Minnesota. On the other hand, some tribes, like the Navajo Nation, are so large they share borders with more than one state; and in the case of the Navajo Nation, it shares borders with Utah, New Mexico, and Arizona. Interestingly, the Navajo Nation also shares borders with the Hopi Tribe as its land mass surrounds the Hopi Tribe.

[35] The Six Nations of the Iroquois Confederacy were the Cayuga, Mohawk, Oneida, Onondaga, Seneca, and Tuscarora.

Are the tribes each unique?

Yes. Tribes are unique entities, which are a collection of people joined by common history, values, customs, and traditions. Each tribe defines itself.

The perception that there are three sovereigns within the United States, therefore, fails to account for the more than 560 sovereign tribes. The premise that the tribal sovereign is one collection of tribes fails to respect the individuality of each tribe. The presumption is not valid that a member of the Choctaw Nation is similar to a member of the Susanville Rancheria or that both tribes share the same history, culture, or tradition. Taking the analysis to another level, referring to the members of 560 Indian nations as one group is as descriptive as referring to all citizens of planet earth as humans. All citizens share the human link, but the broad definition of human fails to account for the distinctions between the Russians, Kenyans, and Brazilians to name a few.

Therefore the laws, policies, norms, and expectations are unique from tribe to tribe; and the assumption that either tribes or Indians are all the same is not valid. If tribes exercise their authority to define their employment rules, the rules created can vary considerably from tribe to tribe. Just as nontribal employers must determine whether they will implement, at will or for cause, an aggressive or rehabilitative stance to alcohol use and how due process is defined, tribal employers must make these employer decisions. However, unlike their nontribal colleagues, tribal employers have numerous more decisions to make regarding the applicability of federal employment laws; and with these choices, substantial differences are realized from tribe to tribe.

Does sovereignty have an impact on a tribal employer's ability to define the terms and conditions of the employment relationship?

Yes. Sovereignty is defining the rules. In the employment context, defining the rules means defining the terms and conditions of the employment relationship. Hiring, firing, preference, overtime pay, access to personnel records, and many more ingredients comprise the terms and conditions of the employment relationship. The sovereignty a tribe possesses and exercises will have an impact on whether the tribe controls few, some, or all of the terms and conditions of the employment relationship. An aspect of whether a tribe possesses and exercises its sovereignty to define the employment relationship is the interaction between the tribe and the federal and state governments.

The relationship between and among these sovereigns generates numerous relevant questions which impact tribal employment practices. Between a tribe and its employee, does the tribe or the state define the employment relationship? What impact does the alphabet soup of federal employment laws (FMLA, OSHA, FLSA) have on employees working for tribes? Is there a status quo? Can the status quo change, and if it can change, how does it change?

There is not a definitive answer to these questions, and therefore, uncertainty plays a role in these important decisions. The arguments which influence, but do not provide definitive answers, to these questions are discussed in the following chapters of this book. When arguments describing the relative merits of the various positions, instead of concrete answers, provide the relevant analysis, uncertainty plays a role.

The role of uncertainty as to the application of federal employment law motivates action by tribes to define the employment relationship since inaction in the face of uncertainty only increases confusion. Moreover, tribal action to define the rules fulfills expectations of an employer to describe the terms and conditions of the employment relationship. However, tribal exercise of lawmaking in this area is not without its risks, which raises numerous interesting questions focusing on both action and inaction.

The questions of action and inaction generate the following inquiries. To what degree may a tribe exercise its sovereignty in the employment arena by defining the terms and conditions of the employment relationship between itself as employer and its employees? The answer or answers lie on a spectrum, which on one end reinforces the tribes' inherent right to exercise its sovereignty by defining the employment relationship while at the other end of the spectrum, the tribe has little sovereignty to exercise. The relevant question becomes, what variables impact a tribe's opportunity to exert or not exert its sovereignty?

The variables which impact the strength of tribes' exercise of sovereignty in the employment arena include this nonexclusive list:

    The law promulgated by the tribe
    Employer activity on or off the reservation
    Employee written consent to the law, the courts, and the rules
    Refusal to accept money with strings attached

> Whether the employee is a member or a nonmember
> Enforcement of tribal employment law
> Addressing the waiver or nonwaiver of immunity
> Understanding when the laws of other sovereigns apply

Because these variables contain a spectrum of questions and answers themselves, the labels do not provide adequate information for leadership to make informed decisions. For example, whether the tribal employer is on or off the reservation generates numerous additional questions, which focus on the nature of the employer's function whether the employees are Indian or non-Indian and the nature of the people served by the employer.

This discussion is an insightful reminder that sovereignty is not a static concept, which either exists or it does not exist. Instead, sovereignty rises and falls with the prudent and poor choices of members electing tribal officials, the actions taken by those officials while in office, the conduct of the employees hired by the tribe to implement policy, and myriad other internal factors. The quantity and quality of sovereignty is also impacted by external factors including other sovereigns.

In short, tribes have control over at least a portion of their sovereignty, and since sovereignty must be exercised for its preservation, a tribe's actions impact the level of sovereignty. Tribal actions, which can increase sovereignty in the employment arena are

1. *Promulgate law and policy*

The variable which creates the most impact in preserving and enhancing tribal sovereignty in the employment arena is promulgating a tribal employment code. Through the employment code, the tribe defines the rules under the law wherein tribal leadership answers numerous questions. For instance, leadership defines whether the tribe will follow federal compensation laws, the type of leave available to employees, whether the tribe uses preference in its hiring practices, and how the tribe defines protected classes of individuals.

By defining tribal employment law, tribal leadership declares the tribe's position on numerous threshold issues. Tribal leadership defines the level of risk by accepting or rejecting federal employment standards. Moreover, leadership provides guidance to governmental and enterprise personnel by promulgating the law, which sets the compass for development of policy for employees. The passage of tribal law fills the "uncertainty" vacuum created by the absence of a clear interaction of tribal, state, and federal employment laws. Accordingly, filling the uncertainty vacuum strengthens a tribe's argument against the application of federal and state laws, which may or may not apply. Creating tribal employment law raises numerous compelling questions; the answers to which will impact where the employer is located on the spectrum of risk.

2. *On-reservation employer activity*

Tribal sovereignty peaks with on-reservation conduct but is not sacrificed by exiting reservation lands. A significant portion of the discussion addressing a tribe's ability to define the rules focuses on whether the employer is on or off the reservation. Geography is important but becoming less critical as a decisive factor. Common sense bolsters the claim that tribes can exert more authority on the reservation as compared to the authority to define the rules sixty miles from the reservation.

Common sense is illustrated by an example. A tribe purchases a golf course within the state, which shares a border with the tribe. The tribe does not sacrifice its sovereignty by leaving its jurisdiction and entering the state, however, the tribe's opportunity to exclusively define its relationship with its employees in the golf course's pro shop is more limited than if those employees worked on the tribe's reservation. The geography discussion below highlights different forms of tribal land, and its impact on the tribe's opportunity to define the rules.

Finally, a nuance on the on-reservation and off-reservation discussion is a split between where the employee works and where the terms and conditions are defined. To the extent that tribal employers hire, review, train, orient, and pay employees on the reservation and assign the employee to work off the reservation may or may not impact the assessment of tribal rulemaking authority.

3. *Employee consent to tribal law and policy*

Adult employees who consent to tribal law and tribal policies deserve the benefit of that bargain. By consenting to tribal employment rules, employees realize the benefits of competitive wages, liberal leave, and meaningful work. Also, in exchange for these benefits, employees consent to the tribe's due process, laws, and courts. Adult employees can work for a tribe, follow its rules, or vote with their feet and work for an entity which is not subject to that tribe's influence. Meaningful consent from employees to tribal rules increases the tribe's opportunity to exercise its sovereignty. A more detailed analysis of this topic is found in chapters 2 and 6.

4. *Not accepting money with strings attached*

Federal government dollars transmitted to tribes oftentimes arrive with strings attached, which require tribes to follow some federal employment laws. There is a trade-off in accepting dollars while at the same time having federal law imposed. Sovereignty is impacted by this trade-off. A more detailed analysis of this topic is found in chapter 2.

5. *Understanding that some federal employment laws do not apply to tribal employers and some others may not apply*

There is a fair level of confusion regarding the applicability of federal employment law to tribal employers. In short, Title VII of the Civil Rights Act of 1964 and the Americans with Disabilities Act do not apply to tribal employers in most instances. The other federal employment laws (FLSA for example) may, or may not, apply to tribal employers. An understanding of these concepts is a prerequisite to good decision making, regarding how the tribe promulgates employment laws and policies. Those decisions inevitably impact the level of sovereignty exerted by the tribe in the employment arena. A more detailed analysis of this topic is found in chapter 2.

6. *Employing tribal members*

Employment litigation has generated numerous written decisions by judges in tribal, state, and federal courts. As a general rule, these decisions scrutinize the relationship between a tribal employer and nonmember of the tribe more than the courts scrutinize the relationship between tribal employer and tribal member employee. Because of this scrutiny, courts permit tribes to exercise more control over tribal member employees and less control over nonmember employees. A more detailed analysis of this topic is found in chapter 6.

7. Not waiving sovereign immunity

A cursory analysis of this variable receives quick acceptance. It makes sense that if the tribe waives immunity it decreases its opportunity to exercise its sovereignty. Reality is more complicated than this cursory view.

Immunity is a defense to a lawsuit, which if effective, causes the court to dismiss the tribe as a defendant. If the tribe through its explicit or implicit actions waives the tribe's immunity from suit in federal or state courts, the tribe exercises less control over the applicable rules. If another sovereign's courts decide what the rules are and who broke the rules, the tribal sovereign is less sovereign.

On the other hand, a tribe can waive its immunity for employment-related actions in tribal court, and that action does not reduce the tribe's sovereignty since the tribe is defining, interpreting, and enforcing tribal law. When tribes promulgate the laws, and tribal courts interpret and enforce those laws, the tribe is exercising more sovereignty and not less.

Therefore, a waiver of immunity permitting courts from other sovereigns to interpret and enforce the law dilutes tribal sovereignty; however, a waiver of immunity permitting tribal courts to interpret and enforce the law exercises sovereignty.

Permitting tribal courts to interpret and enforce the law also increases tribal sovereignty by giving tribal courts the first opportunity to deliver justice, create a record of the facts, and interpret the law (tribal court exhaustion). Furthermore, proceedings in tribal court which supplement sound due process within employer administrative rules (grievances and complaints) mitigates the argument from plaintiffs in federal and state courts declaring that the tribes do not provide a meaningful forum for these disputes, and therefore the federal or state courts must step in. A more detailed analysis of this topic is found in chapter 4.

8. Limiting promises in compacts with other sovereigns

The law requires good faith negotiation between states and tribes regarding the rules when tribal gaming enterprises offer slots, blackjack, and other games. Immunity asserted by state governments presents significant difficulties in enforcing the law's requirement of good-faith negotiation. The law therefore becomes hollow as it provides a right (good-faith negotiation) without a remedy (cannot sue a state for failing to negotiate in good faith). In this legal environment, tribes have "agreed" to varying levels of state rules in exchange for the opportunity to offer Las Vegas-style gaming. The more state rules apply, the less the tribe is defining the rules; and therefore less sovereignty is exercised. Tribes already pay considerable attention to this point. A more detailed analysis of this topic is found in chapter 5.

9. *Reducing promises made to employees which are inconsistent with the tribe's exercise of sovereignty*

Through employee handbooks, well-meaning supervisors, and laminated posters hung in common areas, employers provide promises to employees which may be inconsistent with tribal law. Hanging a laminated poster, notifying employees of protections under federal civil rights and other laws when the tribe may not provide those protections, could permit the intrusion of federal law where it does not apply. A tribe voluntarily following federal civil rights laws is, in itself, an exercise of sovereignty. However, the mixed messages of a handbook pledging allegiance to tribal employment law while at the same time employees are reading laminated posters guaranteeing inconsistent rights dilutes sovereignty. A more detailed analysis of this topic is found in chapters 2 and 6, which reveal that federal employment laws may or may not apply to tribes; and therefore, tribes need to decide whether to meet these standards.

Summary

This list of variables defining the level of sovereignty exercised by tribes is not exhaustive. The list provides a foundation for preserving and enhancing the sovereignty, which permits tribes to define the rules instead of having another sovereign substitute or impose rules on the tribe. A failure to adhere to one or more of the factors discussed above may not waive or remove the tribe's sovereignty. Instead, the ingredients of sovereignty discussed above focus on the idea that sovereignty rises and falls based upon numerous factors. An exact measurement of where sovereignty is at any one time is not possible.

Geography is one of the variables referenced by concluding that an employer's on-reservation activities are more easily protected than an employer's off-reservation activities. Geography's impact on sovereignty is discussed below; and geography, physics, and politics collaborate to present a decent metaphor to describe tribal sovereignty.

There are boulders (tribes) located on a hill (level of sovereignty), and the position of those boulders is impacted by the gravity of history and the exercise of sovereignty by tribes and other sovereigns. More specifically, the geography piece of the metaphor represents a hill with over 560 heavy round boulders, and each bear the name of a tribe and the boulders are located at various altitudes (heights) on the hill. The top of the hill represents sovereignty and the bottom represents no sovereignty.

In our metaphor, the field of physics brings the gravity of history as a force exerting downward pressure on the boulders and positioning those boulders at least partway down the slope. A failure to hold the boulder where it is on the steep hillside results in the boulder rolling to the bottom of the hill.

The third variable in this metaphor is the impact of politics. Whether tribes preserve and enhance their sovereignty is dependent upon the internal politics of the tribe and the external politics of other sovereigns. Therefore whether the boulder will stay where it is or can be pushed back up the hill is dependent in part on tribal, state, and federal politics.

The metaphor does not lend itself to a precise measure of where any particular tribe or tribes as a group are located on the hill. Instead, the metaphor instructs and reconfirms that tribal sovereignty is not static but dependent upon the exertion of tribal members, leaders, and others to preserve and enhance it. In the employment arena, there is an opportunity to push the boulder up the hill by following the nine suggestions above. Unfortunately, inaction by tribal leaders invites action by others; and therefore, a failure to push the boulder in a direction, which enhances sovereignty, by accepting the status quo, will actually permit the gravity of history to continue its downward exertion diluting tribal sovereignty.

What impact does geography have on sovereignty?

Geography has a real impact on the degree of sovereignty a tribal employer may exercise over its employees. A departure of a tribal employer from the reservation creates an opportunity for others to argue a degradation of tribal sovereignty. There are geographical terms used in the book, which deserve definition like "Indian Country," "reservation," "Indian Title," and "fee land." Recent Supreme Court litigation reaffirms that tribes are sovereign on and off their reservations,[36] but that conclusion does not provide insight on the varying degrees of sovereignty a tribe may exert depending upon location.

As location is the three most important things in real estate sales, location for tribal employment law is at least one of the most important variables in determining whether the tribe defines the rules. The borders on maps represented by lines, rivers, and oceans are easy to discern. In most instances, bold lines separate one sovereign from another and those bold lines draw mutual borders terminating the ability of a neighbor from defining the rules for another. Oregon's southern border and California's northern border prevent these neighbors from defining the rules for the other. For tribal sovereigns the border preventing the federal and state governments from defining the rules for the tribe is not as clearly defined as the Oregon-California border. Numerous cases discuss the impact of land and location on whether a tribe can define the terms and conditions. Therefore a primer on relevant geographical terms is in order.

What is Indian Country?

Loosely, Indian Country refers to the lands supervised by the United States set aside for tribes and located inside and outside a reservation. Indian Country can be an important element in determining the nature and extent of authority a tribe has in defining the rules. Within Indian Country, a tribal employer has a better argument that its rules, as opposed to the rules of another sovereign, apply.

The term Indian Country is defined by a federal criminal statute, but courts have used the criminal statute's definition in both criminal and civil contexts.[37] The application of Indian Country to civil matters is important to this analysis since employment laws are civil.

---

[36] *Kiowa Tribe of Oklahoma v. Manufacturing Technologies Inc.*, 523 U.S. 751 (1998).

[37] *South Dakota v. Yankton Sioux Tribe*, 552 U.S. 329, 333 (1998).

Indian Country is defined as:

> (a) all land within the limits of any Indian reservation under the jurisdiction of the United States government, notwithstanding the issuance of any patent, and including rights-of-way running through the reservation; (b) all dependent Indian communities within the borders of the United States whether within the original, or subsequently acquired territory thereof, and whether within or without the limits of a state; and (c) all Indian allotments, the Indian titles to which have not been extinguished, including rights-of-way running through the same.[38]

Application of the definition of Indian Country reveals that Indian Country is all land within a tribe's reservation whether owned by the tribe, Indians, or non-Indians.[39] Subsection (b) includes in Indian Country lands outside of reservations under the supervision of the United States, which includes both trust and nontrust property.[40] The final element of Indian Country includes all trust and all restricted allotments of land located outside a reservation.[41] The difference stems from the idea that trust allotments are owned by the federal government, which are held in trust for the benefit of a tribe; and the restricted allotment is land owned by an Indian, which cannot be sold or leased without the consent of the federal government.

The impact of the Indian Country designation is important. The land within Indian Country and its beneficial owners are exempt from state and local taxes.[42] Tribal members residing in Indian Country are exempt from state income taxes.[43] A state presumptively lacks jurisdiction to enforce its rules within Indian Country.[44] In Indian Country, between employment rules promulgated by tribes and states, tribal rules have primacy.

---

[38] 18 U.S.C.§1151.
[39] *Seymour v. Superintendent*, 368 U.S. 351 (1962).
[40] *U.S. v. South Dakota*, 665 F.2d 837 (8th Cir. 1981), cert. denied 459 U.S. 823 (1983). Also see *Alaska v. Native Village of Venetic Tribal Government*, 552 U.S. 520, 527 n.1 (1998).
[41] *U.S. v. Ramsey*, 271 U.S. 467 (1926).
[42] 25 U.S.C. § 465 (4).
[43] *Oklahoma Tax Commission v. Sac & Fox Nation*, 508 U.S. 114 (1993); *McClanahan v. Arizona State Tax Commission*, 411 U.S. 164, 165 (1973).
[44] *Narragansett Indian Tribe v. Narragansett Electric Company*, 89 F.3d 908, 915 (1st Cir. 1996).

What is an Indian reservation?

An Indian reservation is land set aside for the use, possession, and benefit of a tribe.[45] The right which the tribe holds in reservation land is that of occupancy while the fee (ownership) and disposition (selling the land) remains with the federal government.[46] Indian Country describes a larger subset and includes but is not limited to an Indian reservation. Reservation land is characterized by (1) land held in trust by the federal government, (2) land owned in fee by the tribe or member of the tribe, and (3) land held in fee by nonmembers. Land held in trust is owned by the federal government, and the right of occupancy is granted to the tribe or a member. Land held in fee by the tribe, a member or nonmember, is ownership of the land including occupancy.

What is Indian title?

Indian Title was defined in response to the claim of a non-Indian that he acquired land from an Indian tribe. When the Supreme Court addressed the question if the non-Indian could receive title to property from a tribe, the tribes must then own the land as it is difficult to transfer an interest in something you do not own. The Court's decision was made more difficult by its conclusion that if the tribes owned the land they occupied the United States would be bankrupt if it took the land and compensated the tribes. The Supreme Court held that the tribes did not own the land and therefore, could not sell it to a non-Indian and instead attached a new label to the lands occupied by the tribes—Indian Title.[47]

Indian Title requires four elements:

1. The United States acquired ownership of all the land within the United States by discovery and conquest of the tribes;
2. Indians retain a perpetual right to possess the land unless and until the federal government takes the land;

---

[45] *Minnesota v. Hitchcock*, 185 U.S. 373, 390 (1902). Reservations are created three ways: by treaty until 1871 (See, 25 USC §71; 43 USC §150) by Executive Order and by Statute.

[46] *Northwestern Bands of Shoshone Indians v. United States*, 324 U.S. 335 (1945).

[47] *Johnson v. McIntosh*, 21 U.S. 543 (1823).

3. The right to the land is possessory (like a lease in real property) and therefore the tribe does not own it;
4. The land cannot be sold without the consent of the federal government;

Some of the cases discussed herein reference these geographical concepts. There is much written on each concept; so therefore the intent of these brief descriptions is to provide enough information for a better understanding of those cases.

Geography influences the application of law and its transition from one sovereign to another when employees travel from the state's lands to tribal lands. An example is illustrative.[48] There is a Wisconsin town, which sits on the border between Wisconsin and Minnesota. Most of the town's residents travel across the border into Minnesota to work every day. Wisconsin traffic, employment, and health laws do not apply to these Wisconsin residents during their time in Minnesota. Therefore if the Wisconsin resident speeds to work, is fired, and contracts food poisoning at a Minnesota bar, his remedies for the speeding ticket, wrongful termination, and tort lie under Minnesota law and not the law of his Wisconsin residence. The point is the employee voluntarily consents to the law of the jurisdiction where he drives, works, and imbibes during happy hour. In most contexts, the law holds adults accountable for their decisions as long as no fraud is committed, which led to the adult consenting to the decision. Consistent with this logic, tribal employees acquiesce to tribal law when entering the tribe's jurisdiction through a consensual relationship with the tribe.

---

[48] The illustration alludes to *Worcester v. Georgia*, 31 U.S. 515 (1832) which reinforces tribal jurisdiction within tribal lands.

CHAPTER 2

Do federal employment laws apply to tribal employers?

There is not a neutral answer to the question of whether federal employment law applies to tribal employers. A 1960 United States Supreme Court decision concludes that federal laws, unless specifically exempted from application to tribes, apply to tribes. However, reading this sole precedent is not enough to understand the complicated legal landscape surrounding the question of whether federal employment laws apply to tribal employers. There are numerous cases since 1960, which define the only reasonable response to the question—there is not an answer. However, there are arguments which argue in favor of application of federal employment laws to tribal employers, and there are arguments favoring the opposite conclusion.

As more fully discussed in the first chapter, a tribe's ability to define the rules to the exclusion of other sovereigns, including the federal government is dependent upon numerous variables. Those variables include choices like the acceptance of federal monies, whether the tribe enacts employment codes, and the consent of tribal employees. Whether federal law applies to tribal employers is impacted by those variables and others. This chapter examines this complicated and interesting legal landscape.

What is the legal relationship between tribes and the federal government?

In a word, "complicated with layers of complication."

a. The relationship between tribes and the federal government is complicated

The first layer of complication reveals there is not a relationship between the tribes collectively and the singular federal government but rather 560 relationships between each tribe and the federal government. There are numerous legal principles, which apply in the same general way to all tribes. The basic rule that state law does not apply to tribes is a general rule with almost uniform application regardless of the tribe. Another basic rule is Congress can dilute tribal sovereignty and, as a general rule, it applies uniformly to the tribes.

However, the opposite is true as well. Tribes with treaties guaranteeing specific rights can assert more authority in the exercise of those rights as compared to a tribe, which is not a party to the treaty. Furthermore, federal civil rights laws do not apply to the tribe, but may if the tribe consents to application of the law through a funding agreement of gaming compact.

Second, the federal government is not one entity but instead a collection of institutions and people, which includes Congress, the Executive, and the Courts. Each branch relates to tribes in different ways, and each branch influences the interaction of the other branches with the tribes. A more accurate question is posed by asking about the relationship between a tribe and the various aspects of the federal government. The analysis demands an understanding of the link between the tribe and the *federal governments*. These federal governments interact with tribal employers through the courts, the National Labor Relations Board, The Equal Employment Opportunity Commission, Department of Labor, and laws written by Congress.

The various arms of the federal government can send mixed messages to tribes. The president could declare deference to tribal sovereignty while at the same time, EEOC lawyers are challenging tribal preference. A more acutely inconsistent message is one agency approving a lease while another sues objecting to a provision in the lease.

Third, there are gaps in the laws, which define the relationship between the tribes and the federal government. A principle of federal law is the plenary powers dilution of tribal sovereignty through the enactment of laws, which apply to tribes. When the federal government exercises the plenary power, a specific declaration of its use is presumed. Therefore, when a specific declaration of use is not forthcoming, there is an assumption that Congress did not intend to dilute tribal sovereignty. This chapter explores instances where these rules are jumbled to create a confusing gap in the law. These gaps force tribal leaders to make educated guesses regarding when and if federal laws apply to tribes. Speculation regarding applicability necessarily complicates the analysis. Through these layers of complication, general rules and principles are revealed which define the relationship(s) between tribes and the federal government.

b. *The relationship is influenced by multiple forces*

An understanding of the relationship between the tribes and the federal government requires insight into contradictory and complementary forces working against and for the other. This statement does not assert that tribes and the federal government are the contradictory forces working against the other. Instead, the statement references the collection of consistent and inconsistent rules, agendas, and goals, which impact the relationship between these sovereigns. The mix of ingredients which influence the tribal-federal relationship includes two sovereigns, a trust responsibility, a history of promises kept, a history of promises broken, an Indian population with serious needs, and tribes with unique cultures and traditions older than the United States.

The United States Supreme Court characterizes tribes as domestic, dependent nations.[49] Domestic refers to tribal nations within the United States, and dependent refers to their alleged dependent status upon the federal government.

The Supreme Court asserts that the United States is a discovering and conquering sovereign, and therefore the United States can limit and dilute tribal sovereignty. The power to dilute tribal sovereignty by imposing federal law on tribes is referred to as the plenary power. Plenary power is the full and complete power over tribes, tribal government, tribal members, and their property.[50] The federal government has used its plenary power many times to legislate gaming, crime, dispersal of tribal lands, and the formation of tribal governments. The question in the employment area is whether the federal

---

[49] *Worcester v. Georgia*, 31 U.S. 515 (1832)
[50] *U.S. v. Sandoval*, 231 U.S. 28 (1913).

government has attempted to dilute tribal sovereignty through the use of its plenary power by imposing federal employment laws on tribal employers. The answer is not clear.

There is a trust relationship between the federal government and tribes. The trust relationship can be characterized as between two parties where one holds property for the other; the party holding the property must make choices which benefit the other. The trust relationship between the federal government and tribes means more than the fiduciary duty owed from a possessor of property to its owner. The trust relationship between the federal government and tribes exists even when there is no property interest. A trust relationship demands that the trustee (federal government) place the ward's interests (tribes) ahead of its own. This unique relationship has been characterized as a "semantic knot which is impossible to untie by concentrating on the words used to define the relationship."[51] The trust relationship should give the federal government pause before imposing its employment laws on the tribal sovereign.

The relationship between the federal government and the states impacts the tribes. The states are located on tribal lands and this geographical relationship breeds some harmony and some discord. When tribes and states are advancing their own interests, there are times when inconsistent goals bring consistent trouble. For example, California believed tribes were violating the law by gaming while at the same time tribes believed the establishment of gaming enterprises was consistent with tribal sovereignty. Tribes' inherent right to engage in gaming as an enterprise and the absence of state control was confirmed by the United States Supreme Court in 1987,[52] and a year later, in part because of the assertive objections raised by various states, Congress promulgated the federal tribal gaming law which unequivocally dilutes tribal sovereignty.[53] An aspect of federal gaming law dilutes tribal sovereignty in favor of the states as it requires tribes to obtain the consent of a state before Las Vegas-style gaming is offered. The states comprise a strong lobby in Washington DC and that influence impacts the relationship between the tribes and the federal government. In chapter 3, the question whether state

---

[51] *Alaska Natives and American Laws*, Second Edition, D. Case, D. Volnuck, University of Alaska Press, 2002.
[52] *California v. Cabazon Band of Mission Indians*, 480 U.S. 202 (1987).
[53] Indian Gaming Regulatory Act, 25 U.S.C. § 2701 et seq.

employment law applies to tribal employers is evaluated. Even in those instances where state employment law may not apply, the influence of states to influence the federal government's imposition of federal employment law must be evaluated.

The relationship between the tribes and the federal government is strengthened by the promises kept between these sovereigns and weakened by the promises broken. The pendulum of trust ebbs and flows along the same arc followed by the pendulum of sovereignty. It is difficult to trust another sovereign while it strips you of your rights, but on the other hand, trust returns with comity. Trust is a necessary ingredient of a meaningful relationship, and both tribal and federal sovereignty have an obligation to preserve and enhance the trust between them.

In addition to trust as a necessary ingredient to a successful relationship, insight into each partner's culture is required. Tribes do not always understand the United States, and the United States does not always understand tribes and their members. The federal government endorses the exercise of Indian preference in the workplace, but an aspect of the federal government will not endorse tribe-specific preference in selecting workers. This dichotomy in thought and process is dependent, in part, on limited insight on both sides of the debate.

Has the United States defined its relationship to tribes?

The relationship between the tribes and the federal government is characterized by a nation to domestic-nation relationship where the federal nation can dilute tribal sovereignty, but whether the federal government has diluted the sovereignty is viewed through a prism where the benefit of any doubt creates a presumption that federal laws do not apply to tribes. This relationship has developed over a couple centuries, defined by numerous ambiguous rules, which limits definitive answers regarding the strength of the powers exercised between these sovereigns.

Before the United States was formed, tribes interacted with the Europeans. When Europeans first arrived, there were five hundred nations possessing their own government, culture, and language.[54] When the United States became

---

[54] *Rights of Indians and Tribes* at page 1.

a nation, with the ratification of its Constitution, the new nation formed agreements with the tribes through treaties. Nearly four hundred treaties were signed between the tribes and the federal government.[55]

The United States Constitution is a contract of delegation wherein limited powers are granted to various subunits of the federal government. The Constitution also creates a power-sharing relationship between the federal government and the state governments. As between the federal government and the states, the principle of federalism causes the presumptive delegation of all powers to the states except those reserved for the federal government.

A power reserved to the federal government and specifically its legislative branch is the relationship with the tribes. Early in the Constitution, the power to interact with the tribes is granted to Congress in article 1, section 8, clause 3 (the Commerce Clause) which provides in part:

> Congress shall have the Power . . . to regulate Commerce with foreign Nations, and among the several States and with the Indian Tribes.

Congress is the federal government's agent for dealing with tribal governments. The United States Constitution grants to the Senate and the president the authority to enter into treaties. In addition to the Commerce Clause (quoted above) and the treaty power, the United States Supreme Court has asserted that federal power over tribes is also based upon the federal government's status as a conquering sovereign,[56] and the trust relationship between the tribes and the federal government includes both protection for and power over the tribes.[57] These are the ingredients of the federal government's plenary power over tribes, which permit the federal government to dilute or even extinguish tribal powers.[58] If federal employment laws apply to tribal employers, the plenary power is the conduit, which permits application of federal law.

The plenary power is disputed by tribes. Tribes argue that the Commerce Clause is an internal federal delegation of authority, which does not permit

---

[55] Id. at 46.
[56] *Johnson v. McIntosh*, 21 U.S. 542 (1823).
[57] *U.S. v. Kagama*, 118 U.S. 375, 382 (1886).
[58] *South Dakota v. Yankton Sioux Tribe*, 522 U.S. 329, 343 (1998).

dilution of tribal sovereignty. The tribal governments are not parties to the United States Constitution, so therefore when between the federal government and the states, the federal government is appointed the party to deal with tribes, this delegation of authority appoints an agent for the United States but does not permit dilution of tribal sovereignty.

Moreover, the conquering sovereign argument is not based upon the stubborn facts, which reveal that some tribes were conquered by the federal government but most were not.

Without rejecting the merit of the tribes' objection to the assertion of the plenary power, the reality is the federal government will continue to assert it. The question is whether the federal government asserts the plenary power through the various federal laws, which impact employment relationships. In interpreting whether the federal government has exercised its plenary power by imposing federal employment laws on tribal employers, both the trust responsibility and the canons of construction aid the conversation.

What is the federal government's trust responsibility to tribes, and how does the trust responsibility impact whether federal employment laws apply to tribes?

The trust responsibility imposes upon the federal government the obligation to encourage tribal self-government and preserve tribal assets. The federal trust responsibility has its roots in nation-to-nation dealings with tribes and therefore has been recognized for over two centuries.[59] The federal government's trust responsibility to tribes requires at least two things: (1) the federal government to support and encourage tribal self-government and economic prosperity and (2) when the federal government controls tribal resources like land and minerals, federal officials have a fiduciary duty to tribes.[60] A 1977 United States Senate report characterized the trust responsibility as follows:

---

[59] *Worcester v. Georgia*, 31 U.S. 515 (1832); *Cherokee Nation v. Georgia*, 30 U.S. 1 (1831); These cases discussed the trust relationship in the context of treaties between tribes and the young United States and in Worcester, referring to tribes as domestic dependent nations.

[60] Stephen L. Pevar, *The Rights of Indians and Tribes* (Southern Illinois Press, 2002) at chapter 3, pages 33-34.

> The purpose behind the trust doctrine is and always has been to ensure the survival and welfare of Indian tribes and people. This includes an obligation to provide those services required to protect and enhance Indian lands, resources, and self-government; and also includes those economic and social programs which are necessary to raise the standard of living and social well-being of the Indian people to a level comparable to the non-Indian society.[61]

The trust responsibility is supposed to impose upon federal officials the obligation to read federal law in a way which benefits or favors a tribe.[62] If a reading of a federal statute could lead reasonable persons to more than one conclusion, a court may find statutory ambiguity. If there is a finding of ambiguity, the trust responsibility urges an interpretation, which most benefits the tribes. Common sense also reinforces the idea that an ambiguous statute should be interpreted in a manner which does not benefit the drafter of the law since the drafter is in the best position to write with clarity; and when clarity is not found, the drafter should not be rewarded with an interpretation which favors them. Therefore, the language of federal law, if confusing, should be viewed in a manner which benefits the tribes.

Numerous federal employment laws neither declare application to tribes nor declare an exemption of applicability. These laws are silent on applicability. A logical application of the trust responsibility doctrine to the question of whether federal employment laws, which are silent as to applicability, apply to tribal employers forces the conclusion that the laws do not apply. Under these circumstances, the trust relationship reinforces tribal self-government by deferring to tribal employment laws and policies, which define the terms and conditions of the employment relationship. Said another way, since the trust responsibility is supposed to enhance tribal self-government, the imposition of federal employment laws upon tribes, is inconsistent with that goal.

Sovereignty is dependent in large part on the sovereign's ability to define its own rules and apply those rules to people, places, and things. In other words, sovereignty is increased in the employment context if tribal employers

---

[61] American Indian Policy Review Commission, *Final Report* (Washington DC, Government Printing Office, 1977) at 128-30.
[62] *Ramah Navajo Chapter v. Lujan*, 112 F.3d 1455, 1462 (10th Cir. 1997).

define the terms and conditions of the employment relationship, and conversely, sovereignty is diluted if tribes must accept rules promulgated by other sovereigns. If federal law applies to the relationship between tribal employers and its employees, the tribe's exercise of sovereignty is diminished. Unfortunately, for tribes, the federal trust responsibility does not, by itself, determine which federal rules apply.

What are the canons of construction?

The canons of Indian construction have a similar impact on the interpretation of whether federal law applies to tribes as these canons require reading the law to benefit Indians.[63] When Congress imposed state criminal and civil laws on tribes in certain states,[64] the Supreme Court's interpretation of the statutory language forced it to conclude, after applying the canons, that the federal statute imposed state criminal, but not state civil jurisdiction on the tribes.[65] Likewise when the federal government terminated a tribe and later re-recognized it, courts concluded that the tribe's hunting and fishing rights had not been terminated because the congressional termination of the tribe was clear, but its termination did not expressly terminate the hunting and fishing rights.[66]

The canons of construction make sense since tribes are inherently sovereign. As inherently sovereign, tribes reasonably presume the necessary authority to define the rules. The presumption is limited only in those instances when the federal government exercises its plenary power in a clear manner. The federal government's clarity of action to limit tribal sovereignty is a prerequisite to fundamental fairness. It is, therefore, fundamentally unfair in those instances where the federal government has not explicitly exercised its plenary power by declaring a statute applicable to tribes while at the same time its courts declare rules which force tribes to speculate whether the federal government's inaction effectively limits the tribe's sovereign rights.

---

[63] *Menominee Tribe v. United States*, 391 U.S. 404 (1968)
[64] Public Law 280
[65] *Bryan v. Itasca County*, 426 U.S. 373 (1976); *California v. Cabazon Band of Mission Indians*, 480 U.S. 202 (1987)
[66] *Menominee Tribe v. United States*, 391 U.S. 404 (1968).

The canons and trust relationship do not terminate the speculation regarding the application of federal employment law to tribal employers. More analysis is necessary, and understanding context assists in limiting speculation's range of options. Both the trust responsibility and the canons of construction provide some context for the conversation. Application of the trust responsibility and the canons of construction to whether federal employment laws, which are silent on applicability, apply to tribal employers favor nonapplication.

Are the tribal-federal rules discussed in this chapter applicable to the tribal-state relationship?

Before the question of whether federal employment laws apply to tribal employers is addressed, a brief reminder of the reality that the tribal-state relationship is different from the tribal-federal government relationship is timely.

The relationship between the tribes and the federal government is different than the relationship between the tribes and the states which border tribes. Unlike the federal government, states do not possess a plenary power to dilute tribal sovereignty. Also, states do not derive their authority to govern from the tribes and likewise, tribes derive no power from the states. Similarly, for the tribes to exercise power, they are not dependent on state power.

The sovereignty triangle helps define the relationships among the three sovereigns, which rest at each point of the triangle. Through the sovereignty triangle, geometry helps compare and contrast the relationships among the sovereigns. The sovereignty triangle places the tribes, states, and federal government at each turn of the three-sided object. The leg of the triangle between the federal government and the tribes is different from the leg between the states and the tribes. The tribes start with the presumption of inherent sovereignty in relationship with other sovereigns. That presumption is strong between the tribes and the states, so therefore that leg of the triangle does not invite state intervention in tribal affairs. On the other hand, unlike the states, the federal government can overcome the presumption of tribal sovereignty and therefore, that leg of the triangle may illustrate the federal government's dilution of tribal sovereignty. The natural question in this chapter is whether the federal government leveraged the sovereignty triangle by imposing federal employment laws on tribal employers.

Through these next several sections, the discussion focuses on the relationship between the tribes and the federal government and not with the states.

Under what circumstances do federal employment laws apply or do not apply to tribal employers?

Whether federal employment laws apply to on-reservation governments and tribally owned business enterprises brings together a confluence of factors including tribal law, the principles of sovereignty, the interpretation of relevant federal statutes and case law, and the behavior of the tribe and its agents. This section provides a framework for the discussion.

The analysis of potentially applicable federal law is threefold. First, there are federal laws which specifically exempt tribal employers. Certain federal civil rights laws and the federal law prohibiting discrimination based upon disability do not apply to tribes.

Second, there are federal employment laws which are silent as to their application to tribal employers. For these silent laws, the courts have responded to an interesting series of arguments but have not yielded a definitive answer. In short, there is an argument that the laws which are silent on applicability apply to tribal employers; however, there are arguments the laws do not apply.

Third, as to both the laws which exempt tribal employers and laws, which are silent on applicability, the analysis is not complete without addressing an additional question: Has the tribe, through its behavior, consented to application of federal employment laws?

Which federal laws declare they are not applicable to tribal employers?

Title VII of the Civil Rights Act of 1964 and the Americans with Disabilities Act do not apply to tribal employers.[67]

---

[67] Tribes must recognize that the laws do not apply, however the tribe could agree to follow the law through a funding agreement, gaming or other compact, or other mechanism.

Title VII of the Civil Rights Act of 1964, which prohibits discrimination on the basis of race, religion, gender, and national origin, does not apply to tribes.[68] The reason behind exempting tribal employers from the reach of Title VII was to promote the ability of tribes to control their own enterprises.[69] Under the statutory language, Title VII excludes tribes as defined employers. Title VII's exclusion of Indian tribes as defined employers is explained by a review of legislative history in the words of South Dakota Senator Mundt who introduced the tribal exemption by stating that the exemption was to protect "the welfare of our oldest and most distressed American minority, the American Indians" to allow them to "conduct their own affairs."[70] Senator Mundt also understood that exempting the tribes from the reach of federal law was not limited to governmental operations but also to tribal economic endeavors:

> Let me emphasize that Indian tribes, in an effort to decrease unemployment and in order to integrate their people into the affairs of the national community, operate many economic enterprises, which are more or less supervised by the Indian tribes, the employees serving as apprentices in many instances, and as supervisors and regularly employed and paid employees in others.[71]

---

[68] 42 U.S.C. § 2000, et seq.; *Dille v. Council of Energy Resource Tribes*, 801 F.2d 373 (8th Cir. 1986); *Pink v. Modoc Indian Health Project*, 157 F.3d 1185 (9th Cir. 1998); *Thomas v. Choctaw Management Services Enterprise*, 313 F.3d 910 (5th Cir. 2002); But see, *Tidwell v. Harrah's Kansas Casino Corp.*, 322 F.Supp.2d 1200 (D.Kan. 2004) (sexual harassment); *Hines v. Grand Casinos of Louisiana, LLC*, 140 F.Supp. 2d 701 (W.D.La. 2001) (sexual harassment).

[69] Statement of Senator Mundt, 110 Cong. Rec. 13702.

[70] 110 Cong.Rec. 13702 (1964) *Burns v. Mille Lacs Housing Authority*, 1997 W.L. 882911 (D. Minn. 1997). *Wardle v. Ute Indian Tribe*, 623 F.2d 670 (10th Cir. 1980) (Plaintiff, a nontribal member, employed by tribe as policeman for 17 years, is terminated to make room for employment of tribal members. Complaint falls within Title VII, and it does not apply); But see, *Myrick v. Devils Lake Sioux Manufacturing Corporation*, 718 F.Supp. 753 (D.N.D. 1989) (corporation defendant organized under North Dakota State law with mixed ownership of an Indian tribe (51 percent) and a nontribal entity (49 percent) did not qualify for exemption); *Vance v. Boyd Mississippi, Inc.*, 923 F.Supp. 905 (S.D. Miss. 1996).

[71] Id.

The remarks of one senator certainly do not reflect the reasoning of all senators, but the logic of his argument is a compelling assertion of tribal sovereignty. Furthermore, the legislative history does not segregate governmental functions from economic endeavors, which forces reconsideration of those who argue for less tribal sovereignty in response to the expansion of tribal enterprises.

Additionally, the Americans with Disabilities Act (ADA), which prohibits employers from making decisions based upon an employee's disability, does not apply to tribal employers.[72] The ADA directs employers to make employment decisions without bias against the disabled when the applicant can perform the essential function of the job with, or without, employer assistance. Under the ADA's parlance, employer assistance is called a reasonable accommodation. Reasonable accommodation may be many things including, but not limited to, a change in schedule or hours worked, a piece of equipment, modification of the way a job is performed, and many other options, which assist the worker.

The ADA addresses more than the relationship between employers and employees. Outside the employment context, the Eleventh Circuit Court of Appeals in *Florida Paraplegic* declared that the public accommodation aspect of the ADA applies to tribes.[73] In *Florida Paraplegic*, the court found that Title III of the ADA requires, among other things, that businesses open to the public be accessible to all including persons with disabilities. After applying the *Tuscarora-Donovan* analysis (see next section), the court found that this tribal restaurant was a commercial enterprise open to non-Indians and therefore not a governmental function, excepting application of federal law. However, after declaring the law applicable to

---

[72] 42 U.S.C. § 12111(5)(B)(i) (term employer does not include tribe). Even though Title III of the ADA which requires places of public accommodation to be accessible to persons with disabilities, it does not exclude tribes. The Eleventh Circuit ruled that it cannot be enforced by private persons against Indian tribes in non-Indian forums because Congress did not expressly waive tribal immunity from suit. *Florida Paraplegic Association, Inc. v. Miccosukee Tribe of Indians of Florida*, 166 F.3d 1126 (11th Cir. 1999); *Cano v. Cocopah Casino*, 2007 WL 2164555 (Ariz. 2007).

[73] *Florida Paraplegic Association, Inc. v. Miccosukee Tribe of Indians of Florida*, 166 F.3d 1126 (11th Cir. 1999).

the tribe, the court found that tribal sovereign immunity precluded relief for the plaintiff.

In sum, the ADA, like Title VII, does not define the terms and conditions of the relationship between tribal employers and employees.

When Title VII and the ADA declare tribes are not employers under those laws, tribes sometimes agree to follow the laws in funding agreements or compacts. Legitimate questions flow from these contradictory positions:

> Do Title VII and the ADA apply just to the program which receives the benefit of the federal dollars? Do these laws apply to the tribe? To the tribe's enterprises? Should the employee handbook be modified to reflect these rules? Should the tribe hang the laminated poster providing notice of the federal civil rights?

Risk accompanies every answer to these questions. Risk of noncompliance with the contract comes with failing to hang the poster and make the handbook change while at the same time the tribe risks diluting its sovereignty when it permits the application of federal law in those instances where it does not apply. A definitive answer does not accompany these risks. Instead the future will bring rules articulated by courts and governmental officials which will better define the consequences associated with these complex questions.

At this stage of the discussion, a reminder regarding the separation between the legal and moral questions presented is relevant. The legal question presented is whether the federal government's civil rights laws—prohibiting discrimination based upon race, religion, national origin, gender, and disability—apply to tribal employers via an exercise of the plenary power. The answer is the federal government declared these laws do not apply to tribal employers.

The moral question of whether tribal employers should discriminate against employees of particular races, religions, either gender, those born in another country, or employees which present at the interview with a disability is separate from the legal question of what sovereign defines the rules. No credible moral argument exists, which permits discrimination against those enumerated protected classes. Whether the tribe promulgates employment laws which protect the natural civil rights of tribal employees is *the* moral and practical question.

Under the exemption from Title VII, what is the definition of tribal employer?

Unless modified by agreement or through adoption by the tribe, Title VII does not apply to the tribal employer. Tribal employer is defined broadly to include the tribal government, an enterprise owned by the government, and an entity owned and operated by a tribal consortium. Many courts have drawn an expansive definition of tribe under the Title VII exemption.[74] This expansive view is consistent with the "settled principle of statutory construction that statutes passed for the benefit of dependent Indian tribes are to be liberally construed, with doubtful expressions being resolved in favor of the Indians."[75]

Sage Hospital[76] is a good example of the reasoning behind the application of an expansive definition of tribal employer. The Navajo Nation is divided into chapters (legislative districts), and eight chapters formed a corporation, which provided medical services to members. The corporate board was comprised

---

[74] *Dille v. Council of Energy Resource Tribes*, 801 F.2d 373 (10th Cir. 1986) (collection of 35 tribes in joint venture to manage energy resources). *Taylor v. Alabama Intertribal Council Title IV JTPA*, No. 00-12280 (11th Cir. 7/9/01) *Pink v. Modoc Indian Health Project, Inc.*, 157 F.3d 1185 (9th Cir. 1998) (off reservation health service controlled by tribe exempt as tribal enterprise). *Giedosh v. Little Wound School Bd.*, 995 F.Supp. 1052 (D.S.D. 1997) (on reservation South Dakota corporation exempt); *Setchell v. Little Six, Inc.*, 1996 WL 162560 (Minn. Ct. App. 1996) *Cohen v. Little Six, Inc.*, 543 N.W.2d 376 (Minn. Ct. App. 1997) (raising revenue and redistributing it for the welfare of a sovereign nation is manifestly a governmental purpose. *Id.* at 379. But see, *NLRB v. Chapa De Indian Health Program, Inc.*, 316 F.3d 995 (9th Cir. 2003).

[75] *Three Affiliated Tribes of the Fort Berthold Reservation v. Wold Engineering*, 467 U.S. 138, 149, 104 S.Ct. 2267 (1984).

[76] *EEOC v. Navajo Health Foundation-Sage Memorial Hospital, Inc.*, 2007 WL 2683825 (D. Ariz. 2007); The Court also reasoned that since *Sage Hospital* was a tribal organization under the ISDEAA it supports the idea that it an organization which serves as an arm of the Navajo Nation concluding that Congress' intent was the same in creating ISDEAA and the exemption under Title VII. For a contradictory analysis see *Dawavendewa v. Salt River Project*, 154 F.3d 1117, 1123 (9th Cir. 1998).

of enrolled members of the nation and voting members of the chapters they represent. As to the application of Title VII, the Court concluded:

> Because the hospital has been formed by eight political subdivisions of the Navajo Nation, and those eight chapters select and are represented by members of the hospital's board of directors, the Court finds that the Navajo Nation exercises sufficient control over the hospital to render it a tribal entity for purposes of Title VII.[77]

The Court's conclusion based upon deference to tribal sovereignty is consistent with congressional intent. Whether the employer is the tribe, a tribal subdivision, or a corporation controlled by the tribe, Title VII does not apply.

Do federal employment laws which do not declare application to tribal employers apply to tribal employers?

Most federal employment laws are silent on applicability as they do not declare application to tribal employers nor do the laws declare inapplicability. For example, the National Labor Relations Act, Fair Labor Standards Act, and Family and Medical Leave Act[78] do not address whether they apply or do not apply to tribal employers. Fairness declares that Congress failed to specifically apply federal employment laws to tribes, so therefore the laws do not apply. Fairness met reality; and reality introduced the courts which have spent considerable time interpreting the application of laws, which are silent on the question of application.

What is the *Tuscarora Donovan* analysis?

There is neither an affirmative or negative answer to the question of whether federal employment laws which are silent on application apply to tribal employers. Instead of an answer, there are federal court decisions, which provide a framework for an analysis, which guides the conversation. Two cases from the federal judiciary frame the analysis of whether federal employment laws, which are silent on applicability, apply to tribal employers. Those cases

---

[77] *EEOC v. Navajo Health Foundation-Sage Memorial Hospital, Inc.*, 2007 WL 2683825 (D. Arizona 2007).

[78] This is not an exhaustive list of federal employment laws which are silent on applicability to tribal employers.

are the Supreme Court's *Federal Power Commission v. Tuscarora Indian Nation*[79] and the Ninth Circuit's *Donovan v. Coeur d'Alene Tribal Farm*[80] which provide the framework for the applicability discussion. Pairing these cases and the almost opposite views articulated by these courts, creates what is commonly referred to as the *Tuscarora-Donovan* analysis.

An *answer* to the applicability question does not flow from the *Tuscarora-Donovan* analysis. Instead, the *Tuscarora-Donovan* analysis reveals the facts which courts rely on to decide whether, in particular cases, the federal employment laws apply. This is a distinction with a real difference. Tribal and federal leaders, private business, regulators, directors of human resources, and lawyers want an answer to the applicability question, but those answers are not forthcoming since the analysis presents numerous *arguments* on both sides of this question. Those seeking definitive answers will be met with disappointment, and those seeking ambiguity, uncertainty, and a good fight will find the *Tuscarora-Donovan* analysis an excellent vessel.

Tuscarora is a land condemnation case where the United States Supreme Court confronted the question whether the United States could flood a portion of the tribe's fee lands. The tribe argued against application of the law used to flood the lands, but the Court declared it could flood the lands since tribes must follow laws of general applicability. The Supreme Court reconciled its holding with a contrary line of cases[81] finding other precedents consistent with its reasoning. The line of cases pushing against the Court's holding asserts that tribes may reasonably assume that the federal government has not used its plenary power to dilute tribal sovereignty unless the federal government specifically declares its use of the plenary power in the language of the law.

---

[79] 362 U.S. 99 (1960).

[80] 751 F.2d 1113 (9th Cir. 1985).

[81] General acts of congress did not apply to Indians, unless so expressed as to clearly manifest an intention to include them. *Elk v. Wilkins*, 112 U.S. 94 (1884). There is an old and well-known rule that statutes which, in general terms, divest preexisting rights or privileges will not be applied to the sovereign without express words to that effect. *Leiter Minerals, Inc., v. United States*, 352 U.S. 220, 224-225 (1957); *United States v. Wyoming*, 331 U.S. 440, 449 (1947); *United States v. Stevenson*, 215 U.S. 190 (1909); *United States v. American Bell Telephone Co.*, 159 U.S. 548, 553-555 (1895); *Lewis v. United States*, 92 U.S. 618, 622 (1875).

Put simply, before *Tuscarora,* there were cases where courts found that tribal inherent sovereignty rests on the assumption that only tribal law applies to the exclusion of law imposed by other sovereigns, unless the federal government specifically declares that its law applies. *Tuscarora* undermines the assumption that a specific declaration of applicability is a prerequisite to application. Instead, *Tuscarora* declares general applicability of federal laws.

An illustration of laws of general applicability is useful. Middle April of every year imposes a deadline requiring Americans to disclose intimate financial details regarding the individual's previous year's income and spending to the federal government. In short, most Americans file tax returns, which are sent to the Internal Revenue Service and its state equivalent. Most Americans assume an obligation for payment of income taxes and disclosure of these financial details is necessary to conform to the law, which generally applies to everyone. Consistent with this general assumption, the federal government does not present a special invitation to individual taxpayers declaring applicability of the tax code to those individuals. Instead, taxpayers are to assume the tax code applies to them and therefore, payment of taxes and disclosure of the financial details is necessary. *Tuscarora* places tribes in the same category as all others requiring tribes to assume application of federal tax laws and otherwise.

Tribal leaders view sovereignty as an impediment to the assumption that federal legislation applies to tribes. Leadership asserts that if the federal government exercises its sovereignty and imposes its will on the tribes, the law should demand that the federal government clearly articulate its intent. A failure by the federal government to clearly articulate its intent to apply federal law to tribes permits tribal sovereigns to presume the opposite of general applicability. Tribes assume the law does not apply to tribes *unless* the tribes receive a special invitation from the federal government declaring applicability.

An example reinforces the point. When Congress promulgated the Resource Conservation and Recovery Act of 1976 (RCRA), which aimed to remedy pollution caused by improper disposal of hazardous waste, RCRA permitted suit against any person violating the law, and RCRA defined "person" to include tribes which therefore abrogated tribal sovereign immunity.[82] When

---

[82] 42 U.S.C. §6972 (a)(1)(A), 42 U.S.C. § 6903 (13)(15) repealed; *Blue Legs v. United States Bureau of Indian Affairs,* 867 F.2d 1094, 1097 (8th Cir. 1989).

Congress declares certain laws applicable to tribes (RCRA), the federal government has clearly exercised its plenary powers, but when Congress does *not* include the tribes in the law, the choice is purposeful, and therefore the law does not apply. Common sense endorses the argument as well.

Under the logic of *Tuscarora*, those federal employment laws, which are silent on applicability apply to tribes; so therefore, *Tuscarora* creates a presumption of federal law application. Accordingly, the minimum wage, overtime, child labor, and glass ceiling laws (FLSA), laws addressing collective bargaining between employee representatives and the employer (NLRA), leave for medical issues and expansion of the family (FMLA), and federal safety laws (OSHA) among many others all apply to tribes if the *Tuscarora* decision is read without modification by the later cases.

Tuscarora is not an employment case. The United States Supreme Court, the court which decided *Tuscarora*, has not addressed the question of whether federal employment law applies to tribal employers. Since 1960 when *Tuscarora* was decided, plenty of courts have endorsed, rejected, and shaped *Tuscarora* specifically in the context of tribal employment. The employment case which rejects *Tuscarora* as overreaching was the Ninth Circuit's *Donovan v. Coeur d'Alene Tribal Farm (Donovan)*.[83]

Donovan declares that federal employment laws, which are silent on applicability, do not apply if there is a treaty, which precludes application, the federal law's history (legislative intent) presents arguments against application, or application of the federal employment law invades the essential governmental function of the tribe. The *Donovan* Court asked whether "congressional silence should be taken as an expression of intent to exclude tribal employers from the scope of an Act to which they would otherwise be subject." *Donovan* helps answer whether silence on the question of applicability in laws like FMLA, FLSA, and NLRA is a stark omission of congressional intent to abrogate tribal sovereign immunity. The *Donovan* language, which describes exceptions to the *Tuscarora* assumption of general application of federal law to tribes, is not the model of clarity but it has been interpreted in a manner which is consistent with this summary.

---

[83] 751 F.2d 1113 (9th Cir. 1985)

Under *Donovan*, a law of general application, which is silent on applicability, does not apply to tribal employers when:

1. the law touches exclusive rights of self-government in purely intramural matters;
2. the application of the law would abrogate treaty rights; or
3. legislative history shows that Congress did not intend the law to apply to tribes.

Each of the *Donovan* exceptions is explored and defined below. Note, these exceptions do not apply if Congress explicitly declares the law applies to tribes. Therefore, these exceptions only enter the analysis when the employment statute is silent on whether it applies to tribes. Courts have spent considerable time defining the first *Donovan* exception and less time discussing exceptions two and three.

The essential government function exception to application of federal law

The first *Donovan* exception declares that federal employment laws do not apply to tribes if the federal law touches exclusive rights of self-governance in purely intramural matters. A clearer statement of the relevant question is, Does application of the federal employment law interfere with an essential governmental function of the tribe? If the employer is engaged in an essential governmental function, there is an argument that federal law does not apply. How a court views what is, and what is not, an essential government function is determinative to the legal question of applicability.

Some courts have ruled that wrongful termination actions are internal tribal affairs.[84] Other courts recognize that the activities of tribal government do not fit neatly into categories of government or commercial enterprise. Instead, many activities fall somewhere between government, where tribal sovereignty is at its zenith, to off-reservation commercial activities where sovereignty is at its weakest.

An examination of the cases, which apply the relevant test in determining what is, and what is not, an essential governmental function, reveals some examples which guide the conversation. If the employer is a police department,

---

[84] *Penobscot Nation v. Fellencer*, 164 F.3d 706, 713 (1st Cir. 1999); *EEOC v. Karuk Tribe Housing Authority*, 260 F.3d 1071, 1080 (9th Cir. 2001).

the *Donovan* analysis can provide an argument, which if accepted, precludes application of federal employment law.[85] On the other hand, if the tribal employer does not look like tribal government action but instead is operating a gaming enterprise, the *Donovan* exception may not carry the day.[86] Yet other courts see past the casino lights and focus on the purpose of the enterprise before declaring essential government function or not.

In *Allen v. Gold Country Casino,*[87] the Ninth Circuit Court of Appeals dismissed a civil rights claim, finding that the casino is not a mere revenue producing business but rather an enterprise created under the rubric of federal law which is premised upon the promotion of tribal economic development, tribal self-sufficiency, and strong *tribal* government.[88] Like states engaged in the lottery business, there is an argument that government is business, and business is government. *Allen* recognizes that the inquiry must investigate the real purpose for the revenue generating entity before a fair conclusion regarding the applicability of federal law can be reached.

In distinguishing between governmental action and commercial enterprise, courts look to a variety of factors. Factors weighted toward government activity and, therefore, favor inapplicability of federal law (NLRA does not apply) are

> *Tribal employment ordinance defines the terms and conditions of the employment relationship as a governmental purpose*
>
> *Employment activity occurs on the reservation*
> *Indians are the employees*
>
> *Indians are the recipients of the health care, education, or commercial activity*

---

[85] *Snyder v. Navajo Nation*, 2004 WL 1277031 (9th Cir. 2004).
[86] *San Manuel Indian Bingo and Casino v. NLRB*, 475 F.3d 1306 (DC Cir. 2007);
[87] 2006 WL 2788494 (9th Cir. 2006). Also see, *Chao v. Spokane Tribe of Indians*, CV-07-0354-CI (E.D. Wash. March 5, 2008) (adopts the *Allen* analysis in rejecting application of the FLSA to a tribal gaming enterprise).
[88] The Indian Gaming Regulatory Act and more specifically 25 U.S.C. §2701 (4); §2702 (1).

Tribal funds are used to pay the employees

Employees are employed for a governmental purpose (health care, education)

Factors weighted toward commercial enterprise and application of federal law (NLRA applies) are

Employment activity occurs off the reservation

Non-Indians/nonmembers are the employees

Non-Indian recipients of the health care, education, or commercial activity

Nontribal funds are used to pay the employees

Employees are employed in a tribal business

Beyond these basic elements, tribes argue for a more in-depth analysis of the activity before declaring application of the federal employment law. At first glance, tribal gaming appears to be inconsistent with the tribes' essential government function. Tribal gaming, so the argument goes, is big business and big business is not government. However, a more in-depth analysis reveals that tribes use gaming revenues for governmental purposes like education, health care, and housing. Likewise, states which engage in gaming, and most participate at least through the lottery, do not sacrifice their sovereignty when the lottery generates revenues for education, health care, and housing. The state employee who works for the state-run lottery is subject to the state's rules while working for an employer, which generates money for the state government, and at no time does the state government lose its sovereignty by engaging in the same behavior which, for the tribes, exposes them to this government-enterprise analysis.

The idea that tribal casinos generate money, which permits tribal governments to address significant needs of their members, is underscored by a recent decision finding that the FLSA did not apply to a tribal casino. In *Chao v. Spokane Tribe of Indians*,[89] the court framed the question of whether the regulation of casino employees clearly implicates the tribe's inherent powers of self-government and regulation of intramural matters. In response to the question, the court reasoned that the employment relationship with casino employees is an exercise of self-governance—pointing to the tribe hiring and licensing employees, the consensual nature of the relationship, the casino is owned and operated by the tribe—is in part a product of a government-to-government compact; and the revenues support the economic viability of the tribe. The court further reasoned that application of the FLSA would have significantly more impact on tribal revenue and on the tribe than the intrusion imposed by the application of the NLRA's collective bargaining rules. The court succinctly found

> the Casino is not a mere revenue-producing tribal business. It is created and operated for the primary purpose of supporting the Tribe's government and governmental services. (Internal quotations omitted.)

The *Chao* court emphasized the integration of government and business in its in-depth analysis of whether the tribal casino is an essential governmental function. The employer-employee relationship is between a government and an individual—the employee is free to work for the tribal government or choose another employer, the tribal government licenses the employee, the tribal government compacts with the state to provide a portion of the gaming where the employee works, and the casino revenues are spent by the government on programs which benefit the people the government serves. The court found an abundance of governmental action and concluded it was important to the political integrity of the tribe. On this basis, the magistrate judge rejected application of the FLSA to this tribal employer, but the magistrate's recommendation was rejected by the court which refused to quash the subpoena demanding records relating to an investigation relating to allegations of a violation of federal wage and hour law.

The importance of tribal self-determination and economic development is reinforced by the United States Supreme Court. Self-determination is not

---

[89] *Chao v. Spokane Tribe of Indians*, CV-07-0354-CI (March 5, 2008) (Report and Recommendation for Order Granting Respondent's Motion to Quash, Denying Petition for Enforcement of Subpoena and Dismissing Petition). *Chao v. Spokane Tribe of Indians*, 2008 LEXIS 72687 (E.D.Wa. 2008).

achieved unless the tribe can raise capital and employ tribal members.[90] The generation of revenues from tribal enterprise and the employment of tribal members in the operation of these economic activities are crucial in the achievement of economic self-sufficiency. Eroding tribal self-sufficiency through the application of federal law is inconsistent with these goals.

There are numerous cases which reach the opposite conclusion and hold that when the tribal government engages in business and that business attracts patrons and employees from off the reservation, federal employment laws apply. For example, *San Manuel Indian Bingo and Casino v. NLRB (San Manuel)*[91] held that the National Labor relations Act (NLRA) applies to tribes. A union complained that this California tribe operating a gaming enterprise committed an unfair labor practice in violation of the NLRA by preferring one union over another. In evaluating whether the federal NLRA, which is silent on applicability, should apply to this tribal employer, the court in *San Manuel* evaluated whether its gaming enterprise was an essential government function. If the gaming enterprise was an essential government function, the first *Donovan* exception could apply in making the NLRA moot. The court noted governmental action by the tribe by finding that the government enacted a law which permitted the gaming and negotiated with another sovereign (California) to engage in Las Vegas-style (IGRA's class III) gaming. The court also observed nongovernmental activities by concluding that the gaming was primarily commercial, not a traditional attribute of self-government; the patrons and employees were not members of the tribe; and under the tribal-state compact the tribe enacted a labor law. In a turning point in the decision, the court found:

> the total impact on tribal sovereignty at issue here amounts to some unpredictable, but probably modest, effect on tribal revenue and the displacement of legislative and executive authority that is secondary to a commercial undertaking. We do not think this limited impact is sufficient to demand a restrictive construction of the NLRA.

---

[90] *California v. Cabazon Band of Mission Indians*, 480 U.S. 202 (1987).

[91] *San Manuel Indian Bingo and Casino v. NLRB*, 475 F.3d 1306 (DC Cir. 2007); *Sac and Fox Industries, Ltd.*, 307 NLRB 241 (1992)(NLRA applies to off-reservation tribal enterprises)

Cases evaluating whether *Donovan*'s first exception applies engage in a factual analysis to determine if the employer's activity is an essential government function, which focuses on the tribe's conduct, the source of monies used, location of the activity, and the nature of the employees involved in the entity's function. If the weight of these factors favors the conclusion that the entity is performing an essential government function, the federal law may not apply. On the other hand, if the facts show that the weight of the evidence does not reveal an essential government function, the federal law more than likely applies.

The treaty exception to application of federal law

The second *Donovan* exception finds federal law does not apply to tribal employers when a treaty intervenes. The Tenth Circuit Court of Appeals used the Cherokee Nation's treaty to relieve the tribe of an obligation to respond to an EEOC subpoena in an age discrimination case.[92] The court found that the ADEA was not applicable to this tribal employer because its enforcement would directly interfere with the tribe's treaty-protected right of self-government.

> Article V of the Treaty of New Echota, December 29, 1835, 7 Stat. 478, provides in pertinent part: The United States hereby covenant and agree . . . [to] *secure to the Cherokee Nation the right by their national councils to make and carry into effect all such laws as they may deem necessary for the government and protection of the persons and property within their own country* belonging to their people or such persons as have connected themselves with them; provided always that they shall not be inconsistent with the constitution of the United States and such acts of Congress as have been or may be passed regulating trade intercourse with the Indians . . . .[93]

This Tenth Circuit decision also has an interesting discussion of the role of the canons of construction in the absence of specific legislative language, memorializing an exercise of the federal government's plenary power.

---

[92] *EEOC v. Cherokee Nation*, 871 F.2d 937 (10th Cir. 1989).
[93] Id.

Courts have rejected the use of treaties to preclude application of federal employment law under *Tuscarora-Donovan*. In *Smart v. State Farm Insurance Company*,[94] the Seventh Circuit Court of Appeals found that a treaty, which set aside the reservation for the tribe's use, did not preclude the application of a federal employment insurance benefits law (ERISA) to the tribal employer. Likewise, in *United States Department of Labor v. Occupational Safety and Health Review Commission*[95] the Ninth Circuit Court of Appeals rejected use of the *Donovan* treaty exception based upon a treaty, which permitted the tribe to exclude persons from the reservation. The court held that the exclusion language did not exclude federal employment safety laws (OSHA).

The legislative history exception to application of federal law

The third *Donovan* exception directs a review of legislative history to determine whether Congress, when enacting legislation, intended for application of the legislation to tribes. Courts rely on this exception less than the other exceptions set forth in *Donovan*.[96]

Can tribes rely on the *Tuscarora-Donovan* analysis?

Not only do *Tuscarora* and *Donovan* stand for contradictory principles, the law regarding precedent impacts the risks associated with reliance on the *Tuscarora-Donovan* analysis. Reliance on the *Donovan* reasoning is cautioned by (1) recognizing it is a lower court decision which creates exceptions to a higher court (Supreme Court) decision in *Tuscarora*, (2) courts in other circuits are not controlled by this Ninth Circuit decision, and (3) the Supreme Court can accept or reject the *Donovan* exceptions if a case reaches the Supreme Court for review. Each of these reasons is explained in turn.

The *Donovan* court creates exceptions to a general rule articulated by a higher court, and therefore, reliance on *Donovan* may present a risk. There are three procedural steps for a case in the federal court system. The first step is

---

[94] 868 F.2d 929 (7th Cir. 1989).
[95] 935 F.2d 182 (9th Cir. 1991).
[96] *Lumber Industry Pension Fund v. Warm Springs Forest Products Industries*, 939 F.2d 683 (9th Cir. 1991).

comprised of a district court where trials are conducted and a decision issued. The federal system's second step is comprised of area appellate courts called federal circuits, and the opportunity to appeal a district court decision to a circuit court is automatic if chosen by a party to the lawsuit. The third step in federal procedure permits parties to seek the right to appeal a decision from the circuit courts to the United States Supreme Court. Thousands of requests a year are filed by circuit court litigants but only a few cases are accepted by the Supreme Court.[97]

The *Donovan* analysis is generally accepted by other circuit courts, but those courts are not obligated to follow *Donovan*. A decision of a circuit court provides controlling precedent for only those courts in that circuit and in future cases in that circuit. Accordingly, the Ninth Circuit's *Donovan* decision controls only those courts located in the Ninth Circuit and in future Ninth Circuit cases. The other circuits, and the courts in those circuits, are not obligated to follow the *Donovan* precedent. Nevertheless, several other circuits have adopted the *Donovan* analysis.

Another uncertainty in *Donovan* reliance is recognizing that the law can change course quickly if the Supreme Court receives an opportunity to evaluate the law. If the Supreme Court accepts an appeal from the circuit courts, the Supreme Court decision controls the law in all federal courts (district courts and circuit courts). Accordingly, the law could change with a Supreme Court decision on the issue. If the Supreme Court gets an opportunity to evaluate the merit of *Donovan*, the Court could affirm, reject, or modify its principles. When the Court articulates a standard, it controls all federal courts.

There is another line of reasoning which is more respectful of tribal sovereignty and history. Instead of starting from the *Tuscarora* premise that federal law applies and only if one or more of the *Donovan* exceptions apply is there a reason to exclude federal law, tribes argue the opposite. Start with the premise that tribes define the rules and only apply federal law if Congress has clearly declared the statute's applicability. The ambiguity of congressional silence must

---

[97] The United States Supreme Court 2007 Year-End Report revealed 8,521 filings in 2005 and 8,857 in 2006 while in 2006 the Court heard seventy-eight cases and disposed of seventy-four.

favor the tribes since ambiguous statutes are read in the light most favorable to the tribes.[98] This analysis brings more clarity to employers and employees and more respect to the sovereignty of tribes. The speculation necessary to determine applicability of federal law under *Tuscarora-Donovan* serves no rational constituency.

The *Tuscarora-Donovan* analysis is not the only path taken by courts in evaluating whether federal laws, silent on applicability, apply to tribes. Some courts have focused on tribes as sovereigns and tribal interest in self-determination. For example, in *Taylor v. Ala. Intertribal Council Title IV JTPA*,[99] the court precluded the employee's claim based upon the tribes' strong interest in self-government. The *Taylor* Court cited *Morton v. Mancari*,[100] wherein the United States Supreme Court recognized that an *Indian tribe's strong interest in internal self-government* prevents parties from raising employment discrimination claims alleging injury from the use of Indian preferences for jobs when the federal government administrates Indian affairs.

Likewise, in *NLRB v. Pueblo of San Juan*[101] the court reasoned that the silence of Congress regarding applicability to tribes "is insufficient to establish an abrogation of traditional sovereign authority." The court also noted Congress's specific exemption of applicability to tribes in Title VII and observed that Congress has the means of raising its hand and declaring the target of its law. When Congress declares its laws apply to tribes, the law applies; or when Congress declares inapplicability (Title VII), the law does not apply. The *San Juan* court says it well:

> The exclusion of Indian tribes from the employment discrimination statutes illustrates congressional intent not to interfere in employee-management disputes on reservations. In *EEOC v. Cherokee*

---

[98] *County of Yakima v. Confederated Tribes & Bands of the Yakima Indian Nation*, 502 U.S. 251, 268 (1992); *EEOC v. Cherokee Nation*, 871 F.2d 937 (10th Cir. 1989).

[99] 261 F.3d 1032, 1035-36 (11th Cir. 2001) (tribal employer insulated from employment discrimination claim under 42 U.S.C. § 1981).

[100] 417 U.S. 535, 551-555, 94 S.Ct. 2474, 41 L.Ed.2d 290 (1974).

[101] 280 F.3d 1278 (10th Cir. 2000)

Nation,[102] we considered the ADEA, which is silent as to tribes, and Title VII, which excludes tribes, and concluded that the close relationship of these statutes indicates that Congress did not intend for the ADEA to apply to tribes; absent express statutory inclusion.

The United States Supreme Court has reinforced this argument by finding that clear expression of congressional intent is necessary before construing a statute applicable to a tribe.[103] Starting from the premise that the law does not apply unless and until Congress declares application appeals to common sense and sovereignty.

Moreover, the argument that following *Tuscarora's* dictates of general applicability is diminished by an understanding of how courts write decisions. The general applicability language in *Tuscarora* was in the discussion part and not in the part where the court set forth its decision (holding) on the issue. Dictum is that portion of the written decision where courts discuss their analysis before getting to the bottom line. *Dictum* or *obiter dictum* is Latin for "a remark by the way." The bottom line of a written judicial decision is its holding. The holding expresses the rule of law in the case while obiter dictum explains the reasoning. *Tuscarora's* "general applicability" dictum was not necessary to the holding because the statute in question (Federal Power Act) specifically addressed tribes, and therefore congressional intent could be measured in statutory language, making the announcement of a general rule applying to all statues unnecessary.

Even if *Tuscarora* is diminished, until a clearer test is established the *Tuscarora-Donovan* analysis is the legal analysis followed. Several circuits have adopted the reasoning set forth in *Donovan*. Below is a categorical overview of some of the decisions using the *Tuscarora-Donovan* analysis to assess whether federal employment law applies to tribal employers.

Does the National Labor Relations Act (NLRA) apply to tribal employers?

The NLRA does not declare applicability or nonapplicability to tribal employers so therefore, its text is silent on applicability. In determining

---

[102] 871 F.2d 937 (10th Cir. 1989).
[103] *White Mountain Apache Tribe v. Bracker*, 448 U.S. 136 (1980).

whether it applies, courts apply the factors raised in the *Tuscarora-Donovan* analysis. The NLRA is a depression-era law, which formulates rules relating to the collective bargaining process between an employer and a representative of the employees. The NLRA therefore addresses the relationship between an employer and union or unions representing some or a majority of the workforce.

The success and growth of tribal gaming has highlighted the question of whether the NLRA applies to tribal employers. A tribal gaming trade group calculates several hundred thousand employees work in tribal casinos.[104] For decades, the National Labor Relations Board, the federal agency in charge of enforcing the NLRA, declared the NLRA inapplicable to tribes.[105] A change in that position has generated a fair amount of litigation.[106]

The case which generated significant attention is *San Manuel Indian Bingo and Casino v. NLRB (San Manuel)*,[107] which held the NLRA applies to tribes. A union complained that this tribe, operating a gaming enterprise, committed an unfair labor practice in violation of the NLRA by preferring one union over another. In evaluating whether the federal NLRA—which is silent on applicability—should apply to this tribal employer, the court in *San Manuel* evaluated whether its gaming enterprise was an essential government function. If the gaming enterprise was an essential government function, the first *Donovan* exception could apply in making the NLRA moot. The court noted governmental action by the tribe in finding the government enacted a law which permitted the gaming and negotiated with another sovereign

---

[104] See, National Indian Gaming Association's *www.indiangaming.org*.

[105] *Fort Apache Timber Co.*, 226 N.L.R.B. 503 (1976)(NLRB ruled tribal business a subdivision of the United States and therefore outside the scope of the NLRA).

[106] *San Manuel Indian Bingo and Casino v. NLRB*, 475 F.3d 1306 (DC Cir. 2007); Sac & Fox Industries, Ltd., 307 N.L.R.B. 241 (1992)(NLRA applies to off-reservation tribal enterprises); See also, *Yukon Kuskokwim Health Corp.*, 328 N.L.R.B. 761 (1999)(off reservation health care facility operated by tribal consortium). *NLRB v. Chapa De Indian Health Program, Inc.*, 316 F.3d 995 (9th Cir.2003)

[107] *San Manuel Indian Bingo and Casino v. NLRB*, 475 F.3d 1306 (DC Cir. 2007)

(California) to engage in Las Vegas-style (IGRA's class III) gaming. The court also observed nongovernmental activities by concluding the gaming was primarily commercial, not a traditional attribute of self-government; the patrons and employees were not members of the tribe; and under the tribal-state compact, the tribe enacted a labor law. In a turning point in the decision, the court found the total impact on tribal sovereignty at issue here amounts to some unpredictable, but probably modest, effect on tribal revenue and the displacement of legislative and executive authority that is secondary to a commercial undertaking.

The court found that the tribe's commercial activity trumped the tribe's essential governmental function and, once the court reached this conclusion, the issue was decided. This conclusion by the court is a "tell" which defined its reasoning. In poker, a "tell" is a habit which permits the other players to discern whether your all-in bet is the sign of a strong hand or a bluff. The *San Manuel* court bet the pot with this statement, which revealed its strongly held opinion that the NLRA applied to the gaming enterprise.

Tribes are taking proactive steps to address the issues raised in *San Manuel*. In response, tribal employers are

1. Promulgating employment laws which exercise the tribe's sovereignty and self-determination in the employment arena.

There are arguments for and against the application of federal employment laws to tribal employers. As these arguments do not present a definitive answer to the question, tribal exercise of authority in the employment arena defines the tribe's view under the law.

2. Reviewing solicitation policies and practices, which may impact the reach of unions attempting to organize tribal employees.

Permitting employees and vendors to sell cookies and knives in the workplace enables the argument from unions that equal access to employees is consistent with federal law.

3. Drafting right-to-work ordinances, which give employees the right to join or decline joining a union, recognized as the bargaining agent.

Tribal governments may promulgate laws, which relieve employees of the obligation to join a union which bargains on behalf of the employees.[108] This principle is referred to as right to work, which declares that no person shall be required as a condition of employment to join or financially support a union representing employees.

4. Determining where the tribe exceeds expectations in wages and benefits and sharing the information with employees.

Tribal employers are frequently the employer of choice in the area because of the competitive wages and benefits provided to employees.[109] Furthermore, providing meaningful due process through grievance and complaint procedures educates employers regarding areas of potential improvement in the work environment. Communicating these benefits to employees generates gratitude for the tribal employer.

5. Emphasizing and reinforcing the safety programs utilized by tribal employers.

Workplace safety is an employer's imperative which, if not satisfied, will be an issue used by prospective unions to generate support from employees.

6. Modifying gaming commission regulations to address the licensure of unions and their representatives.

Gaming regulators license employees, gaming enterprises, and vendors. Some gaming regulators are requiring unions to seek and obtain a license as the employee's representative.

---

[108] This is an exercise of inherent sovereignty which happens to be endorsed by a federal court at *NLRB v. Pueblo of San Juan*, 276 F.3d 1186 (10th Cir. 2002). The Ho-Chunk Nation promulgated right to work in its employment laws. Ho-Chunk Nation Personnel, Employment and Labor Code, chapter 1, section 6(f) (appendix A).

[109] See the significant benefits provided by the Ho-Chunk Nation. Ho-Chunk Nation Personnel, Employment and Labor Code, chapter 4, section 16, 17, 18, 19, 20, 21, 22, 23, 24, 25, 26, 27, 28 (appendix A). The employee benefits section of the law consumes seventeen pages of law (not including wages) and provides world-class benefits.

7. Reinforcing the jurisdictional powers of the employer.

The delegation of authority to tribal courts to hear employment-related claims and the consent of employees and others to the tribal court's jurisdiction is important.

Application of the NLRA will continue to generate attention for collective bargaining reasons and for the broader application question of federal law.

Does the Fair Labor Standards Act (FLSA) apply to tribal employers?

The FLSA is a federal statute, which combines five federal laws addressing issues like child labor, equal pay, minimum wage, and overtime compensation. The FLSA does not, in its text, define its applicability to tribal employers; however, courts have evaluated the question. FLSA is a law of general applicability,[110] and therefore, the *Tuscarora-Donovan* analysis defines applicability to tribal employers. Whether federal employment laws apply to tribal employers is a function of the facts and the court's interpretation of the law.

In a case involving tribal police officers,[111] the court concluded that the FLSA did not apply. In this case, the court observed that the FLSA contains an express exemption for state and local law-enforcement officers. Since law enforcement is an essential governmental function, the FLSA did not apply even when tribal police officers left the reservation to assist with judicial proceedings.

In *Reich v. Great Lakes Indian Fish and Wildlife Commission*,[112] the federal Department of Labor attempted to enforce a subpoena under the auspices of the authority granted by the FLSA and more specifically its overtime compensation provision, which requires employers to pay certain employees one and one-half times the employee's hourly rate in excess of a forty-hour workweek. The employer, the Great Lakes Indian Fish and Wildlife Commission is a consortium of thirteen tribes. The commission was created by the member tribes to protect the tribes' treaty rights. The

---

[110] *Rutherford Food Corp. v. McComb*, 331 U.S. 722 (1947).
[111] *Snyder v. Navajo Nation*, 2004 WL 1277031 (9th Cir. 2004).
[112] 4 F.3d 490 (footnote: 7th Cir. 1993)

employees in question performed a number of functions including the protection of treaty rights, enforcement of limitations imposed upon hunting and gathering under the treaties, and protection of the tribal members exercising these rights. The commission employees were also cross-deputized under state law. The Department of Labor conceded that had the employees been state workers, calculation of overtime would have been under a formula which accounted for the concentrated long hours worked by employees during the hunting and gathering seasons; but since the FLSA did not mention tribal employers, the exemption which permitted this more flexible calculation of overtime, the tribal employer could not benefit from the exemption. The steep challenge for the DOL in its analysis is arguing for application of the law when the text is silent and using that silence to penalize the tribe from exercising a statutory exemption. Congress's failure to mention tribes in the statute was a signal that the law was not intended to apply to tribes.

In addition to the facts in the case, the Court took comity into account in evaluating whether the FLSA applied to commission employees. Comity requires sovereigns to treat other sovereigns with respect, which requires the exercise of forbearance in applying federal law to the central regulatory functions of a tribe. In so many words, the Court recognizes and respects tribal exercise of self-determination and its necessary corollary sovereignty.

The Court also noted and rejected the DOL's argument that payment of overtime necessarily benefits employees. The Court observed that by requiring the payment of overtime compensation, it increases the cost of labor which may cause "disemployment." Additionally, the Court rejected the idea that a failure to pay overtime evidences the commission's disloyalty to its employees. These paternalistic assertions are based upon the premise that Congress knows better than tribal governments.

The Court limited its holding to law enforcement employees performing governmental functions. *Reich* does not hold that the FLSA does not apply to tribal employers. Instead, *Reich* holds that the FLSA does not require the payment of overtime to employees of tribes furthering the government functions of the tribe or, in this case, tribes. Interestingly, *Reich* involves commission employees who spent considerable time off reservation in the performance of their duties.

In *Chao v. Matheson*,[113] the court evaluated whether the FLSA applies to an on-reservation private business owned by a member of the tribe. The business owners argued that the payment of wages is intramural to the tribe and should be subject to tribal, not federal, law. Based upon *Donovan* language, the *Chao* court rejected the argument drawing on the idea that commercial activity does not fit within the intramural exception. The business owners cited two cases[114] arguing where a treaty exists between a tribe and the federal government, unless Congress expressly applies federal law to tribes there is a valid presumption that the law does not apply to the "treaty tribe."[115] The court rejected the treaty argument and found the FLSA applicable to this on-reservation private business. Interestingly, the court noted that unlike *NLRB v. Pueblo of San Juan*,[116] the tribe had not enacted a law, which competed with the federal law, so therefore an act of the tribal government was not at issue. Had the tribe enacted a wage law, it may have created an obstacle for the court to consider consistent with *Donovan*'s essential government function exception.

In a casino case a federal judge rejected a magistrate's conclusion that the FLSA does not apply. In *Chao v. Spokane Tribe of Indians*,[117] the magistrate framed the question of whether the regulation of casino employees clearly implicates the tribe's inherent powers of self-government and regulation of intramural matters. In response to the question, the magistrate reasoned that the employment relationship with casino employees is an exercise of

---

[113] 2007 W.L. 1830738 (W.D. Wash. 2007)
[114] *United States v. Lara*, 541 U.S. 193 (2004); *National Labor Relations Board v. Pueblo of San Juan*, 276 F.3d 1186 (10th Cir. 2002).
[115] This argument is logically appealing since tribes are sovereign, the federal government may exercise its plenary power and a general assumption that its laws not only apply generally but also to the tribes all but removes the sovereign-to-sovereign relationship between tribes and the federal government.
[116] 280 F.3d 1278 (10th Cir. 2000)
[117] *Chao v. Spokane Tribe of Indians*, CV-07-0354-CI (March 5, 2008) (Report and Recommendation for Order Granting Respondent's Motion to Quash, Denying Petition for Enforcement of Subpoena and Dismissing Petition). The district court judge rejected the magistrate's recommendation and enforced the subpoena. 2008 U.S. Dist. LEXIS 72687 (September 24, 2008). Also see, *Lobo v. Miccosukee Tribe of Indians of Florida*, 2008 WL 2222074 (11th Cir. 2008) (FLSA does not apply).

self-governance, pointing to the tribe hiring and licensing the employees, the consensual nature of the relationship, the casino is owned and operated by the tribe, is in part a product of a government-to-government compact, and the revenues support the economic viability of the tribe. The magistrate further reasoned that application of the FLSA would have significantly more impact on tribal revenue and on the tribe than the intrusion imposed by the application of the NLRA's collective bargaining rules. The magistrate succinctly found the Casino is not a mere revenue producing tribal business. It is created and operated for the primary purpose of supporting the Tribe's government and governmental services. (Internal quotations omitted).

The *Tuscarora-Donovan* analysis forces the analysis of a variety of facts in determining whether a tribal employer is government or commercial in nature. How much weight is given to a fact versus another heavily impacts the court's decision.

In *Chao v. Spokane Tribe of Indians*, the purpose of the gaming enterprise weighed heavily in the magistrate's final analysis. The magistrate noted that the employer-employee relationship was between a government and an individual; the employee was free to work for the tribal government or choose another employer, the tribal government licenses employees, the tribal government compacted with the state to provide a portion of the gaming where the employee works, and the casino revenues were spent by the government in programs, which benefit the people the government serves. The magistrate found an abundance of government action and concluded this action was important to the political integrity of the tribe, but the district court judge quashed the magistrate's recommendation.

Does the Family and Medical Leave Act (FMLA) apply to tribal employers?

The FMLA provides unpaid leave to employees when a child is added to the family or the employee, or her family, encounters a serious health condition. FMLA is required of companies which employ more than fifty employees[118] but only for those employees who are employed for more

---

[118] 29 U.S.C. § 2611(4) (i).

than a year, and work in excess of 1,250 hours.[119] When these thresholds are reached, the employees are entitled to twelve weeks of unpaid leave for defined medical conditions and for the birth or adoption of a child. Qualified employees receive leave for their own medical issues and those of their children, spouses, and parents. FMLA's goal is to balance the demands of the workplace with the needs of families, to promote the stability and economic security of families, and to promote national interests in preserving family integrity.[120] Consistent with this goal, employees returning from leave are entitled to the job they worked before the leave, and the employer is obligated to maintain pre-leave health benefits.

FMLA has generated controversy over the years. Employers complain that employees abuse FMLA by claiming vague and chronic maladies, and employees respond by claiming that employers are scrutinizing leave requests by forcing employees to obtain second and third medical opinions to support these medical requests.[121] Within tribal government, the question is whether the FMLA applies, and if so, how much more is expected of the tribal employer when the leave request is presented. The question is relevant since tribal employers are known to provide liberal leave for employees for a wide range of purposes. Many tribes grant bereavement, cultural, religious, military, disability, and education leave. Tribes oftentimes grant leave covered by FMLA whether the federal law applies or not.

When promulgating FMLA, Congress was silent on the applicability question and did not declare FMLA applicable to tribes. Congressional silence extended to its failure to explicitly declare the law inapplicable to tribes. Accordingly, the *Tuscarora-Donovan* analysis is used to determine whether tribal employers must adhere to its leave requirements.

An agency of the federal government believes FMLA applies to tribes.[122] The federal government's Department of Labor, which is responsible for enforcing

---

[119] 29 U.S.C. § 2611(2).
[120] 29 U.S.C. § 2601 (b)(1).
[121] *Wall Street Journal*, November 21, 2007 "Is Family Leave Act Too Soft or Too Tough?"
[122] Department of Labor asserts applicability at 60 C.F.R. 2181.

FMLA, asserts that FMLA applies to tribal employers and the DOL can enforce the law. The Supreme Court has already addressed FMLA's impact on state employers. States can assert immunity to FMLA self-care suits,[123] but not to the family care provisions in the law.[124]

The Second Circuit has ruled that tribal casino employers are immune from a claim under the FMLA even when the tribal employer consented to FMLA application in the employee handbook. An employee of a tribal casino had approved leave to care for a family member and upon return from the leave, he was terminated. The case was thoroughly litigated,[125] and in each, the employee asserted that through the tribe's adoption of the FMLA in its employee handbook as company policy, the tribe consented to be "subjected" to the remedies under the FMLA. The courts rejected the assertion by finding the inclusion of FMLA rights in a handbook, not a clear waiver of immunity.[126] In another East Coast case, the federal court rejected these same arguments and the additional assertion that a tribe's limited waiver of immunity between itself and the state in a gaming compact created a waiver of immunity as to employee-plaintiffs.[127] The FMLA was also addressed in a case raising the tribal court exhaustion doctrine.[128]

The tribe's version of FMLA was the subject of *Barthelet v. Mashantucket Pequot Gaming Enterprise*[129] wherein the tribal court rejected an employee's argument that time-out on worker's compensation leave could be used to qualify the employee for the 1,250-hour threshold required under the tribe's leave law.

The FMLA was applied to a private management contractor operating a tribal gaming enterprise. A federal district court permitted a FMLA claim

---

[123] *McKlintic v. 36th Judicial Circuit Court*, 508 F.3d 875 (8th Cir. 2007).
[124] *Nevada Department of Human Resources v. Hibbs*, 538 U.S. 721 (2003).
[125] *Chayoon v. Reels*, 3-02CV1358 (JCH)(D.Conn. March 12, 2003); *Chayoon v. Chao*, 355 F.3d 141 (2d Cir. 2004); *Chayoon v. Sherlock*, 89 Conn. App. 821 (Conn. App. 2005).
[126] Id.
[127] *Myers v. Seneca Niagara Casino*, 488 F.Supp.2d 166 (NDNY, 2006).
[128] *Sharber v. Spirit Mountain Gaming, Inc.*, 343 F.3d 974 (9th Cir. 2003).
[129] 33 ILR 6061 (Mash.Tr.Ct. 2006).

in *Johnson v. Harrah's Kansas Casino Corp.*[130] wherein Harrah's executed a contract with the Prairie Band Potawatomi, which permitted Harrah's to manage the tribal gaming enterprise in exchange for a fee. The question presented by the case was whether the tribe's sovereign immunity extended to and protected Harrah's. Harrah's argued *Indian Country, U.S.A. Inc. v. Oklahoma ex rel. Oklahoma Tax Commission*[131] wherein a federal court found that tribal sovereign immunity protected a tribal gaming enterprise operated by a nontribal entity.

The *Johnson* court reasoned that for sovereign immunity to apply, Harrah's had to be a subordinate economic entity to the tribe. In ruling whether Harrah's was a subordinate economic entity of the Prairie Band Potawatomi, the court evaluated numerous factors:

1. the announced purpose for which the entity was formed,
2. whether the entity was managed to form or exploit specific tribal resources,
3. whether federal policy designed to protect Indian assets and tribal cultural autonomy is furthered by the extension of sovereign immunity to the entity,
4. whether the entity is organized under the tribe's laws or constitution rather than federal law,
5. whether the entity's governing body is comprised mainly of tribal officials,
6. whether the tribe has legal title or ownership of the property used by the entity,
7. whether tribal officials exercise control over the administration or accounting activities of the organization,
8. whether the tribe's governing body has power to dismiss members of the organization's governing body,
9. whether the entity generates its own revenue,
10. whether a suit against the entity would impact the tribe's fiscal resources and whether it may bind or obligate tribal funds.

---

[130] 2006 WL 463138 (D.Kan. 2006)
[131] 829 F.2d 967 (10th Cir.1987), cert. denied, *Okla. Tax Comm'n v. Muscogee (Creek) Nation*, 487 U.S. 1218, 108 S.Ct. 2870 (1988).

The court placed paramount importance on the tenth factor. In evaluating all of the factors, the Court found against Harrah's ability to assert the defense of sovereign immunity.

In another Harrah's case, the court addressed the intersection between tribe-specific preference and the FMLA. In this tribal gaming case where some of the casino employees were transitioned from the management company to employees of the tribe, there was an employee on leave who was given the opportunity to apply for a new position but neglected to apply. The employee on leave did not apply because he anticipated that the open position would be filled by a tribal member under the tribe's preference policy. An employer is not required to grant an employee an FMLA leave "any right, benefit, or position to which the employee would have been entitled to, had [he] never taken leave."[132] Therefore, an employer has no duty to restore an employee to his previous leave if it can prove that the employee would have been removed from that position if he had not taken the protected leave.

Does the Age Discrimination Employment Act (ADEA) apply to tribal employers?

Federal law prohibits age discrimination through a couple statutes. The ADEA[133] applies to employers, employment agencies, and labor organizations. The Age Discrimination Act of 1975[134] prohibits age discrimination in those entities accepting federal funds. The definition of employer in Title VII and ADEA are nearly identical except that Title VII, which was enacted before ADEA, excepts tribal employers.

Federal law limits when employers may take age into account when making employment-related decisions. ADEA is silent on applicability; therefore, courts use *Tuscarora-Donovan* to answer the applicability question. Courts considering application of the ADEA to tribal employers have rejected application.[135]

---

[132] 29 U.S.C. §2614 (a) (3) (B); *Yashenko v. Harrah's NC Casino Company*, LLC, 352 F. Supp. 2d 653, 657 (W.D.N.C. 2005).

[133] 29 U.S.C. § 621-34.

[134] 42 U.S.C. § 6101-07.

[135] In *EEOC v. Fond du Lac Heavy Equipment & Construction Co.* 986 F.2d 246 (8th Cir. 1993)(focused on general sovereignty principles); *EEOC v. Cherokee*

In *EEOC v. Fond du Lac Heavy Equipment and Construction Company, Inc.*, the Eighth Circuit Court of Appeals found the employment dispute to be internal to the tribe since, in part, the employee was a member of the tribe, and the employer enterprise was located on the reservation. Whether the employee's age is a relevant consideration should be determined by reflecting on the tribe's rules, and therefore, application of the federal age discrimination law would dilute tribal sovereignty.

After citing *Fond du Lac* the Ninth Circuit in *EEOC v. Karuk Tribe Housing*,[136] held the federal age law did not apply to this internal matter to the tribe, which related to the tribe's self-governance. The court noted that the employer was the government, providing homes for members, under the auspices of a federal program, which recognized self-determination and self-governance.

In *EEOC v. Cherokee Nation*,[137] the Tenth Circuit found the ADEA a statute of general applicability, which did not apply to tribes because Congress did not clearly exercise its authority to impose the law on tribal governments. The absence of a declaration of applicability of federal law to tribes endorses the presumption of nonapplicability. This general rule wrenches out of the analysis some of the uncertainty associated with determining whether federal law applies.

However, in *Cano v. Cocopah Casino*,[138] the district court permitted a pro se[139] plaintiff to amend the complaint holding the ADEA may apply since a commercial venture that provides services in the open market and employs both tribal members and non-Indians is not government in action. Although the profits resulting from casino operations are presumably important to the tribe and provide funding for purely intramural matters, the actual operations and employment of workers at the Casino do not appear to touch on any "exclusive rights of self-governance in purely intramural matters." The court

---

Nation, 871 F.2d 937 (10th Cir.1989)(federal law does not apply because of treaty language); *EEOC v. Karuk Tribe Housing Authority*, 260 F.3d 1071 (9th Cir. 2001); *Curtis v. Sandia Casino*, 2003 WL 21386332 (10th Cir. 2003).

[136] 260 F.3d 1071 (9th Cir. 2001).
[137] 871 F.2d 937, 938 (10th Cir.1989)
[138] 2007 WL 2164555 (D. Ariz. 2007).
[139] Party not represented by a lawyer in the proceedings.

found that the casino appears to function "simply as a business entity that happens to be run by a tribe or its members."

Do Sections 1981, 1983, and 1985 apply to tribal employers?

During the Civil War era, Congress enacted several laws protecting newly freed slaves from discriminatory treatment. These laws include Section 1983,[140] which prohibits violations of federal constitutional protections by persons acting under color of state law; Section 1981,[141] which prohibits race discrimination in contracts; and Section 1985,[142] which prohibits conspiracies to deprive individuals of equal protection under the law. Tribes, tribal officials, and subdivisions of tribal governments are not subject to suit under these laws.[143] Unless acting in concert with state officials, Indian authorities cannot be said to act "under color of state law" because tribes are not states.[144]

Does the Occupational Safety and Health Act (OSHA) apply to tribal employers?

Federal law imposes safety standards for workers and whether federal safety laws or tribal safety laws apply to a tribal employer[145] is a function of the

---

[140] 42 U.S.C. § 1983

[141] 42 U.S.C. § 1981

[142] 42 U.S.C. § 1985

[143] *Nero v. Cherokee Nation of Oklahoma*, 892 F.2d 1457 (10th Cir. 1989) (tribe not subject to race discrimination claims under Sections 1981, 1985); *Wheeler v. Swimmer*, 835 F.2d 2569, 262 (10th Cir. 1987) (tribe not subject to claims under Section 1985 for alleged wrongful conduct of tribal election); *Wardle v. Ute Indian Tribe*, 623 F.2d 671 (10th Cir. 1980) (tribe not subject to Section 1981 claim for terminating white police officer); *Montgomery v. Flandreau Santee Sioux Tribe*, 905 F.Supp. 740, 745 (D.S.D. 1995) (tribe not subject to Section 1985 claim). But see, Allen v. Mayhew, 2008 WL 223662 (E.D.Cal. 2008)(alleged race discrimination suit not dismissed against certain individuals).

[144] See, *R.J. Williams v. Fort Belknap Housing Authority*, 719 F.2d 979, 982 (9th Cir. 1983). But see, Aleman v. Chugach, 43 I.L.R. 2141 (4th Cir. 2007).

[145] The Ho-Chunk Nation protects its employees under tribal law. Ho-Chunk Nation Personnel, Employment and Labor Code, Chapter 1, Section 6(c)(Appendix A).

Tuscarora-Donovan analysis. The *Donovan* part of the *Tuscarora-Donovan* analysis is an OSHA case where the Ninth Circuit held that OSHA applied after declaring that none of the exceptional circumstances existed.[146] The Ninth Circuit Court of Appeals again reached the same result six years later.[147]

The Tenth Circuit reached the opposite conclusion finding that OSHA did not apply to a tribal entity.[148] In a case which does not apply *Tuscarora-Donovan*, the Tenth Circuit Court of Appeals ruled that application of OSHA to a tribally owned on-reservation business violated the tribe's treaty rights.[149] The Court found that limitations on tribal self-government could not be implied, and since OSHA did not declare application to tribes, it did not. Additionally, the court noted the tribe's inherent right to exclude non-Indians from tribal lands is an inherent attribute of sovereignty.

Does the Employment Retirement Income Security Act (ERISA) apply to tribal employers?

ERISA is a federal law that sets minimum standards for most voluntarily established pension and health plans in private industry to provide protection for individuals in these plans. ERISA requires plans to provide participants with plan information including important information about plan features and funding, provides fiduciary responsibilities for those who manage and control plan assets, requires plans to establish a grievance and appeals process for participants to get benefits from their plans, and gives participants the right to sue for benefits and breaches of fiduciary duty.[150] The Seventh Circuit

---

[146] *Donovan v. Coeur d'Alene Tribal Farm*, 751 F.2d 1113 (9th Cir. 1985).

[147] *United States Department of Labor v. Occupational Safety & Health Review Commission*, 935 F.2d 182 (9th Cir. 1991)(OSHA applied to an on-reservation tribally owned timber mill which employed a significant number of non-Native Americans and sold its goods off reservation).

[148] *Reich v. Mashantucket Sand & Gravel*, 95 F.3d 174 (2nd Cir. 1996)(applying OSHA to a tribally owned business).

[149] *Donovan v. Navajo Forest Products Industries*, 692 F.2d 709 (10th Cir. 1982); Note this case predates *Donovan v. Coeur d'Alene Tribal Farm*, 751 F.2d 1113 (9th Cir. 1985).

[150] Summary of ERISA from the Department of Labor;

and Ninth Circuit have held that ERISA applies to tribal employers.[151] Other courts have reached the opposite conclusion.[152]

These decisions may have limited value as precedent since Congress amended ERISA under the Pension Protection Act of 2006. Under the law change, ERISA applies to tribes unless there is a separately established health plan for its employees performing essential governmental functions like police and firefighting. ERISA applies to plans, which apply broadly to employees who are engaged in commercial activity even if the commercial activity is an essential governmental function:

> The term "governmental plan" includes a plan which is established and maintained by an Indian tribal government (as defined in section 7701(a)(40) of Title 26), a subdivision of an Indian tribal government (determined in accordance with section 7871(d) of Title 26), or an agency or instrumentality of either, and all of the participants of which are employees of such entity substantially all of whose services as such an employee are in the performance of *essential governmental functions* but not in the performance of commercial activities (whether or not an essential government function).[153] (Emphasis added.)

Tribes are reviewing plan documents to determine compliance with ERISA and Internal Revenue Code compliance, understanding fiduciary

---

[151] *Smart v. State Farm Insurance*, 868 F.2d 929 (7th Cir. 1989); *Lumber Industry Pension Fund v. Warm Springs Forest Products Industries*, 939 F.2d 683 (9th Cir. 1991). In *Smart*, the court imposed a burden on the Chippewa tribe to demonstrate that application of ERISA on the tribe would modify a treaty right or statute or an essential tribal right of self-governance or intramural matter.

[152] *Colville Confederated Tribes v. Somday*, 96 F.Supp.2d 1120 (E. D. Wash, 2000); Also see *Prescott v. Little Six*, Inc., 387 F.3d 753, 757 (8th Cir. 2004) where the Eighth Circuit Court of Appeals directed dismissal of an ERISA claim when deferring to a tribal court holding that the retirement plans were not authorized under tribal law. The Court did not find ERISA inapplicable to this tribal employer. Rather, the Court held that the employer did not authorize establishment of the plan challenged under ERISA.

[153] 29 U.S.C. § 1002 (32).

responsibility as plan administrators, filing the required governmental reports and communicating with employees. Litigation has and will be generated addressing the reach of ERISA to tribal employers.[154]

Before the Pension Protection Act of 2006, ERISA was the subject in *Prescott v. Little Six*[155] wherein a tribe established a corporation responsible for operating on reservation tribal casinos. ERISA was the topic but deference to earlier tribal court factual findings played the central role in the case. Executives of the corporation drafted employee benefit plans but the plans were never formally approved. When the executives were replaced, the new Board of Directors specifically refused to adopt the draft plans. The tribal court dismissed plaintiffs' claims concluding that no plans existed under which plaintiffs could assert claims. Thereafter, plaintiffs filed an action in federal district court. The tribe presented three arguments in support of its motion to dismiss plaintiffs' suit: (1) the tribal corporation possesses sovereign immunity, (2) federal district court must defer to the tribal court's determination that no ERISA plans were created, and (3) the federal court lacks jurisdiction because ERISA does not apply to the tribal corporation. The Eighth Circuit concluded that the tribal court properly determined that the legal status of the tribal corporation's draft benefit plan was a question of tribal, not federal law. The tribal corporation is governed by tribal law, which permits tribal corporations to delineate operating rules in articles of incorporation wherein officer compensation may be fixed. Interpreting these rules, the tribal court determined that the corporation's board must approve of executive compensation, and the board did not approve of the compensation sought by the executives.

Can a tribe consent to the application of federal employment laws?

Yes. There are at least two gradations of this answer. The first gradation of this answer covers meaningful consent where tribes embrace federal employment law for the competitive reason of attracting workers who

---

[154] *Dobbs v. Anthem Blue Cross and Blue Shield*, 2007 WL 2439310 (D. Colo. 2007); on remand from 475 F.3d 1176 (10th Cir. 2007).

[155] 387 F.3d 753 (8th Cir.2004); Also see, *Koopman v. Forest county Potawatomi Member Benefit Plan*, 2006 WL 1785769 (E.D.Wis. 2006)(tribal court exhaustion doctrine triggered)

expect federal standards or because the federal government has articulated a fair standard, which should be replicated. For these reasons, tribes may voluntarily consent to the application of some or all of federal employment laws. Under the same reasoning, tribes could also voluntarily consent to the application of laws promulgated by other tribes, states, and other sovereigns.

The second gradation of this answer speaks to whether tribal consent to the application of federal law is real or a concession in a negotiation where bargaining power is stronger for the nontribal party. To the extent that a tribe consents to the application of federal employment laws in exchange for the receipt of federal monies, tribes are at a disadvantage because those federal funds are necessary to operate critical programs. Tribes also cry foul in these circumstances since under the trust relationship between tribes and the federal government, the monies should be forthcoming without any strings attached.

Likewise, in negotiating a gaming compact, states have required tribal adherence to federal and state employment laws, which is inconsistent with Indian Gaming Regulatory Act's requirement of good faith negotiation.[156] Under these circumstances, tribes do not consent in a meaningful way to the application of state employment laws, but instead tribes concede the point in exchange for the benefit of Las Vegas-style gaming. Emerging from this analysis is the conclusion that consent is not equal under all circumstances. What the law views as consent can be the voluntary and enthusiastic embrace of federal employment law, but on the other hand, consent can be the reluctant concession to a zealous state official requiring the application of federal law.

Whether following federal law follows an embrace or concession, the law enforces contractual obligations. Whether an enforceable obligation will overcome the assertion of immunity is another question, which is part of the ultimate analysis regarding culpability.

a. *Acceptance of federal funds*

There are more questions than answers to what happens if a tribe promises to follow federal employment laws in exchange for federal funds, and thereafter, the tribe breaks its promise or is alleged to have broken its promise. The

---

[156] 25 U.S.C. § 2710 (d)(3)(A).

consequences of accepting federal funds which are conditioned upon certain behavior and a break of that conduct include, but may not be limited to, denial of similar funds in the future, reimbursement of the funds given, and liability to employees who are protected by the employment laws. This third instance was tested in *Sanderlin v. Seminole Tribe of Florida*.[157]

In *Sanderlin*, the court concluded that the acceptance of federal funds, which required a tribal promise to follow federal law did not act as a waiver of the tribe's sovereign immunity. Jerry Sanderlin, a police officer with the Seminole tribe, was injured on the job. Mr. Sanderlin argued that the tribe terminated the employment relationship when, as a result of an injury, he could not perform the job.[158] The tribe had previously accepted $189,000 from the federal government for a drug rehabilitation program, and the tribe consented to the federal government's request to follow certain federal employment laws. One law the tribe was to follow prohibited employers from terminating employees because of the employee's disability. The court wrestled with whether the tribe's promise to follow federal disability discrimination law trumped the tribe's assertion of sovereign immunity. The Eleventh Circuit Court of Appeals sided with the tribal employer by dismissing Mr. Sanderlin's claim based upon the tribe's asserted immunity.

The Eleventh Circuit Court cited the United States Supreme Court[159] for the proposition that tribal sovereign immunity protects a tribe from suit unless the federal government authorizes suit or the tribe waives its defense. In evaluating whether the federal government has permitted suit against tribes, the law is to be viewed in a light most favorable for the benefit of the tribe.[160]

In response to Mr. Sanderlin's argument that the tribe waived its immunity when the tribe accepted federal funds and agreed to follow federal law, which prohibits discrimination on the basis of disability, the court was not persuaded, concluding that waivers must be unequivocal and therefore cannot be implied based on the tribe's actions (agreement to follow federal law). The court also

---

[157] *Sanderlin v. Seminole Tribe of Florida*, 243 F.3d 1282 (11th Cir. 2001).
[158] Id.
[159] *Kiowa Tribe of Oklahoma v. Manufacturing Technologies, Inc.*, 523 U.S. 751, 754 (1998).
[160] *Montana v. Blackfeet Tribe of Indians*, 471 U.S. 759, 766 (1985).

found that tribal law asserted immunity from suit and declared the immunity could not be waived absent explicit consent from the tribal government.[161]

The *Sanderlin* case was decided years ago and that precedent may not survive scrutiny today. In *Sanderlin*, the court followed the idea that the tribe's immunity was not waived by its promise to follow arguably applicable federal employment law. Fifty-three days after the Eleventh Circuit Court of Appeals issued the *Sanderlin* decision, the United States Supreme Court found a tribe waived its immunity indirectly by agreeing to arbitrate a dispute in a construction contract.[162] Since the Supreme Court found a tribe indirectly waived its immunity through an arbitration agreement, there is risk of it finding a tribe waiving its immunity by agreeing to follow federal employment laws. Accordingly, blind reliance on *Sanderlin* must be cautioned.

Tribal governments interact with the federal government to create and enhance tribal housing under the Native American Housing and Self-Determination Act (NAHASDA). NAHASDA imposes federal civil rights and minimum wage requirements for construction of tribal homes.[163] The Eighth Circuit rejected the waiver of immunity argument in *Dillon v. Yankton Sioux Tribe Housing Authority*[164] wherein a former employee argued that when the tribal housing authority entered into an agreement with the federal government, promising to abide by various civil rights statutes, it therefore effectively waived its sovereign immunity. In its agreement with the federal government, the contract signed by

---

[161] Also see *Dillon v. Yankton Sioux Tribe Housing Authority*, 144 F.3d 581 (8th Cir. 1998) for a similar argument in a race discrimination suit wherein the federal court rejected an employee's argument that the tribe's acceptance of federal housing dollars in exchange for an agreement to follow federal antidiscrimination law meant that the tribe waived its immunity.

[162] *C & L Enterprises, Inc. v. Citizen Band Potawatomi*, 532 U.S. 411 (2001)

[163] 25 U.S.C. § 4112(c) (5) (A); 25 U.S.C. § 4114(b) (3). Also see 24 C.F.R. § 1000.16 (e).

[164] 144 F.3d 581 (8th Cir. 1998) (receipt of federal financial assistance from Department of Housing & Urban Development and therefore must comply with federal civil rights laws and therefore waiver of sovereign immunity); *Guthrie v. Circle of Life*, 176 F.Supp. 2d 919 (D.Minn. 2001)(acceptance of Individuals with Disabilities Education Act (IDEA) funds does not constitute a waiver of tribal sovereign immunity).

the housing authority agreed to specific federal regulations, but the court found no provision in the regulations mandating a waiver of sovereign immunity.

b. *The Indian Self-Determination Act*

What is known as the Indian Self-Determination Act is actually the Indian Self-Determination and Education Assistance Act of 1975 (ISDA).[165] ISDA is referred to as 638 contracts or 638 funds because the federal government promulgated the law at Public Law 93-638 which was codified (placed in the official statutes) at 25 U.S.C. §450. The ISDA is federal law, which delegates authority and the responsibility for certain contracts to tribal governments. This delegation of authority from the federal government to tribal government is an opportunity for the tribe to increase tribal self-determination by administering a program itself instead of having the program administered by a federal agency. Through ISDA contracts, tribes operate health clinics, law enforcement, water treatment facilities, and schools to name a few.[166] Acceptance of monies under the ISDA does not abrogate tribal sovereign immunity. Therefore, even if an employee argues a violation of federal employment law, there may not be a forum for the dispute.[167]

c. *Promises in an employee handbook and on a laminated poster*

Sovereigns write their own rules, and therefore tribes certainly can voluntarily utilize those laws promulgated by another sovereign. Between the federal and state governments, most tribes view their primary relationship with the federal government. If tribes adopt employment law from another sovereign, most tribes look first to other tribes, and then to the federal government's body of law. Some tribal leaders believe many of the federal government's employment laws make sense for moral and economic reasons. Moreover, employers do not make moral decisions by excluding employees based upon religion, national origin, gender, race, disability, age, or other federally protected classes. If a tribe decides the federal government's antidiscrimination laws make sense, the tribe can incorporate those principles into the fabric of the tribe's employment practices. The question becomes, where should the tribe incorporate these federal principles?

---

[165] 25 U.S.C. §450 et seq; Public Law 93-638.
[166] T. Johnson and J. Hamilton, "Self-Governance for Indian Tribes: From Paternalism to Empowerment," 27 Conn. L. Rev. 1251 (1995).
[167] 25 U.S.C. §450n (1).

There are choices for memorializing federal law into the fabric of the employment relationship. If the tribe chooses to incorporate federal law, promulgating it as a tribal law or ordinance is the best choice. Sovereigns exercise their sovereignty by writing and enforcing laws. Appendix A includes the Ho-Chunk Nation's employment law, which is an excellent example of a tribe exercising its sovereignty in the employment arena.[168]

The second place to incorporate federal law into the terms and conditions of the employment relationship is the specific employer's employee handbook since placing federal law in the tribe's employee handbook generates a promise from employer to employee. Whether the promise is enforceable in a court is impacted by whether the tribe creates an avenue for relief and whether the tribe asserts the defense of immunity to an action naming the tribe. A tribal employer could grant to its employees an avenue for relief by including a grievance procedure, administrative review by a regulator or, if jurisdiction exists, tribal court.

The question of immunity was addressed in a tribal employment case[169] assessing whether incorporating federal law into an employee handbook served to waive the tribe's sovereign immunity. The court stated that courts have consistently applied two complementary principles to waivers of immunity: (1) a sovereign's waiver must be unambiguous, and (2) a sovereign's interest encompasses not merely whether it may be sued, but where it may be sued. The Connecticut court found the tribe's employment forms did not provide a clear waiver of sovereign immunity.

d. *Promises in a gaming compact*

The federal government promulgated the Indian Gaming Regulatory Act (IGRA) in 1988 to construct a three-sovereign cooperative which regulates gaming. Tribes must comply with the minimum standards imposed by IGRA

---

[168] The Navajo Nation has comprehensive employment laws including, but not limited to its Navajo Preference in Employment Act, 15 N.T.C. §601 et seq.

[169] *Chayoon v. Sherlock*, 2005 WL 1473902, 877 A.2d 4 (Conn. App. 2005) citing *Garcia v. Akwesasne Housing Authority*, 268 F.3d 76, 86 (2nd Cir. 2001). *Chayoon v. Reels*, 3-02CV1358 (JCH)(D.Conn. March 12, 2003); *Chayoon v. Chao*, 355 F.3d 141 (2d Cir. 2004); *Myers v. Seneca Niagara Casino*, 488 F.Supp.2d 166 (N.D.N.Y. 2006).

and demonstrate compliance through the adoption of a comprehensive law approved by the chairman of the National Indian Gaming Commission (NIGC). Specifically, these goals are achieved through IGRA's operational section 2710, which (1) enumerates the minimum standards for tribal gaming and (2) requires the tribe to submit its comprehensive gaming law to the chairman of the NIGC for approval.[170] IGRA defined categories of gaming with corresponding delegation of jurisdiction to tribal, state, and federal entities. For instance, traditional games were left to tribal oversight, bingo shared by tribes and the federal government while Las Vegas-style gaming (slot machines and blackjack) delegated to both states and tribes. Before a tribe can offer Las Vegas-style gaming, the tribe and state must reach an agreement called a tribal-state compact. These compacts vary significantly from state to state and can vary from tribe to tribe within the same state.[171]

Some compacts include a promise from the tribe to follow state and federal employment laws, covering those employees hired by tribal gaming enterprises. The standard compact between the State of California and tribes located within that state includes promises from the tribes to follow a portion of the state's human rights act, meet minimum worker's compensation standards, and some federal employment laws.[172] Incorporation of state employment law is not the norm since most compacts do not address the issue.

Tribes operating gaming enterprises under the Indian Gaming Regulatory Act are confronted with the argument that there is enough waiver of immunity to enforce IGRA compliance.[173] Enforcement by employees of compact required employment law will be tested in the future.[174]

---

[170] 25 U.S.C. §2705 (a)(3); 25 U.S.C. §2710.
[171] The tribal-state compacts can be found in the reading room at *www.nigc.gov*.
[172] California compacts, paragraphs 10.2(g) (human rights), 10.3 (workers compensation and unemployment compensation) and 10.7 (labor relations).
[173] *Mescalero Apache Tribe v. State of New Mexico*, 131 F.3d 1379 (10th Cir. 1997); *Maxam v. Lower Sioux Indian Community of Minnesota*, 829 F.Supp. 277 (D.Minn. 1993); Ross v. Flandreau Santee Sioux Tribe, 809 F.Supp. 738 (D.S.D. 1992); But see, *Davids v. Coyhis*, 869 F.Supp. 1401 (E.D. Wis. 1994)(no waiver of immunity).]
[174] The issue was tangentially addressed in *Myers v. Seneca Niagara Casino*, 488 F.Supp.2d 166 (N.D.N.Y. 2006) wherein the court rejected an equivalency argument that a limited waiver to the state also waived immunity as to employees.

Are there federal laws, which specifically apply to tribal employers?

Yes. The federal government has promulgated laws, which reinforce the civil rights of people interacting with tribes, by imposing background standards for tribal employees who interact with children and for required reporting of abuse and neglect of Indian children.

The Indian Civil Rights Act[175] (ICRA) takes an approximation of the United States Bill of Rights and imposes them on tribes. For tribal employers that part of ICRA, which generates interest, are the guarantees of due process and equal protection of the law. ICRA provides that no tribe shall deny to any person within its jurisdiction the equal protection of its laws or deprive any person of liberty or property without due process of law.[176]

The reach of certain federal rights was limited in Indian Country. The Supreme Court recognized that tribes are "distinct, independent political communities, retaining their original natural rights" to govern themselves[177] and later underscored that sovereignty by holding that tribes are not obligated to conform their governments to the standards imposed on state and federal governments.[178] From these principles, federal courts could not get involved in intertribal disputes even if the tribes violated federal standards.[179] Allegations of an absence of civil rights between tribes and members led Congress to pass ICRA.

ICRA requires tribal employers to provide due process and equal protection when making employment decisions. Limiting health care benefits to male

---

[175] ICRA is located at 25 U.S.C. §1301 et seq.
[176] 25 U.S.C. §1302(8).
[177] *Worcester v. Georgia*, 31 U.S. 515, 559 (1832)
[178] *Talton v. Mayes*, 163 U.S. 376 (1896).
[179] *Santa Clara Pueblo v. Martinez*, 436 U.S. 49 (1978); Congress has waived tribal sovereign immunity under ICRA only for habeas corpus relief. *Santa Clara Pueblo*. Federal courts lack subject matter jurisdiction to hear claims under ICRA against tribes for declaratory relief (the employee's personnel file shall be given to them)(*Ordinance 59 Association v. United States Department of Interior*, 163 F.3d 1150, 1154 (10th Cir. 1998) or monetary damages (employee claim for back pay for example) (Olguin v. Lucero, 87 F.3d 401, 404 (10th Cir. 1996).

employees, rejecting Asian job applicants, and promoting blue-eyed employees only are examples of unequal protection of the law. As to due process, employers may be required, under ICRA, to provide a fair mechanism for considering the employee's version of events in determining whether termination of employment is selected. Both the statutory law and the courts' interpretation of the law fail to provide much guidance on what equal protection and due process mean for tribal employers.

Even if the law was clear regarding employee rights the protected employee may not have the ability to enforce their rights. Said another way, employees can have rights without a remedy. One variable in limiting an employee's opportunity to enforce ICRA rights is the lack of federal court jurisdiction articulated by *Santa Clara Pueblo v. Martinez*.[180] In most instances, federal courts cannot hear ICRA disputes if the tribal defendant raises an immunity defense. Immunity even protected a tribal employer from the allegation that tribal employees pointed firearms at a colleague at the time the worker's employment was terminated.[181]

There is a limited exception to the general rule that federal courts do not have jurisdiction to hear ICRA claims when the claim is against the tribe. Under *Dry Creek Lodge*,[182] a plaintiff may bring a suit for damages against a tribe or tribal official under limited circumstances in federal court. Eligibility for assertion of a federal court claim requires a plaintiff to show (1) the dispute involves a non-Indian party, (2) a tribal forum is not available, and (3) the dispute involves an issue falling outside internal tribal affairs. These exceptions are discussed in chapter 4.

Are tribal employers required to perform background investigations when employees interact with children?

Some federal employment laws explicitly apply to tribal employers. The federal government has promulgated a law, which has direct application to

---

[180] *Santa Clara Pueblo v. Martinez*, 436 U.S. 49 (1978)
[181] *Mullins v. Sycuan Band of Kumeyaay Nation*, 2008 WL 2745260 (S.D. Cal. 2008).
[182] *Dry Creek Lodge, Inc. v. Arapahoe & Shoshone Tribes*, 623 F.2d 682 (10th Cir. 1980).

employees, which have regular contact with or control over children. The law has a couple monikers including the Indian Child Protection and Family Violence Prevention Act or Public Law 101-630.[183] Since the label 101-630 is the label most frequently used on the ground, it is the label used here.

Under federal law, the character of certain present and future tribal employees must be evaluated to mitigate the risks of retaining and hiring employees who may harm children while in the workplace. For instance, tribes accepting monies under Indian Self-Determination and Education Assistance Act or Tribally Controlled Schools Act of 1988 shall conduct character investigations of present and future employees who will have regular contact or control over children.[184] Employees who have regular contact or control over children may include social workers, teachers, physicians, nurses, pharmacist, speech pathologist, medical clerk and dental hygienist. A case by case analysis is necessary in determining what positions fall within the contact or control positions.

For contact or control positions, at a minimum the character assessment must deny employment to those individuals with felonies and a collection of certain misdemeanors. The law states:

> The minimum standards of character that are to be prescribed under this section shall ensure that none of the individuals appointed to positions described in subsection (a) of this section have been found guilty of, or entered a plea of nolo contendere or guilty to, any felonious offense, or any of two or more misdemeanor offenses, under Federal, State, or Tribal law involving crimes of violence; sexual assault, molestation, exploitation, contact or prostitution; crimes against persons; or offenses committed against children.[185]

There is not a grandfather provision in the law so therefore workers employed before the law was promulgated in 1990 are subject to the character investigation even if the employee was convicted of a crime, which predates

---

[183] 25 U.S.C. §3201 et seq.
[184] 25 U.S.C. §3207 (c).
[185] 25 U.S.C. §3207 (b).

the law.[186] Moreover, rehabilitated employees do not receive a second chance since the law's disqualifying criteria does not permit evidence of mitigation to establish an employee's fitness for continued employment.[187]

Layered over 101-630 is the Crime Control Act[188] which applies to federal agencies, facilities operated by the federal government and facilities operated under contract with the federal government. Indian Health Service clinics fall into facilities operated under contract with the federal government. The crime Control Act extends the requirement of background investigations beyond employees to contractors and volunteers. The Crime Control Act precludes from employment those convicted of crimes of violence, sex crimes, offenses involving a child victim and drug offenses. Moreover, the law may preclude someone involved in an incident which has not been adjudicated.

In this arena of uncertainty as to the application of federal employment laws, what options are presented to the tribes?

There are several options, which reveal tribal leadership's appetite for sovereignty and conversely, leadership's risk tolerance. The more a tribe pushes the envelope of sovereignty, the more risk of a lawsuit or regulatory challenge in the short term and conversely, the tribe which does not push the envelope of sovereignty the less risk in the short term.

In these statements, there is the qualifier "in the short term." There is a compelling argument, which asserts that short term risk avoidance where a tribe fails to assert its sovereignty and write its own rules eventually permits the erosion of tribal sovereignty at its core. The erosion of sovereignty stemming from a failure to exercise it will have long-term negative implications for tribes. Accordingly, gauging long term and short-term risk is necessary to the analysis.

As the following discussion reveals, a tribe's choice not to meet the minimum requirements of federal employment law (pay minimum wage for

---

[186] *Delong v. Department of Health and Human Services*, 264 F.3d 1334 (Fed. Cir. 2001), cert. denied 122 S.Ct. 2661 (2002).
[187] Id.
[188] 42 U.S.C. § 1304 et seq. is also referred to as Public Law 101-674.

instance) may result in greater short-term risk through a lawsuit generated by an employee or the intervention of a federal governmental agency. On the other hand, a dilemma is created by acquiescing to the federal government's employment laws, creating an expectation of following federal law, which certainly leads to an expectation that employees are not following tribal law. Does the tribe react to the short-term risk of an expensive lawsuit by meeting the minimum standards of federal employment law recognizing that mitigating this short-term risk may create the larger and more dangerous long-term risk of sacrificing sovereignty at its core? The question has at least four answers, which ask tribal leadership to engage in a trade-off of risk aversion for the safety of compliance. Those four options are discussed below.

Option 1: Follow federal employment law

The option, which brings the safest short-term risk through the avoidance of a private lawsuit or federal government intervention, is to simply follow federal employment laws. This option does not enhance sovereignty if sovereignty is defined by a tribe's exercise of its rule and law making authority. Therefore, what appears to be risk aversion in the short-term may in the long view increase the risk of the imposition of federal employment law.

Option 2: Promulgate tribal employment laws which meet the minimum requirements of federal employment laws

The second option reaches for the relative safety of conforming to the minimum requirements of federal law without following the actual federal law. For example, the FMLA requires employers to grant twelve weeks of unpaid leave to employees after a year of employment if the employee encounters a serious health condition. After understanding the risks, the tribe could reject application of FMLA while at the same time meeting the requirements of the law. By adopting standards, which meet or exceed federal law, the tribe is exercising its sovereignty since the tribe's court, grievance committee, and tribal council interpret and apply tribal law. Furthermore, since the employee receives the same leave the employee would have received had the tribe simply followed the FMLA, there is reduced harm, which may form the basis of a lawsuit initiated by the employee. Risk is reduced through the reduction of harm to the employee.

Option 3: Promulgate tribal employment laws which reflect the tribe's values and some of the federal government's good ideas

When tribes break the tether to federal law, the tribe is asserting its sovereignty. If tribal law does not meet the minimum requirements of potentially applicable federal law the tribe's assertion of its sovereignty increases its short-term risk of litigation. For instance if the FMLA applies to tribes and the tribe permits six instead of twelve weeks of unpaid leave, an employee could litigate the missing six weeks. Litigation costs, the potential for a verdict against the tribe, and the time consumed by litigation are unwanted liabilities. However, the assertion of the tribe's rule-making authority, without deference to federal law, is an exercise of inherent sovereignty. Litigation management is about balancing risk and reward.

Option 4: The tribe does what it wants, when it wants; and federal employment laws are not relevant to the discussion

The fourth choice for a tribal leader is to conclude that absent a clear declaration from the federal government's legislative branch directing tribes to follow federal employment laws, the tribe will not pay attention to the federal government's rules on the issue. There is an argument that option 3 and option 4 generate the same potential liability. Once a tribe falls below the federal minimum standards, the risk of liability arises if the federal standards apply. From a liability assessment perspective, options 3 and 4 may present the same degree of risk. However, from the perspective of inherent sovereignty, where the tribe's values dictate the conversation, the absence of a conversation regarding federal standards permits greater clarity in drafting tribal laws with allegiance to tribal values. To the extent that a tribe choosing option 3 does adopt some, but not all of the federal employment standards, there is a difference between options 3 and 4.

What does your vote mean?

Years of presenting the four options in response to employment hypotheticals yields an interesting response from groups. These nonscientific surveys of groups where everyone votes for one of the four options reveals a couple generalizations. First, in most groups, the responses generate a bell curve, which swells the number of votes for options 2 and 3. Second, the most risk-adverse group is experienced human resources professionals. Third, the most risk-tolerant groups are tribal council members and those individuals serving tribal boards.

Behind these votes is a predisposition for human resources professionals to follow the rules and make decisions, which keep employers out of trouble. Furthermore, elected officials and board members almost always possess an increased awareness of the importance of sovereignty and therefore the results are weighted toward the risk tolerant end of the spectrum.

The other theme which flows from the hypothetical is the realization that preservation of sovereignty comes with a price. If sovereignty were a static idea not requiring action to preserve and enhance it, choosing the most sovereign option would always be the choice for tribal leadership. However, tribal leaders understand, as do the voters, there is a trade-off with every choice. For example, compliance with the FLSA's overtime standards reduces the risk of a regulatory audit or private enforcement action but crowds out the opportunity for tribes to exercise their sovereignty by defining the overtime rules free from the federal government's perspective. The trade-off is the benefit of less risk in exchange for the detriment of less sovereignty. Increased sovereignty comes with a price and therefore, tribal leaders must make choices by gauging the risk and reward of these important trade-offs.

CHAPTER 3

Do state employment laws apply to tribal employers?

As a general rule, state law does not apply to tribes. Geographic proximity and shared borders between a state and a tribe does not change the rule that the federal government, under its constitution, has the relationship with tribes. The United States Constitution, which delegates limited powers to the federal and state sovereigns, delegates the relationship with tribes to the federal government, and does not contemplate the assumption of authority by states over tribes. To the extent that the federal government shares with states its authority to engage in a relationship with tribes this can and has altered the basic assumption that state law does not apply to tribes. There are exceptions to this general rule of nonapplication. This chapter explores the foundation of the general rule and, in turn, addresses the exceptions to the general rule.

What is the legal relationship between tribes and the state governments?

The foundation of the relationship between the tribes and the United States *and* the tribes and the various states starts with the premise that tribes defined the rules before the existence of the United States of America. The history, which defines tribal-state relations, both in and outside the courts, is marked by serious mistrust. The relationship between tribes and states is impaired by history, which is characterized by the Supreme Court's observation that:

> The people of the States where [Indians] are found are often their deadliest enemies.[189]

After America was formed and its Constitution ratified, the United States Supreme wrestled with the principle of tribal sovereignty when a non-Indian entered Cherokee Nation land in violation of the State of Georgia's law, requiring non-Indians to seek and obtain permission from the state.[190] The case, *Worcester v. Georgia*, evaluated the question of between an Indian tribe and the State of Georgia which government had the authority to regulate the conduct of non-Indians on Indian lands?

The United States Supreme Court found the State of Georgia did not have authority to regulate the Cherokee Nation's decision to admit or deny individuals from entering Cherokee Nation lands. Because of its relevance to the present-day relationship issues between the states and the tribes, *Worcester v. Georgia* is cited frequently by courts and litigants for the general proposition that tribes define the rules and state law does not control. This oft-cited case delivered the most cited language in federal Indian law when the Supreme Court excluded states exercise of power of tribal affairs:

> The Cherokee Nation, then, is a distinct community, occupying its own territory, with boundaries accurately described, in which the laws of Georgia can have no force.

Almost 130 years later, the United States Supreme Court diluted the *Worcester* clear separation between the tribes and states by limiting the application of state law on the reservation when state action infringed on the right of reservation Indians to make their own laws and be ruled by them. The Supreme Court explained the infringement test in *Williams v. Lee*[191] which diminishes the bright line between tribes and states in favor of a fuzzy test evaluating under what alleged important circumstances does state law apply on the reservation. The assumption of tribal sovereignty, which precluded the application of state law, was further diluted in a case which supported sovereignty but shuffled the analysis to an examination of whether federal law preempted state law. The preemption analysis forces a mushy balancing of federal and state interests:

---

[189] *United States v. Kagama*, 118 U.S. 375, 384 (1886).
[190] *Worcester v. Georgia*, 31 U.S. 515, 559 (1832).
[191] 358 U.S. 217 (1959).

State jurisdiction is preempted by the operation of federal law if it interferes with or is incompatible with federal and tribal interests reflected in federal law, unless the state interests at stake are sufficient to justify the assertion of state authority.[192]

From this language, clarity is not the driving force behind the preemption doctrine. The preemption test favors the application of federal over state interests as the federal government has a significant interest in encouraging tribal self-government.[193] More recently, the United States Supreme Court reaffirmed *Worcester* to the extent that "state law is generally inapplicable" to on-reservation conduct, but the Court did not erect a barrier to the intrusion of state laws.[194] Preemption squeezes a tribe seeking self-determination by asking the tribe to favor federal law to crowd out state law, but at the same time, the tribe is motivated to reject federal law since the tribe relies on its inherent sovereignty to define its own rules.

When courts engage the preemption analysis, at least two factors impact the strength of the tribal and state interests. Tribal interests are stronger when evaluating on-reservation activity, involving tribal members, and states assert an increase in authority when dealing with nonmembers and off reservation behavior. Between these bookends, the strength of tribal sovereignty is driven by the facts, which place sovereignty's strength within the spectrum between member activity on the reservation and nonmember activity off the reservation.

When tribal leaders define the employment rules, in most instances leadership starts from the premise that state law does not apply. From *Worcester v. Georgia* and *Williams v. Lee*, tribal employers assert that tribal employers, not the States where the tribes are located, define the terms and conditions of the employment relationship. As coequal sovereigns, tribes cannot define employment laws for the states where the tribes are located and conversely, the states cannot define the legal relationship between the tribes and their employees.

---

[192] *New Mexico v. Mescalero Apache Tribe*, 462 U.S. 324, 334 (1983).
[193] *California v. Cabazon Band of Mission Indians*, 480 U.S. 202, 216 (1987).
[194] *Nevada v. Hicks*, 121 S.Ct. 2304 (2001).

The point is strengthened when viewed from the perspective of relationships between states. States do not determine the law in other states whether those states have common boundaries or are separated by a thousand miles. From that perspective, the State of Minnesota cannot define employment law for its neighbor Wisconsin, its non-neighbor Oregon or its neighbor the Prairie Island Indian Community. The rules of reciprocity also apply. Since Minnesota cannot define the rules for Wisconsin, Oregon, or Prairie Island Indian Community, those sovereigns cannot define the rules for Minnesota.

The effectiveness of a state's argument for the assertion of state rules in state courts applied to tribal employers is further diluted by the exercise of tribal authority over employees within the tribe's jurisdiction. The exercise of tribal jurisdiction stems from inherent sovereignty and secondarily from the United State's Supreme Court's recognition of tribal authority reaching member and nonmember employees under the reasoning in *Montana v. United States*.[195] When tribes exercise their federally endorsed right of inherent sovereignty as to all employees, there is a valid assumption that states are foreclosed from exercising state rules. Permitting both tribal and state assertion of authority concurrently multiplies employer and employee confusion based upon an effort to conform to two sets of rules, which may or may not be aligned.[196] The natural corollary to *Montana* is the assumption that state employment rules are squeezed from the relationship between tribal employer and employee.

Accordingly, as a general rule, state courts do not possess the power to hear cases involving tribal employers and employees.[197] Accordingly, state human

---

[195] 450 U.S. 544 (1981); *Montana* is not a case addressing employment issues; however, the *Montana* principles deal with the question of whether tribal rules apply to tribal employees.

[196] *Rodriguez v. Wong*, 82 P.3d 263, 267 (Wash. App. 2004) (Allowing the complaining employee to sue in state court directly affects the tribe's political integrity as it would force the tribe to abandon its government. The court used the same reasoning to reject shared or concurrent jurisdiction of the tribe and state).

[197] *Rodriguez v. Wong*, 82 P.3d 263 (Wash. App. 2004); But see, *Gavle v. Little Six, Inc.*, 555 N.W.2d 284 (Minn. 1996)(state courts can consider civil claims regarding acts outside reservation)

rights laws,[198] workers compensation statutes,[199] state collective bargaining rules,[200] and state rules which guaranty overtime compensation after eight working hours in a day do not apply to tribal employers.

Are there exceptions to the rule that state employment laws do not apply to tribal employers?

Yes. The Supreme Court found that state jurisdiction does not cease at the state-reservation line. The *Worcester* border separating tribes from states where state law does not apply is a fading line on the map. Under *Worcester*, the line was bold, separating Georgia from the Cherokee Nation when the Supreme Court declared exclusive jurisdiction for the Cherokee Nation. Tribes take less solace in *Nevada v. Hicks*[201] where the court asserted that state sovereignty does not end at the reservation boundary. *Hicks* found that state officials investigating off reservation crimes can enter tribal lands to execute a warrant finding that tribal land ownership is an important factor but not dispositive.[202] On-reservation conduct between Indians does not invoke state jurisdiction; but when nonmembers are involved, the state's regulatory interest rises.

Tribal employees are subject to state laws limiting the service of alcohol, state income taxes, the reach of a state subpoena, and other protections. State law

---

[198] *Penobscot Nation v. Fellencer*, 164 F.3d 706 (1st Cir. 1999) (tribe not subject to state antidiscrimination law in terminating non-Indian nurse at tribal health center).

[199] *Tibbetts v. Leech Lake Reservation Business Committee*, 397 N.W.2d 883, 887 (Minn. 1986)(sovereign immunity bars application of state worker's compensation statute). The Ho-Chunk Nation promulgated its worker's compensation law as part of its employment code. Ho-Chunk Nation Personnel, Employment and Labor Code, chapter 5, section 35 (appendix A).

[200] State right-to-work laws are of no effect in federal enclaves such as Indian reservations, see *Lord v. Local Union No.2088, IBEW*, 646 F.2d 1057, 1062 (5th Cir.1981) (finding state right-to-work law inapplicable in federal enclave in spite of § 14(b) of the NLRA), cert. denied, 458 U.S. 1106, 102 S.Ct. 3483, 73 L.Ed.2d 1366 (1982); *New Mexico Fed'n of Labor v. City of Clovis*, 735 F. Supp. 999, 1002-03 (D.N.M.1990) (indirectly noting the inapplicability of state right-to-work laws in federal enclaves).

[201] *Nevada v. Hicks*, 121 S.Ct. 2304 (2001).

[202] Also see, *Inyo County v. Paiute-Shoshone Indians*, 538 U.S. 701 (2003).

can be extended to the tribal employee by a tribal-state compact or by the voluntary application of a workers' compensation statute.

Can state laws apply to tribal employers under tribal-state compacts?

State employment laws apply to some tribal casinos through an agreement between the state and the tribal government. A compact is an agreement between sovereigns, and many tribal-state compacts are the product of federal gaming law. The federal law, which governs many aspects of tribal gaming, is the Indian Gaming Regulatory Act (IGRA). In the operative section of IGRA, the most lucrative gaming opportunities require consent from the state where the tribe is located.[203] This lucrative or Las Vegas-style gaming is defined as class III gaming. There are more than 230 compacts between tribes and states, and the terms in those compacts vary greatly from state to state and from tribe to tribe.[204]

Tribes compact[205] with states and other sovereigns wherein tribes agree to a variety of conditions including the application of state employment law. Through compacts, tribes have adopted state human rights laws,[206] workers compensation,[207] unemployment compensation,[208] and other

---

[203] 25 U.S.C. §2710.

[204] The federal regulator which enforces the Indian Gaming Regulatory Act is the National Indian Gaming Commission (NIGC). NIGC hosts an informational website which includes details regarding gaming tribes. The website is located at *www.nigc.gov.*

[205] A compact is an agreement between sovereigns. In the gaming context tribes and states compact to memorialize the rules when tribes engage in Las Vegas-style (class III) gaming. 25 U.S.C. §2710;

[206] See, Compact between Picayune Rancheria of Chukchansi Indians of California and the State of California (2000). Most California compacts require tribal gaming enterprises to apply rules at least as stringent as the state rules prohibiting discrimination on the basis of race, religion, color, national origin, gender, sexual orientation and disability. The compacts can be viewed in the Reading Room of the NIGC's website located at www.nigc.gov.

[207] See, Compact between Omaha Tribe of Nebraska and the State of Iowa (1999).

[208] See, Compact between Omaha Tribe of Nebraska and the State of Iowa (1999).

laws.[209] In chapter 4, the available forums for employment-related disputes is discussed since application of federal law does not require a federal court to hear the dispute, nor does it require a tribe to have the federal court address its conflicts.

What is the influence of insurance on the application of state law?

Incorporation of state law in an insurance contract may create an exception to the general rule that state law does not apply. In a couple of workers' compensation cases, the contractual choice of law was the definitive factor in the case where one insurance policy incorporated Oklahoma law[210] and the other incorporated tribal law.[211]

What impact do federal worker's compensation rules have on the application of state rules?

The mix of federal land and tribal sovereignty leads to a more complicated analysis in evaluating whether state workers compensation laws apply on the reservation. State workers compensation laws apply on the reservation to private entities but not to tribal governments and their wholly owned entities. Federal law extended the reach of state workers' compensation laws to federal lands. Indian reservation trust land is federal property, and therefore state laws apply to those lands.[212] Therefore, private business entities performing work on the reservation must comply with state workers compensation laws.[213] However, state workers compensation laws do not apply to on-reservation

---

[209] See, Compact between Mashantucket Pequot Tribe and the State of Connecticut (1991) (regulates health, safety and traffic); Compact between Southern Ute Indian Tribe and the State of Colorado (1995)(regulates safety standards).

[210] *Squirrel v. Bordertown Bingo*, 125 P.3d 680 (Okla. App. 2005).

[211] Hall v. Cherokee Nation, 162 P.3d 979 (Okla. App. 2007).

[212] 40 U.S.C. § 290.

[213] *Industrial Commission v. Indian Country Enterprises, Inc.*, 944 P.2d 117 (Idaho 1997); *Begay v. Kerr-McGee Corp.*, 682 F.2d 1311 (9th Cir. 1982)(Arizona workers compensation law applied on Navajo reservation); *Workforce Safety & Insurance v. JFK Raingutters*, LLC 34 I.L.R. 5218 (N.D. 2007).

tribes or wholly owned tribal entities since federal law did not abrogate sovereign immunity.[214]

Does Public Law 280 permit states to impose state employment laws to on-reservation tribally owned or operated entities?

No. As coequal sovereigns, as a general rule, states cannot impose their laws and rules on tribes located within the boundaries of those states. This general rule can be modified by the federal government.

Through the United States Constitution, the relationship with tribes is between the federal government and tribes. Article I, Section 8 of the United States Constitution delegates to the federal government the authority to regulate commerce with Indian tribes. Think about the United States Constitution as a three party agreement. The citizens of the United States are the first party; the federal government, the second party; and the states, the third party. A constitution is by definition, a document which delegates limited powers. In the United States Constitution, the federal government is delegated the authority to deal with the tribes and the states are delegated no relationship. Also remember that the tribes are not a party to the United States Constitution and therefore, were not given an opportunity to negotiate the product or consent to its terms. Since states were not delegated any authority relating to tribes, state governments have limited authority over tribal affairs.[215]

Through an exercise of its plenary power, the federal government can impose its rules on tribes.[216] In 1953, the federal government imposed state law on tribes located in a handful of states by enacting Public Law 83-280, which is

---

[214] 40 U.S.C. § 3172; *Middletown Rancheria of Pomo Indians v. Workers Compensation Appeals Board*, 60 Cal. App. 4th 1340 (1998); *Tibbets v. Leech Lake Reservation Business Commission*, 397 N.W.2d 883 (Minn. 1986).

[215] *Washington v. Confederated Tribes of Colville Indian Reservation*, 447 U.S. 134, 154, 100 S.Ct. 2069, 2081 (1980).

[216] *Worcester v. Georgia*, 31 U.S. 515 (1832); *Menominee Tribe v. U.S.*, 391 U.S. 404 (1968).

commonly referred to as PL 280.²¹⁷ Note PL 280 is not an action by states to impose state law on the reservation but rather the federal government applying state law on the reservation. This is a distinction with a difference. Those states included Alaska, California, Minnesota, Nebraska, Wisconsin, and Oregon. When enacted, state criminal and civil laws applied to Indian Country.²¹⁸ Since enactment the law's impact has evolved.

Several decades later, the United States Supreme Court limited 280's application to the criminal context in a case called *Bryan v. Itasca County*.²¹⁹ In *Bryan* the court found congressional clarity in the imposition of state *criminal* law on the reservation, but did not find a clear delegation of state *civil* law to the reservation. The Court followed *Bryan v. Itasca County* in *California v. Cabazon Band of Mission Indians* in 1987 by declaring California's attempt to exercise its 280 jurisdiction could not close tribal gaming operations operating inconsistently with state "criminal" laws.²²⁰ The word "criminal" deserves its quotation marks when a state declares behavior criminal, but allows and engages in the same behavior (gaming)—the declaration of a crime lacks substance. Like *Bryan*, the *Cabazon* court found that states cannot use PL 280 to regulate tribal government on-reservation civil activities.

An excellent example of an on-reservation civil activity is the employment relationship between the tribes and its employees. Employers trade green dollars for employee time and effort, which is a civil contract between consenting parties. State employment laws are civil in nature, so therefore,

---

²¹⁷ 18 U.S.C. §1162; 28 U.S.C. §1360. Legislative history shows that the federal government was concerned about curbing crime, reducing the use of federal law enforcement, and assimilation of Indians into the larger community.

²¹⁸ Indian Country is defined by 18 U.S.C. §1151.

²¹⁹ *Bryan v. Itasca County*, 426 U.S. 373 (1976); *Bryan* did not emasculate all of civil state jurisdiction from P.L. 280 since tribal members residing on tribal lands can still use state courts to address certain civil matters.

²²⁰ California v. Cabazon Band of Mission Indians, 480 U.S. 202 (1987); Under *Cabazon* there is a question whether states can impose civil rules on the reservation impacting non-Indians when the infringement/preemption tests are not violated.

Public Law 280 does not open the door to application of these civil laws to on-reservation tribal employment practices.[221]

Can tribes voluntarily apply state law?

Some tribes consent to the application of state law for convenience or for competitive reasons. Tribes utilize state workers compensation laws because some tribes have not promulgated laws to protect their workers. Or in an effort to attract the best employees available, providing state workers compensation protection is a protection which attracts and keeps good employees. In other words, these laws may make tribal employers more competitive to some employees.

Are the rules different for tribes in Oklahoma?

The tribes located in Oklahoma have a unique history with the United States. The tribes owned Oklahoma before it was a state and through the ebb and flow of history the tribes in Oklahoma had sovereignty taken and restored. Today, the tribes in Oklahoma are sovereign and enjoy the same immunity from suit as other federally recognized tribes said the United States Supreme Court in 1991.[222] The Supreme Court found that the tribes exercise "inherent sovereign authority over their members and their territory."[223] As a result, the state of Oklahoma lacks civil jurisdiction over Indians on tribal lands.[224] Without civil jurisdiction, Oklahoma follows the general rule precluding state employment laws.

Are the rules different for tribes in Connecticut?

In Connecticut, there are both federally recognized tribes and tribes seeking federal recognition.[225]

---

[221] *Middletown Rancheria of Pomo Indians v. WCAB*, 60 Cal. App. 4th 1340 (Cal. App. 1998); *Tibbetts v. Leech Lake Reservation Business Committee*, 397 N.W.2d 883, 887 (Minn. 1986)

[222] *Oklahoma Tax Commission v. Citizen Band Potawatomi Indian Tribe*, 498 U.S. 505 (1991).

[223] Id. at 509.

[224] *Oklahoma Tax Commission v. Sac and Fox Nation*, 508 U.S. 114 (1993).

[225] The tribes seeking federal recognition are Historic Eastern Pequot tribe comprised of the Paucatuck Eastern Pequot tribe and the Eastern Pequots, the Paugussett triben and the Schaghticoke tribe.

a. *Mashantucket Pequot Tribe.* The Mashantucket Pequot tribe was recognized by Congress in the 1983 Connecticut Land Claims Settlement Act (the "Act").[226] The Connecticut Supreme Court found that the language of the Act was ambiguous and held that Connecticut has criminal[227] and civil regulatory jurisdiction[228] over the Tribe.
b. *Mohegan Tribe.* In the Mohegan Nation of Connecticut Land Claims Settlement Act,[229] Congress defined the relationship between the tribe, state and federal government.

Are the rules different for tribes in New York?

The discussion relating to Public Law 280 parallels the status of tribes located in the state of New York. The federal government promulgated law for the tribes in New York, which is similar to Public Law 280.[230] In *Bryan v. Itasca*,[231] the United States Supreme Court ruled that Public Law 280, which is a similar federal delegation of power to other states, ruled that Public Law 280 did not permit states to exercise civil jurisdiction over the tribes. Experts argue that *Bryan v. Itasca's* limitation of Public Law 280 delegation of authority similarly limits the delegation of civil jurisdiction of New York over the tribes located in New York.[232] Employment laws are civil laws and if New York's version of Public Law is similarly limited, New York cannot impose its employment laws on tribes located in New York.

Are the rules different for Pueblos in New Mexico?

History started and ended with independent and sovereign Pueblos which dealt with the governments of Spain, Mexico, and the United States. The Pueblos located in New Mexico preexisted the arrival of Europeans. The Spanish recognized Pueblo land as did Mexico after it gained its independence.

---

[226] 25 U.S.C. § 1751 et seq.
[227] *State v. Spears*, 662 A.2d 80 (Conn. 1995), cert. denied, 516 U.S. 1009 (1995).
[228] *Charles v. Charles*, 701 A.2d 650 (Conn. 1997), cert. denied, 523 U.S. 1136 (1998).
[229] 25 U.S.C. § 1775.
[230] 25 U.S.C. §232; *People v. Edwards*, 432 N.Y.S.2d 567 (App. Div. 1980).
[231] 426 U.S. 373 (1976).
[232] *Rights of Indians and Tribes* at 309.

The Treaty of Guadalupe Hidalgo between Mexico and the United States granted the territory of New Mexico to the United States. In 1876, the United States Supreme Court ruled that the Pueblos were not Indian tribes,[233] and the same court reversed itself in 1913.[234] The Pueblos own their land but that does not diminish the federal government's trust responsibility.[235]

Are the rules different in Alaska?

The Alaska Native Claims Settlement Act (ANCSA)[236] settled land claims between the federal government and Alaska natives. Alaska native villages are incorporated under state law and own land with borders established by ANCSA. The land is not Indian Country[237] so therefore, the Alaska tribes could not exercise governmental powers over these lands. However the Alaska tribes are sovereign powers under federal law and can enforce their rights.[238] Whether Alaska tribes can define and enforce employment rules will be further determined by the tribes and the courts.

---

[233] *U.S. v. Joseph*, 94 U.S. 614 (1876).
[234] *U.S. v. Sandoval*, 231 U.S. 28 (1913).
[235] *U.S. v. Candelaria*, 271 U.S. 432 (1926); *Lane v. Pueblo of Santa Rosa*, 249 U.S. 110 (1919).
[236] 43 U.S.C. § 160-28.
[237] *Alaska v. Native Village of Venetie Tribal Government*, 522 U.S. 520 (1998).
[238] *In re C.R.H.*, 29 P.3d 849, 851 n.5 (Alaska 2001).

CHAPTER 4

Where are disputes between tribes and employees heard and what law applies?

Workplace disputes range from an objection to the paint on an office wall to the theft of an employer's computer, or the termination of an employee. Some disputes receive formal due process from an employer or governmental agency and other disputes generate little employer response. Tribal employees will encounter processes for informal complaints, formal grievances, opportunities for tribal court review; and in some instances, other sovereigns (states and the federal government) may have the power to provide due process. This chapter evaluates numerous questions, which fit under the larger category of employment-related disputes. For instance, this chapter asks,

> *Between on-reservation tribal employers and their employees, if there is an employment dispute, where is the dispute heard?*
>
> *Who hears the dispute?*
>
> *What law applies to the dispute?*
>
> *Can the dispute be heard in state and federal courts?*
>
> *Can a tribal employer raise the immunity defense if sued in tribal, state, or federal court?*
>
> *For crimes committed by employees at work, which sovereign has the authority to enforce the law?*

Do tribal employers use informal and formal internal dispute resolution mechanisms?

Yes. Tribal employers understand that communication is at the core of successful relationships, which include the connection between tribal employers and employees. Tribal employers use grievances, complaint processes, informal dispute resolution techniques, mediation, and peacemaking to resolve employment disputes. These mechanisms are sometimes a product of tribal law but more frequently, the subject of a provision in the employee handbook.

Tribal employers use the same grievance procedures used by other sophisticated business enterprises. Those grievance procedures vary from tribe to tribe just as the procedures vary from business to business. For instance, tribes utilize summary grievance proceedings where a human resources official presents the dispute and its relevant documents to a review board and thirty minutes later, due process is delivered in the form of a final decision. On the other hand, tribal employers may permit a contested hearing where the aggrieved employee cross-examines witnesses, testifies on his own behalf, and has the right to appeal an adverse decision to the tribal court. Other tribes reject these options for a more traditional model which gives employees an opportunity to meet with decision makers, tell their story, and seek resolution.

The Ho-Chunk Nation, for example, has developed a sophisticated combination of statutory law, common law, and policy, which provide due process to employees in a variety of employment-related disputes. The nation's Department of Personnel (DOP) is the intersection where tribal employees meet due process. The DOP administers a mediation service which when used may resolve the dispute before a more formal grievance procedure is exercised by the employee. If a grievance is requested, the DOP is actively involved in facilitating the procedure.

The Ho-Chunk Nation's grievance procedure[239] consists of

---

[239] The author is grateful for the cooperation of the Ho-Chunk Nation in permitting the publication of its laws and policies, which are contained in appendix A. The nation's grievance policy can be found at Ho-Chunk Nation Personnel, Employment and Labor Code, chapter 5, section 34 (appendix A).

1. A suggestion to the employee to informally discuss the matter with the supervisor;
2. To initiate the grievance process the employee completes and files a form, which describes the dispute;
3. DOP collects information from the employer and employee and may attempt to mediate the dispute;
4. Serious disputes are defined and automatically qualify for a hearing and less serious disputes do not qualify for a hearing;
5. The nation has promulgated rules regarding a grievance hearing. Those rules detail the order of proceedings, which party has the burden of proof, an informal evidentiary standard and many other necessary provisions;
6. The grievance panel's decision is subject to review by a Ho-Chunk Nation regulator in charge of enforcing the nation's employment laws, and that decision is subject to an appeal to the nation's courts.

Through these procedures, the Ho-Chunk Nation provides an abundance of due process to employees from the more informal uses of mediation to the formal contested adversary proceeding. Employer due process is not just a grievance hearing after a work-related dispute arises, employer due process is a more comprehensive proposition.

An expanded definition of due process in the tribal workplace is helpful in reducing tribal politics, increasing employee performance, and limiting potential liability. Due process is partially delivered to employees through a grievance procedure, but the grievance hearing is effective only when the employer articulates employee standards and holds employees to those standards. When employers fail to define standards at the start of the employment relationship, workplace decisions are impacted by the vagaries of politics and popularity instead of by clearly defined rules. Accordingly, tribal employers provide due process to employees:

1. Through employee handbooks, job descriptions, and other employer documents providing written rules, which map the path to success and failure in the workplace;
2. Frequently communicating those rules and expectations through orientation, training, coaching, and discipline;
3. Uniform enforcement of the rules;

4. Providing an objective individual or body to evaluate workplace disputes which has the authority to make decisions loyal to the rules, but may be unpopular with tribal leadership.

To summarize, due process means

> Written rules
> Communicated to employees
> Applied fairly, and
> An opportunity to be heard by an independent body.

The last ingredient, an opportunity to be heard, is provided by tribal employers through complaint processes, grievances, peer review panels, tribal council oversight, tribal court review, and other ways.

Tribal grievance proceedings benefit from following best practices:

1. Obtain employee consent to tribal due process;
2. Train supervisors to embrace the due process provided by the employer;
3. Train peer review panels to understand their delegated authority;
4. Reduce the number of steps in a grievance to the amount which delivers meaningful due process;
5. Reduce the time grievance procedures consume;
6. Do not permit any employees or elected officials to circumvent the process;
7. Consider limited tribal court review of grievance decisions.

When disputes cannot be resolved through internal employer mechanisms like grievances or when employers fail to provide administrative processes to address disputes, employees will seek relief in courts, arbitration proceedings, or regulatory bodies. The questions of what entity can hear an employment dispute and what law applies to the matter is dependent on a variety of factors.

Can tribal employers and employees agree to arbitrate employment-related disputes?

Yes. Beyond the borders of Indian Country, employers frequently require employees to raise employment disputes before neutral private parties called arbitrators,[240] and this process of arbitration can certainly be used in Indian Country to address disputes between tribes and employees. In employment, home purchases and vendor contracts, arbitration is chosen as an alternative to a lawsuit before a court. There are advantages and disadvantages to arbitration just as there are advantages and disadvantages to judicial proceedings. Some tribes have enacted laws, which address alternative resolution processes. These laws deal with the enforceability of arbitration agreements between employer and employee, owner and vendor and consumer and manufacturer. A typical provision requiring arbitration may read

> Any controversy or claim arising out of or relating to this employment contract shall be settled by arbitration administered by the American Arbitration Association under its National Rules for the Resolution of Employment Disputes and judgment upon the award rendered by the arbitrator(s) may be entered in any court having jurisdiction thereof [or tribal court].

Arbitration can have several benefits for employers and employees. On the benefit side, arbitration can be less expensive, faster, and provide expertise in decision-makers which enhances the opportunity for justice. On the other hand, arbitration is still expensive, provides limited appellate review, and does not permit access to a jury. Employers are attracted to arbitration because arbitrators are perceived as more objective than juries which can devastate an employer with a huge award of punitive damages. Employees may be less inclined to see arbitration as a tool for changing an employer's poor practices in response to an incentive driven award.

Some tribes do not have tribal courts and therefore, arbitration can be a good choice for delivering due process in those instances where employment disputes arise. Appointment of an arbitrator to hear employment-related disputes can serve as a permanent solution or a temporary bridge while the tribe creates and delegates authority to a tribal court.

Frequently, informal due process in Indian Country looks like arbitration but has another label. For example, gaming commission license revocation

---

[240] Theodore Eisenberg, Elizabeth Hill, *Employment Arbitration and Litigation: An Empirical Comparison*, Research Paper 65, New York University School of Law (2003).

hearings, and patron exclusion proceedings are similar to arbitration. Frequently, these hearings operate under arbitration rules and the participants' experience is the same. The primary difference between an arbitration and a license revocation hearing is a private party is the arbiter in an arbitration while a governmental official is the "arbiter" in a license revocation proceeding.

In Indian Country, there is a layer of complication with the enforcement of an arbitration award. Outside the tribal context if an adverse arbitration award is not satisfied, the prevailing party seeks a judgment from a court. The United States Constitution and laws of the states require enforcement of arbitrator decisions in the jurisdiction where the dispute is heard and importantly where the arbitration is not held. Therefore, an arbitration held in Sante Fe can be enforced in Sante Fe and it can be enforced in Florida.

Within the tribal context, the same process is available by taking the arbitration award and seeking a tribal court judgment which should be forthcoming if the court has jurisdiction to enforce the award. If the judgment debtor has assets, wages, or property within the tribal court's jurisdiction, satisfaction is relatively straightforward. On the other hand, if the judgment debtor does not possess assets under the court's jurisdiction, the tribal court judgment is transferred to a state court under the principles of comity and full faith and credit. Whether a state court will accept a tribal court judgment is a product of state law and judicial discretion and therefore, specific analysis of the relevant jurisdiction is necessary.

Between states, full faith and credit of another state's judicial directive is required.[241] Tribal court judgments are granted full faith and credit or comity by state courts just as tribal courts recognize state court judgments. Comity attempts to solve the challenge when laws do not have effect beyond the reach of the sovereign which is the source of the law but nevertheless enforce a just result.[242] The importance of tribal courts and the dignity federal courts give their decisions weight in favor of comity.[243]

---

[241] United States Constitution, Art. IV § 1; 28 U.S.C. § 1738.
[242] *Hilton v. Guyot*, 159 U.S. 113 (1895).
[243] *Bird v. Glacier Electric Cooperative, Inc.*, 255 F.3d 1136, 1142 (9th Cir. 2001).

What legal forums exist to hear and decide employment disputes between tribal employers and their employees?

The answer will focus on the jurisdiction of tribal, state, and federal courts. Of course, tribal employers, like their nontribal counterparts, can utilize consensual private party dispute resolution like arbitration. Those alternatives are addressed in the previous section of this chapter.

Do tribal courts possess jurisdiction over employment-related disputes?

Yes. Tribal courts have jurisdiction over employment-related disputes. The United States Supreme Court has endorsed the inherent authority of tribes to evaluate conflicts by holding that tribal courts are appropriate forums for the exclusive adjudication of disputes affecting important personal and property interests of Indians and non-Indians.[244] Courts created by tribes are delegated authority to adjudicate a wide variety of issues just as the state and federal courts perform similar functions. The conversation regarding the exercise of authority by tribal courts is guided by two threshold questions dealing with the nature of authority granted by the tribe to its courts and a line of United State Supreme Court cases which evaluate whether, and over whom tribal courts can exercise power.

The first threshold question is whether the tribe has delegated to its courts the authority to hear employment-related claims. Tribal courts vary in the way they are organized, the power delegated to them, and the rules and laws applied. Generally, tribal courts are either a product of the tribe's constitution[245] or of an ordinance promulgated by the tribal council. Through these constitutions and ordinances, powers are delegated to the tribal court and whether the court can entertain an employment-related dispute is an answer found in these organic documents. These organic documents may define the nature of the relief a court can grant; whether immunity can be asserted and the extent of the court's jurisdiction over members and nonmember employees.

---

[244] *Santa Clara Pueblo v. Martinez,* 436 U.S. 49, 65 (1978).
[245] Not all tribes have constitutions. The Navajo Nation does not have a constitution and instead has a significant body of laws, traditions, and customs.

A second threshold question is whether the employer has attempted to preclude claims in court by providing other relief in the form of arbitration or more limited due process. For instance, some tribal employers attempt to eliminate claims to courts by making grievance procedures the exclusive remedy for employees seeking due process. There is a substantial body of nontribal common law, and a developing body of tribal common law, which address whether employee claims can be limited in the amount of due process and the path taken by due process. For instance, can a tribal employer preclude a tribal court claim through employee consent to a final grievance decision? Moreover, can a binding arbitration clause in an employment contract serve as the exclusive forum for disputes or are judicial remedies always available? The analysis must begin with determining whether tribal constitutional, statutory, or common law grant to employees due process rights (as one example) which a tribal employer attempts to limit through employee consent to an exclusive grievance procedure. In the absence of substantive legal rights granted by the tribe, the employee's consent to fundamentally fair rules should not receive much scrutiny from the courts.

Further development of these questions exceed the scope of this book, however, consenting adult employees have a choice of working for an employer and accepting the due process provided or reject these rules by selecting another employer. If an employer seeks competent employees, the marketplace is an excellent arbiter by forcing employers to grant real due process and access to fundamental fairness.

When a tribe provides a judicial forum to hear employment disputes how does it work?

If there is a tribal court, which has the authority to hear an employment dispute, the relevant question quickly becomes

> *Does the tribal court have the exclusive authority to hear disputes to the exclusion of state and federal courts?*

Whether the tribal court has jurisdiction is a complicated analysis which traces itself through several path-making cases in the federal court system. Before reviewing the cases from which the rules emerge, a statement of the general rules is beneficial.

The rules presume the employer is the tribe or a subdivision of the tribe and the employment activities are mainly confined to the reservation. These general rules further divide the analysis between employees who are members of the tribe and employees who are not members of the tribe. Employees who are not members of the tribal employer are referred to as nonmember employees. Nonmember employees can be Indians who belong to a tribe which is not the tribal employer or the employee may be a non-Indian. The three columns below help discern the general rules which ask these questions:

> *Is there a presumption that the tribal court has the power to hear the dispute? See Presumption of Jurisdiction below.*
>
> *Can the tribal court hear the dispute if the employee consents to the court's power? See Consent to Jurisdiction below.*
>
> *Even if the employee does not consent to the tribal court's power to hear the dispute, is the tribe's jurisdictional integrity important enough to assume jurisdiction? See Jurisdictional Integrity below.*

Those general rules are

Group	(1) *Presumption of Jurisdiction*	(2) *Consent to Jurisdiction*	(3) *Jurisdiction Integrity*
Tribal member Employees	Yes	Yes Unnecessary?	Yes Unnecessary?
Nonmember Employees	No	Yes	Maybe

Tribal member employees

General rule 1: Tribal courts can hear employment disputes between tribal member employees and the tribal employer.[246] A tribe has the power to delegate to its courts the authority to address disputes between the tribe and its

---

[246] *Diver v. Peterson*, 524 N.W.2d 288, 290 (Minn.Ct.App. 1994).

members. Therefore, tribal member employees are subject to the jurisdiction of the tribal court or other tribal forum. As the chart reveals, for tribal member employees, the tribe's jurisdictional powers are at its zenith and employee consent may not be necessary. However, for tribal member employees the presumption of jurisdiction is enhanced by employee consent.

Employees who are not members of the employer tribe

Less certainty accompanies the determination of whether a tribe can exercise jurisdiction over disputes between a tribal employer and an employee who is not a member of the tribe. Remember, nonmember refers to Indians from tribes which are not the employer tribe and to non-Indians. As the chart reveals there is not a presumption of tribal court jurisdiction for nonmember employees. As a result, consent of the employee is central to overcoming the presumption of no jurisdiction. If the employee argues lack of consent the tribe may still assert jurisdiction under a political integrity test.

General rule 2: Tribal courts can hear employment disputes between nonmember employees and the tribal employer when the tribal employer proves the employee voluntarily submitted to tribal jurisdiction through a consensual agreement.

General rule 3: If the tribal employer cannot prove a commercial consensual agreement between employee and employer, the tribal employer must demonstrate that the employment activities of these nonmembers have a direct effect on the political integrity, economic security, or health and welfare of the tribe.

General rules 1, 2, and 3 summarize the United States Supreme Court decision in *Montana v. United States*.[247] In *Montana*, the Court creates two paths for analysis of jurisdiction over nonmembers.

Tribes overcome the presumption against the authority of tribal courts to hear employment (civil) disputes involving nonmembers by meeting one or both of the *Montana* tests. Those *Montana* tests are

---

[247] 450 U.S. 544 (1981)

1. Tribes can exercise civil jurisdiction when nonmembers are involved if the nonmember consented to the tribe's authority; or
2. Tribes can exercise civil jurisdiction when nonmember behavior threatens or has a direct effect on the political integrity, economic security, or health and welfare of the tribe.

Tribal employers can therefore implement rules and provide dispute mechanisms which require adherence by all tribal employees (members, nonmembers, Indians, and non-Indians) when the tribal employer seeks and obtains meaningful consent to those rules and procedures from tribal employees. Consent is an ordinary mechanism valued by the law under many circumstances beyond employment. The law bolsters the value of consent when it enforces various rules imposed by banks, neighborhood associations, the municipal pool, and private schools.

This first rule under *Montana* could serve tribal employer and employee in most instances since consent is the essence of all employment relationships. Employees consent to the employer's use of their time and skills in exchange for green dollars and two consecutive days off each week. The benefit of this bargain attracts competent employees and tribal jurisdiction over disputes when the relationship sours.

The second *Montana* rule also makes sense. When people interact with tribes but do not explicitly raise their hand and consent to tribal jurisdiction, the tribe still needs to have the power to deal with disputes when those disputes are important to the tribe. In a case decided after *Montana*, the Supreme Court stated that to meet this test the tribe's interests must be demonstrably serious which is imperiled by the nonmember.[248] According to the Supreme Court, the safety of tribal roads was not enough to meet this stringent test,[249] nor access to tribal fire and police protection.[250] The *Montana* exceptions did not justify the application of tribal employment laws to the construction of a highway on a state right-of-way.[251] The second *Montana* test is difficult

---

[248] *Brendale v. Confederated Tribes and Bands of Yakima Indian Nation*, 492 U.S. 408 (1989).
[249] *Strate v. A-1 Contractors*, 520 U.S. 438 (1997).
[250] *Atkinson Trading Company, Inc., v. Shirley*, 121 S.Ct. 1825 (2001),
[251] *Montana Department of Transportation v. King*, 191 F.3d 1108 (1999).

for tribes to prove and because employment relationships are the essence of consent, *Montana's* "consent" test is the focus of most decisions in the employment arena.

Montana has created a legacy where subsequent courts do not defer to tribal sovereignty by assuming the tribe has the power to address disputes with nonmember employees. Instead, courts start from the opposite conclusion and find that tribal courts do not have the power to address these disputes unless the tribe proves jurisdiction exists. This presumption against tribal jurisdiction is important to the analysis.

This legacy was reinforced sixteen years after *Montana* when the Supreme Court, in a nonemployment case, held that tribal courts, as a presumptive matter, do not have jurisdiction over nonmembers.[252] Presumption is an important issue for courts since it gives the court a starting place in its analysis and answers the question of which party to a dispute has the obligation to prove a fact or legal principle. In this instance, with the presumption that tribal courts do not have the power to hear disputes between tribal employers and nonmember employees, the obligation is on the tribal employer to overcome the presumption of nonjurisdiction by demonstrating it meets one of the *Montana* exceptions which justify tribal court jurisdiction. These jurisdictional issues are almost always addressed early in the case and therefore will more than likely be raised and heard long before a trial which evaluates the merits of the dispute.

Historically, in addition to how an employee fits into the member and nonmember dichotomy, status of the land where the dispute occurs is an important element in gauging the strength of tribal jurisdiction. An on-reservation employer can exert its rules over employees with greater strength than a tribal employer can exert itself located sixty miles from the reservation boundary. Therefore in the employment context, the location of human resources where employees are terminated could be a factor in determining whether the tribe has jurisdiction to hear the litigation stemming from the discharge.

Status of land, however, is less important under reasoning of a more recent court decision. The Supreme Court wrote that the presumption of nonjurisdiction over nonmembers should apply regardless of the status of the

---

[252] *Strate v. A-1 Contractors*, 520 U.S. 438, 445 (1997).

land where the act occurs.[253] The court reinforced its decision by asserting that less focus on the status of the land makes sense because where land status is dispositive, the rules are more difficult to administer and give little notice to nonmembers. If this trend continues placing less emphasis on whether the employer is reservation based or involves fee or nonfee land, the *Montana* exceptions will continue to be used since the consent analysis does not need a connection to land to be useful.

An analytical headache causes significant cognitive dissonance over the status of lands when the federal government forced tribes to leave their lands, live on reservations, which were later chopped up in a mixture of land owned by tribes, the federal government, individual Indians, and non-Indians.[254] Because the federal government created a hodgepodge of land status between these diverse ownership interests, the earlier court decisions made difficult decisions resting in part on land status. Now the Supreme Court trend is away from a focus on the status of land to an analysis which focuses on the parties to the dispute.

Additional dissonance stems from the Supreme Court's rejection of a land status analysis which was created by federal policy and in the course of rejecting the analysis, the Supreme Court dilutes tribal sovereignty by creating a presumption *against* tribal jurisdiction. Common sense and historical principles certainly argue for a presumption in favor of tribal court jurisdiction for disputes occurring on tribal land whether the disputing parties are members or nonmembers. The presumption of tribal court jurisdiction is more compelling when tribal employees consent to the tribal employer's rules.

---

[253] *Nevada v. Hicks*, 121 S.Ct. 2304 (2001).

[254] The Allotment Act is the General Allotment Act or Dawes Act codified at 25 U.S.C. § 331 et seq. That Act had far reaching implications in the analysis of courts. See, *Merrion v. Jicarilla Apache Tribe*, 455 U.S. 130 (1982)(tribe has taxing authority over tribal lands leased by nonmembers) and compare that to *Atkinson Trading Company v. Shirley*, 121 S. Ct. 1825 (2001) (Tribe has no taxing authority over nonmember activities on land held by nonmembers in fee). *Oliphant* which addresses tribal criminal jurisdiction over non-Indians was not based upon the status of lands. Both *Montana* and *Strate* rejected tribal authority to regulate nonmember activities on land over which the tribe could not assert a landowner's right to occupy or exclude.

The Supreme Court in *Nevada v. Hicks* discussed *Montana* and tribal court jurisdiction over disputes arising from consensual agreements and the *Hicks* court quoted *Montana* as follows:

> To be sure, Indian tribes retain inherent sovereign power to exercise some forms of civil jurisdiction over non-Indians on their reservation, even on non-Indian fee lands. A tribe may regulate, through taxation, licensing, or other means, the activities of nonmembers who enter consensual relationships with the tribe or its members, through commercial dealings, contracts, leases, or other arrangements.[255]

Importantly the *Hicks* court, in distinguishing the *Hicks* facts from the *Montana* facts, asserted that *Montana* was "referring to private individuals who voluntarily submitted themselves to tribal regulatory jurisdiction by the arrangement that they (or their employers) entered into."[256] *Montana* finds and *Hicks* reinforces principles which when applied to employment relationships conclude that employees working for tribes voluntarily submit themselves to tribal jurisdiction and therefore disputes arising between employer and employee can be heard in tribal court.[257] Employees who execute a clear acknowledgement of tribal court remedies strengthen the tribal employer's claim that employees voluntarily submit themselves to tribal jurisdiction. Employee acknowledgement or consent to tribal court jurisdiction is discussed in chapter 6, which also includes a sample acknowledgement.

---

[255] *Hicks* at 371 citing *Montana*, 450 U.S. at 565.

[256] *Hicks* at 372.

[257] In *Plains Commerce Bank v. Long Family Land and Cattle Company, Inc.*, 128 S.Ct. 2709 (2008) the United States Supreme Court did not find a consensual relationship between a bank and a tribe justifying tribal court jurisdiction under *Montana*. The decision focused on the tribe's power to exercise power over fee land owned by nonmembers. Since this nonmember fee land was not in the tribe's control, the sale of the land did not trigger jurisdiction for the tribal court. The distinction between the sale of land and conduct between tribal employer and employee is well established and therefore *Plains Commerce Bank* should not impact the exercise of jurisdiction by tribal courts over employment disputes.

In a case involving two nonmember employees of a tribal gaming commission, the state court found it lacked jurisdiction because the tribe's assertion of jurisdiction triggered both *Montana* exceptions.[258] Because the claims of racial discrimination from employee against his supervisor were in the employment context, claims arising from employment met the *consent* test. Furthermore, the tribe met *Montana's* political integrity test which secured tribal jurisdiction. The political integrity test was met since the tribe exercised its sovereignty by promulgating law asserting its jurisdiction and policies to guide employment conduct.

Consensual relationships provide a sufficient link from a tribe to a nonmember therefore supporting the tribe's exercise of jurisdiction. This proposition was tested when a tribe altered the rules regarding the negotiation of union collective bargaining agreements by giving employees a choice to join or not join a union representing the employees in the bargaining agreement. The term open shop refers to a workplace where employees are not obligated to join a union which represents the employees and the term closed shop denotes workplaces where joining the union which represents the employees as a prerequisite to employment. *NLRB v. Pueblo of San Juan*[259] involves commercial dealings of a non-Indian company which owned and operated its business under a consensual agreement with the Pueblo. The agreement, in the form of a property lease, required the company to give preferential hiring to tribal members and it prohibited closed shops as to tribal members. A similar right-to-work provision, expanded to include all employees, was subsequently codified by the Pueblo Tribal Council.

Importantly the court found that the tribe's sovereign status was directly related to its ability to generate revenues through the regulation of commercial activities on the reservation. Lease provisions which restrict closed shops and give preferential hiring to tribal members are internal economic matters which directly affect a sovereign's right of self-government. Importantly, the court recognized the direct link between defining the terms and conditions of the employment relationship, the generation of revenues through economic enterprise and the preservation of tribal sovereignty. This important link has

---

[258] *Rodriquez v. Wong*, 2004 WL 49662 (Wash. Ct. App. 2004).
[259] 280 F.3d 1278 (10th Cir. 2000)

been lost in cases minimizing the link between sovereignty and the economic vitality of tribal commercial enterprise.[260]

The law recognizes the link between defined employment rules and the preservation of tribal sovereignty. Tribes reinforce these legal principles by entering into consensual agreements with employees. Tribes and tribal employees have a contract wherein the tribal employer gives money and other benefits to employees who trade time and talent. Employers define the terms and conditions of the employment relationship in employee handbooks. Employers universally declare in employee handbooks that a contract does not exist between employer and employee but that declaration is not true. A contract does exist between employers and employees and these contracts are the consensual agreements, which reinforce tribal jurisdiction.

In addition to consensual agreements, tribes can define the civil rules for nonmembers within the reservation on fee and trust lands when the conduct impacts the tribe's political integrity, economic security, health or welfare of the tribe.[261] Again the ability of a tribe to define the rules between tribal employer and employee meets this test.[262]

Lack of consent may create challenges for tribal employers under some circumstances. For example, workplace colleagues who are perpetrator and victim of sexual harassment are subject to the tribe's consensual jurisdiction. However, when the perpetrator is not an employee or otherwise consents to the tribe's jurisdiction, the tribe's assertion of jurisdiction may not be endorsed by the *Montana* analysis. In those circumstances where consent is the key pre-requisite to the exercise of tribal authority over nonmember tribal employees, what is the impact on the tribal employer's authority over

---

[260] *San Manuel Indian Bingo and Casino v. NLRB*, 475 F.3d 1306 (D.C. Cir. 2007).

[261] *Id.*

[262] There is an abundance of post-*Montana* decisions interpreting these tests. Those cases include *Strate v. A-1 Contractors*, 520 U.S. 438 (1997)(auto accident on state right of way within reservation did not grant tribal jurisdiction); *Atkinson Trading Company v. Shirley*, 532 U.S. 645 (2001)(tribe could not impose tax on non-Indian doing business within reservation); *Plains Commerce Bank v. Long Family Land and Cattle Company, Inc.*, 128 S.Ct. 2709 (2008)

nonemployee victims of harassment? The consent analysis can lead to some odd results. For instance, a patron at a convenience store located on tribal land who is refused service by a tribal employee may have entered into a consensual relationship with the tribe conferring tribal authority over the resulting dispute. However, the nonmember police officer responding to the fight which erupts between the convenience store manager and patron is probably not operating under these rules if the officer violates the civil rights of the store employee.[263]

Employee consent to tribal rules should be given considerable weight in determining whether the tribe's rules apply to the employment relationship. Irony percolates to the surface when courts limit the application of the tribe's authority as to nonmembers who are not coerced to accept the competitive wages, benefits and training provided by tribal employers. These consenting employees choose tribal employers, accept these numerous benefits, but when "justice" is not found these consenting employees sometimes ask another sovereign to rescue them from the application of tribal law. Economists speak in terms of opportunity costs which essentially requires a trade off in the selection of choice A over choice B. Opportunity cost highlights the give and take of the marketplace where contracting parties select A for the benefits promised while at the same time understanding that the benefits of B will not be realized. Tribal employees should benefit from the competitive wages provided and the justice dispensed by the tribe's courts. Both logic and economic principles should preclude an employee from choosing tribal employment and its benefits but rejecting the accepted rules once a dispute arises.

If the tribe does not have a tribal court, does the tribe have jurisdiction over employment-related disputes?

The tendency to link jurisdiction exclusively to courts tracks the thought process into the wrong direction. Whether a tribe has the power to hear and decide an employment-related dispute is a separate question from what forum will the tribe provide this opportunity? For all practical purposes, the question is linked to sovereignty. If the tribe can and does define the rules governing the employment relationship, the tribe's mechanisms apply for addressing disputes stemming from the employment relationship.

---

[263] *Nevada v. Hicks*, 121 S.Ct. 2304 (2001).

The question of jurisdiction precedes the question of forum. Jurisdiction is the power to hear the dispute; and forum is the person, committee, judge, family member, regulator, or administrator hearing the dispute. Generally, tribal employers include a grievance procedure for employee workplace disputes which may, or may not include a right to appeal the administrative decision (decision by the grievance process) to a tribal council[264] or tribal court. Traditional tribes may give employees an opportunity to be heard in forums which reflect the tribe's traditions and customs. Tribes may delegate the evaluation of these disputes to arbitrators, tribal council, regulatory bodies, or other internal entities.

Tribes use Tribal Employment Rights Ordinances (TERO), requiring the hiring of tribal members at competitive wages by outside firms working within the tribe's jurisdiction. As discussed in chapter 6, TERO and the regulator, which enforces TERO, can also provide a forum to address disputes for employees and tribal employers. TERO regulators frequently are best equipped to understand tribal employment law, share an objective view toward a dispute, and provide meaningful due process.

Do state courts possess jurisdiction over tribal employment-related disputes?

Generally, state courts do not have the power to hear claims against tribal employers.[265] The authority of states to exercise jurisdiction within its borders is, limited by the United States Constitution's delegation of authority as to Indians to the federal government.[266] Accordingly, federal law defines the limits of state court authority over civil matters arising in Indian Country.

---

[264] *Lawrence v. Barona Valley Ranch and Casino*, 64 Cal.Rptr.3d 23 (Cal.App. 2007)
[265] *Rodriquez v. Wong*, 82 P.3d 263 (Wash. App. 2004).
[266] Article I, section 8, clause 3 provides that "Congress shall have the Power . . . to regulate Commerce with foreign Nations, and among the several States, and with the Indian Tribes." Article II, section 2, clause 2 gives the President and the Senate the power to make treaties with Indian Tribes. See, *Worcester v. Georgia*, 31 U.S. 515, 559 (1832).

When the state of Georgia attempted to exercise jurisdiction within the Cherokee Nation, the United States Supreme Court rejected Georgia's assertion of power in *Worcester v. Georgia*.[267] As a general rule, state officials may not exercise authority within Indian Country unless Congress (the federal government) grants that authority.

More recently, the Supreme Court reinforced this principle by holding that a non-Indian could not sue an Indian in state court in connection with an event arising in Indian Country.[268] Tribal sovereignty is in part dependent upon not allowing state authority to go beyond state boundaries. If state laws are asserted beyond state boundaries, the laws infringe on tribal sovereignty. To safeguard against the infringement of state authority and the commensurate dilution of tribal sovereignty, the Supreme Court did not permit a state court to address an Indian Country dispute.

When tribal employers are sued in state courts, these sovereignty principles are used to address whether state courts possess power to hear the case (jurisdiction). Connecticut courts found that the tribe's establishment of a tribal gaming court with exclusive jurisdiction over employment matters enhanced the tribe's assertion of sovereign immunity when the gaming enterprise's former employee commenced an action in state court. In *Davidson v. Mohegan Tribal Gaming Authority*[269] plaintiff was employed by the tribal casino, needed dental surgery, asked for leave, and was denied. When plaintiff had the surgery, he missed work and therefore, violated the tribe's attendance policy and was terminated. The tribal court lawsuit was dismissed because it was filed late and the employee commenced an action in Connecticut state court. The state court dismissed the suit in response to the tribe's assertion of sovereign immunity. Importantly the state court noted that the tribe did not waive its immunity and probably enhanced its sovereignty by establishing a gaming court with "exclusive jurisdiction for the tribe for disputes arising out of or in connection with the gaming..." contracts, customers, employees, and others. The court also rejected the argument that since the casino is commercial in nature and purportedly

---

[267] 31 U.S. 515 (1832)
[268] *Williams v. Lee*, 358 U.S. 217 (1959).
[269] 2006 WL 2289781 (Conn. App. 2006)

not tribal it loses its sovereignty. Also in this case ICRA state court subject matter jurisdiction did not exist.

In *Riggs v. Bishop Paiute Gaming Corporation*,[270] a California state court dismissed employee claims for sexual harassment, discrimination, and other actions finding that the gaming corporation's assertion of sovereign immunity was valid. The Court rejected the employee's claim that sovereign immunity was waived by the tribe when it agreed in a tribal-state compact to follow employment laws at least as stringent as state and federal law. However, California found a waiver in an employment case when the employer executed an employment contract which incorporated a dispute mechanism permitting litigation in a tribunal of competent jurisdiction in any forum; whether tribal, state, or federal.[271]

Even if the tribe waives immunity for tort claims to the monetary limits of insurance coverage, the waiver does not equate to acquiescence of state court jurisdiction.[272] Sovereign immunity removes from the state court the power to hear or decide the issue raised in the litigation.[273]

State jurisdiction over a tribal employer was found in a case which focused on the employer's off-reservation behavior. In *Wright v. Collville Tribal Enterprise Corporation*[274] plaintiff was employed by a tribally owned off-reservation corporation. The corporation was formed under tribal law. Plaintiff raised a racial discrimination claim by alleging he was called "white bitch" and that some of his tribal member colleagues drove his car without his permission. He complained to his supervisors several times but despite assurances that

---

[270] 2003 WL 205183 (Cal. App. 2003)

[271] *Rivera v. Hopland Band of Pomo Indians Economic Development Corp.*, 2007 WL 2310773 (Cal. App. 2007).

[272] *Campo Band of Mission Indians v. Superior Court*, 39 Cal.Rptr.3d 875 (Cal. App. 2006).

[273] *Puyallup Tribe, Inc., v. Washington Department of Game*, 433 U.S. 165, 172 (1977).

[274] 127 Wash. App. 644, 111 P.3d 1244 (Wash. 2005); Also see, *Gavle v. Little Six, Inc.*, 555 N.W.2d 284 (Minn. 1996); But see, *Ogden v. Iowa Tribe of Kansas and Nebraska*, 250 S.W.3d 822 (MO App. 2008)(wrongful discharge claim finding no waiver of immunity as to off-reservation truck stop).

the behavior would not be tolerated, it continued. Wright quit and sued the corporation and his supervisor. Wright asserted race discrimination, racial harassment, and hostile work environment under Washington State Law. He also alleged negligent supervision and negligent infliction of emotional distress. Defendants' asserted the defense of sovereign immunity and objected to the Court's jurisdiction. The court concluded that neither tribal corporation nor supervisor were cloaked by the tribe's sovereign immunity. The question of whether the tribe's sovereign immunity applies is whether the tribe is the real party in interest defined by whether the tribe's assets are at risk in the suit. If the tribe's assets are at risk the tribe enjoys the benefit of immunity, however, if the tribe's assets are not at risk immunity does not apply.

Do federal courts possess jurisdiction over tribal employment-related disputes?

Maybe. The federal courts are limited by the authority delegated to the courts and by tribal sovereign immunity and the doctrine of tribal court exhaustion.

In civil proceedings, federal court jurisdiction is limited to claims which arise under federal law or to disputes which give one of the parties to the dispute the "home court" advantage. Where the dispute is governed by federal law the federal courts call this federal question jurisdiction.[275] Under federal question jurisdiction, the assertion of a state law sexual harassment claim is not enough for federal courts to assert jurisdiction.[276]

In home court advantage cases where citizens from different states are engaged in a dispute, the Minnesota resident, for example, has a perceived advantage in Minnesota state courts and his foe from Wisconsin has a perceived advantage

---

[275] 28 U.S.C. § 1331 or 1343; See, *Sharber v. Spirit Mountain Gaming, Inc.*, 65 Fed. Appx. 151 (9th Cir. 2003), reversed on other grounds 343 F.3d 974 (9th Cir. 2003); *Dobbs v. Anthem Blue Cross & Blue Shield*, 475 F.3d 1176 (10th Cir. 2007); *Oklahoma Tax Commission v. Graham*, 489 U.S. 838, 841 (1989)(the possible existence of a tribal immunity defense does not convert state law claims into federal question); *Ferguson v. SMSC Gaming Enterprise*, 475 F.Supp.2d 929 (D.Minn. 2007).
[276] *Rueles v. Eagle Mountain Casino*, 2006 WL 547964 (E.D.Cal. 2006).

in Wisconsin state courts. The federal courts can hear the dispute between the Minnesota and Wisconsin residents and even though the court may physically be located in either state, because the court is part of the federal system, there is a perception that the home court advantage is mitigated. This form of federal court jurisdiction is called "diversity of citizenship."[277]

Through these two sources of jurisdiction, federal courts can hear disputes which focus on federal statutes like the Fair Labor Standards Act (federal question jurisdiction) or a dispute which does not involve a federal law but is between citizens of different states (diversity jurisdiction).

Unincorporated tribal employers cannot sue or be sued in federal court under diversity jurisdiction as the tribe is not a citizen of the state.[278] Even if a federal court has the power (jurisdiction) to hear a dispute involving a tribal employer, sovereign immunity can raise a hurdle to the suit.[279] The sovereign immunity defense precludes suit either because the court does not have the delegated authority to hear the dispute or the tribal defendant does not consent to the lawsuit. If applicable, the defense of sovereign immunity concludes the lawsuit as to the immune party without further analysis of culpability. Said another way, the immunity defense stops the lawsuit without any analysis of the immune party's responsibility for the alleged wrongdoing. Like other sovereigns, the immunity defense is a necessary corollary to tribal sovereignty and self-determination.[280]

---

[277] 28 U.S.C. § 1332

[278] *Ninigret Development Corp., v. Narragansett Indian Wetuomuck Housing Authority*, 207 F.3d 21, 27 (1st Cir. 2000); *Romanella v. Hayward*, 114 F.3d 15, 16 (2d Cir. 1997); Gaines v. Ski Apache, 8 F.3d 726, 729 (10th Cir. 1993); *Standing Rock Sioux Indian Tribe v. Dorgan*, 505 F.2d 1135, 1140 (8th Cir. 1974); *Barker-Hatch v. Viejas Group Baron Long Capitan Band of Digueno Mission Indians*, 83 F.Supp.2d 1155, 1157 (S.D.Cal. 2000); *Calumet Gaming Group-Kansas, Inc., v. Kickapoo Tribe*, 987 F.Supp. 1321, 1324-25 (D.Kan. 1997); But see, *Warn v. E. Band of Cherokee Indians*, 858 F.Supp. 524, 526 (W.D.N.C. 1994); *Tribal Smokeshop, Inc. v. Alabama-Coushatta Tribes*, 72 F.Supp.2d 717, 718 n. 1 (E.D.Tex. 1999). Under the Maine Indian Settlement Act of 1980 the law expressly applies diversity jurisdiction to Maine tribes. *Atkins v. Penobscot Nation*, 130 F.3d 482, 485 (1st Cir. 1997).

[279] *Adams v. Moapa Band of Paiute Indians*, 991 F.Supp. 1218 (D.Nev. 1997).

[280] *Three Affiliated Tribes v. Wold Engineering*, 476 U.S. 877, 890 (1985).

Congress can, but has not, waived tribal immunity in employment matters. Contrary to waiver of immunity, Congress has preserved tribal immunity under a federal program which permits tribes to use federal dollars in running certain tribal programs.[281] Immunity applies to suits brought by nonmembers.[282]

As an example of immunity, in *Willis v. Bashas Inc.*[283] Plaintiff an African American sued an on-reservation grocery store which refused to hire him because he was not Navajo. Defendant grocery store followed Navajo preference as it was a requirement of the lease Defendant executed. Plaintiff proceeded in the suit under Title VII of the Civil Rights Act of 1964. In response to Defendant's motion to dismiss, the Court refused deciding that it could proceed without the Navajo Nation as a party Defendant but would tailor any judgment in the case respecting the Navajo Nation's immunity and noting that there may be little left to litigate.

In *Cohen v. Winkleman and Comanche Nation College,*[284] plaintiff entered into a three year employment contract with the tribal college. The contract could be terminated for cause or on thirty days written notice, but in the latter situation plaintiff was entitled to the monies due and owing under the contract. The agreement explicitly applied Comanche law and required suit to be heard in the tribal court. The federal court dismissed the breach of contract claim on immunity grounds.

Sovereign immunity can have adverse consequences for the employees commencing suit and the lawyers signing pleadings, which start these actions. Lawyers commencing actions in federal court, without performing the requisite due diligence in evaluating whether the federal court possesses jurisdiction to hear a dispute, can be sanctioned by the court when the tribe seeks dismissal of the claim. The rules of civil procedure require lawyers to file claims only after the lawyer does her homework in evaluating the facts and the law. If the lawyer believes, after performing the necessary research, there

---

[281] Indian Self-Determination and Education Assistance Act of 1975, 25 U.S.C. § 450n(1); *Demontiney v. U.S.*, 255 F.3d 801 (9th Cir. 2001).
[282] *Lineen v. Gila River Indian Community*, 276 F.3d 489 (9th Cir. 2002); *Wilson v. Turtle Mountain Band of Chippewa Indians*, 459 F.Supp. 366 (D.N.D. 1978)
[283] 2006 WL 1328833 (D.Ariz. May 15, 2006).
[284] 428 F.Supp.2d 1184 (W.D. Okla.2006).

is a claim the lawyer is permitted to file suit in court. The rules of procedure, however, permit courts to sanction lawyers for failing to perform the requisite due diligence before asserting claims.[285]

The lack of power to hear a case in federal court may, or may not, create circumstances where employees are without a forum to enforce their rights. For example, the tribe could voluntarily follow the federal leave law, grant access to tribal court for employees who believe there is noncompliance and follow the tribal court's decisions. Under this voluntary scenario, the law would apply and there is an enforcement mechanism. If the tribe does not voluntarily follow the law and provide for tribal court review, are there times when laws apply but there is not the means for enforcing these rules? Yes. The United States Supreme Court has said there is a difference between the right to demand compliance with the law and the means available to enforce the law.[286]

A promise to follow federal law and alleged failure does not obviate immunity. In *Chayoon v. Sherlock*,[287] The court addressed whether incorporating federal law into an employee handbook serves to waive the tribe's sovereign immunity. The court stated that courts have consistently applied two complementary principles to waivers of immunity: (1) a sovereign's waiver must be unambiguous, and (2) a sovereign's interest encompasses not merely whether it may be sued but where it may be sued.[288] The tribe's employment forms do not provide a clear waiver of sovereign immunity.

Even if the federal court possesses the power to hear an employment-related dispute, there may be an obligation to first present the dispute to a tribal court. The doctrine which describes this obligation to give tribal courts the first opportunity to deliver justice is called tribal court exhaustion. The "exhaustion" reference captures the idea that parties to a dispute must first exhaust any available tribal court remedies before another sovereign's courts

---

[285] *Gallegos v. Jicarilla Apache Nation*, 2003 WL 22854632 (10th Cir. 2003)(federal civil rights claims); *Charland v. Little Six, Inc.*, 112 F.Supp.2d 858 (D. Minn. 2000)(frivolous claim under Title VII).

[286] *Kiowa Tribe v. Manufacturing Tech. Inc.*, 523 U.S. 751 (1998).

[287] 2005 WL 1473902 (Conn. App. 2005).

[288] Citing *Garcia v. Akwesasne Housing Authority*, 268 F.3d 76, 86 (2nd Cir. 2001).

can entertain the dispute. The leading tribal court exhaustion case is the United States Supreme Court decision in *National Farmers Union Insurance Company v. Crow Tribe*.[289]

Can a tribe be sued over an employment related dispute?

Yes. Tribes can be sued over employment-related disputes. Whether the tribal employer can defend itself on the merits of the claim, seek dismissal under immunity or jurisdictional grounds, or assert the tribal court exhaustion doctrine are separate questions.

Employees within tribal jurisdictions commence employment-related suits against tribes arguing tribal law. The Ho-Chunk Nation,[290] Navajo Nation,[291] and Grand Ronde tribes,[292] to name a few, permit employee actions against the tribal employer and have employment codes which define the parameters of employee rights, due process and procedure.[293] For example, Grand Ronde law waives immunity allowing judicial review of final employment decisions made by governmental and enterprise employers within the tribe's jurisdiction.[294] A final employment decision is the result of the administrative grievance process granted to tribal employees and employees can appeal the grievance decision to the tribal court for review.[295]

---

[289] 471 U.S. 845 (1985).

[290] *Warner v. Ho-Chunk Nation*, SU 06-5 (Ho-Chunk Nation Supreme Court 2007); *Twin v. Ho-Chunk Nation*, SU 05-09 (Ho-Chunk Nation Supreme Court 2006).

[291] *Hood v. Navajo Nation Head Start*, SC-CV-11-05 (Navajo Nation Supreme Court 2005).

[292] Employment Action Review Ordinance § 255.5(c).

[293] For example the Navajo Preference in Employment Act, 15 NTC 7 (1990) is a comprehensive law which defines tribe specific preference, delegates authority to a regulator and provides specific hearing procedures for Commission oversight of the process.

[294] Id.

[295] *McCallister v. Spirit Mountain Gaming, Inc.*, 33 ILR 6057 (Grand Ronde Tr.Ct. 2005)(Employee pursued a hostile work environment claim asserting tort claims under another tribal law, and the court rejected the claims by holding the employee's exclusive remedy was the tribe's employment specific ordinance).

These examples raise the interesting question of whether tribes should assert the defense of sovereign immunity to employment claims. Without diminishing tribal governments' prerogative to make independent decisions, there are compelling reasons for tribal employers to permit employment actions against the tribe in tribal courts or tribal administrative forums. When tribes fail to provide due process and fundamental fairness to tribal employees the tribe will (1) fail to attract the best employees, (2) increase uncertainty in the workplace, (3) attract interest from federal regulators, and (4) present opportunities for costly litigation. By giving employees an opportunity for due process within the parameters of tribal administrative and judicial rules, the tribes' best interests can be served. If tribes permit employment-related suits in tribal forums, damages can be limited under the law.

The issue which raises serious tribal sovereignty questions is whether tribes can be sued in state or federal courts over employment-related matters.

Can a tribe assert the defense of sovereign immunity in response to an employment related dispute?

Unless the tribe has waived its immunity defense, tribes can raise immunity in tribal, state, and federal courts causing the lawsuit to end without evaluation of the merits or substance of the dispute.

Tribal sovereign immunity is governed by federal law.[296] Indian tribes have long been recognized as possessing the common-law immunity from suit traditionally enjoyed by sovereign powers.[297] The analysis begins with the premise that tribes are "domestic dependent nations" which exercise inherent sovereign authority over their members and territories.[298] Tribal sovereign

---

[296] *Kiowa Tribe of Oklahoma v. Mfg. Technologies, Inc.*, 523 U.S. 751, 754, 118 S.Ct. 1700, 140 L.Ed.2d 981 (1998).

[297] *Santa Clara Pueblo v. Martinez*, 436 U.S. 49, 58, 98 S.Ct. 1670, 56 L.Ed.2d 106 (1978); *Oklahoma Tax Commission v. Citizen Band, Potawatomi Indian Tribe [of Oklahoma]*, 498 U.S. 505, 509, 111 S.Ct. 905, 112 L.Ed.2d 1112 (1991); *United States v. United States Fidelity & Guaranty Co.*, 309 U.S. 506, 512, 60 S.Ct. 653, 84 L.Ed. 894 (1940).

[298] *Oklahoma Tax Commission v. Citizen Band, Potawatomi Indian Tribe [of Oklahoma]*, supra, at 509, 111 S.Ct. 905, citing *Cherokee Nation v. Georgia*, 30 U.S. (5 Pet.) 1, 17, 8 L.Ed. 25 (1831)." *Kizis v. Morse Diesel International, Inc.*, supra, 260 Conn. at 52-53, 794 A.2d 498.

immunity is dependent upon neither the location nor the nature of the tribal activities.[299] An Indian tribe is subject to suit only when Congress has authorized the suit or the tribe has waived its immunity. However, such waiver may not be implied, but must be expressed unequivocally.[300] The Supreme Court has refused to find a waiver of tribal immunity based on policy concerns, perceived inequities arising from the assertion of immunity, or the unique context of a case.[301] However, the Supreme Court did find an implied waiver of immunity when the tribe agreed to a standard arbitration clause in a construction contract.[302]

The leading case on the standard for congressional abrogation of tribal sovereign immunity is *Santa Clara Pueblo v. Martinez.*[303] In this Indian Civil Rights Act case, the tribe denied membership to the children of female members while permitting membership for children of male members of the tribe. The membership criteria were inconsistent with the equal protection of law guaranteed by ICRA. The court found that even if the law applied the tribe's sovereign immunity was not abrogated since the court could not find evidence supporting unequivocal intent to abrogate which is necessary before the court can find that the tribe lost the opportunity to assert the immunity defense. Therefore even if a statute applies to a tribe it does not mean that Congress abrogated tribal immunity in adopting it.[304] Said another way, whether a tribe is subject to a statute and whether a tribe may be sued for violating the statute are entirely different questions.[305]

---

[299] *Kiowa Tribe of Oklahoma v. Mfg. Technologies, Inc.,* supra 523 U.S. at 760, 118 S.Ct. 1700 (applying tribal sovereign immunity to claim of breach of commercial contract executed off reservation).

[300] *Kizis v. Morse Diesel International, Inc.,* supra, 260 Conn. at 54, 794 A.2d 498.

[301] *Ute Distribution Corp. v. Ute Indian Tribe,* 149 F.3d 1260,1267 (10th Cir.1998), citing *Kiowa Tribe of Oklahoma v. Mfg. Technologies, Inc.,* supra, 523 U.S. at 758, 118 S.Ct. 1700.

[302] *C & L Enterprises, Inc., v. Citizen Band Potawatomi Indian Tribe of Oklahoma,* 121 S.Ct. 1589 (2001) (contract stated that arbitration award could be enforced in any court having jurisdiction).

[303] 436 U.S. 49 (1978).

[304] *Kiowa Tribe of Oklahoma v. Manufacturing Tech, Inc.,* 523 U.S. 751 (1998).

[305] *Florida Paraplegic Association v. Miccosukee Tribe,* 166 F.3d 1126, 1130 (11th Cir. 1999).

The Supreme Court stated there are reasons to doubt the wisdom of tribal sovereign immunity, for example, the fact that it "can harm those who are unaware that they are dealing with a tribe, who do not know of tribal immunity, or who have no choice in the matter, as in the case of tort victims."[306] To the extent, however, that "[t]hese considerations might suggest a need to abrogate tribal immunity," courts must defer "to the role Congress may wish to exercise in this important judgment."[307] When used by employees who reap the benefits of competitive wages and health care from their tribal employers, these arguments against immunity are convenient uses of employee amnesia asserting no former knowledge of the status of their employer as a tribe.

Although the initiation of a lawsuit by a tribe may constitute consent, the corresponding waiver of tribal sovereign immunity has been held not to extend beyond the court's adjudication of the merits of that particular controversy.[308] Moreover, tribal sovereign immunity bars even compulsory counterclaims filed against a tribe in an action commenced by the tribe.[309]

---

[306] *Kiowa Tribe of Oklahoma v. Mfg. Technologies, Inc.*, supra, at 758, 118 S.Ct. 1700.

[307] Id.

[308] See *Three Affiliated Tribes of the Fort Berthold Reservation v. Wold Engineering, P.C.*, 476 U.S. 877, 891, 106 S.Ct. 2305, 90 L.Ed.2d 881 (1986) (tribes' access to sue in state court may not be conditioned on global waiver); *Schaghticoke Indians of Kent, Connecticut, Inc. v. Potter*, 217 Conn. 612, 622 n. 9, 587 A.2d 139 (1991) (tribal action in state court insufficient to constitute consent); *McClendon v. United States*, 885 F.2d 627, 630 (9th Cir.1989) (plaintiff tribes consent only to risk of adverse determination).

[309] See *Oklahoma Tax Commission v. Citizen Band, Potawatomi Indian Tribe of Oklahoma*, supra, 498 U.S. at 509, 111 S.Ct. 905 (tribes possess immunity from cross-suits. Articulating a narrow exception to the foregoing rule, the United States Supreme Court has held that a defendant in a tribal action may assert counterclaims against the tribe to set off the tribe's claims and limit its recovery. See *United States v. United States Fidelity & Guaranty Co.*, 309 U.S. at 511-12, 60 S.Ct. 653; *Jicarilla Apache Tribe v. Andrus*, 687 F.2d 1324, 1344 (10th Cir.1982); *Frederick v. United States*, 386 F.2d 481, 488 (5th Cir.1967). This "recoupment-counterclaim exception" is also found in state sovereign immunity jurisprudence. See, e.g., *United States v. Forma*, 42 F.3d 759, 764-65 (2d Cir.1994). In both state and tribal sovereign immunity cases, however, the

Whether asserted by tribal, state, or federal sovereigns, the sovereign immunity defense is a powerful tool which sometimes is endorsed by fairness and equity and at other times inconsistent with those principles.

Immunity is a necessary defense for tribal employers when employees sue their tribal employers in state or federal courts after consenting to exclusive remedies made available by the tribal employer. These circumstances arise when the employee reports to work after accepting a job, participates in employee orientation, executes the acknowledgement memorializing consent to the exclusive application of tribal rules and forums which include a grievance procedure, but thereafter when the employee believes his rights are trampled, the local state or federal court seems more fair. Litigation in that local state or federal court violates the employee's promise to only use the tribe's forum and it directly challenges the tribe's sovereignty. Under these circumstances, the use of immunity by the tribal employer may be the only way to realize the benefit of the bargain wherein the employer traded competitive wages for employee consent to tribal rules.

There may be instances where the use of immunity in tribal court leaves the claimant without a remedy. For instance, an employee tells a long and credible story enumerating complaints about her working conditions which violate the employer's handbook, specific standard operating procedures, and explicit provisions of the law. The employee has, consistent with policy, presented numerous complaints to the employer's human resources department regarding the poor conditions and the multiple breaches of law and policy. The human resources department has taken no apparent steps to deal with these serious complaints and the employee sues the tribal employer. Before the employer presents a response or answer to the complaint, without confirming or denying the allegations in the complaint, and without addressing the employee's complaints, the employer requests the court to dismiss the complaint. The court hears no evidence, does not conduct a trial, but rules that the sovereign cannot be sued. The lawsuit ends without the court evaluating the merits of the complaint. Tribal, state and federal sovereigns possess a powerful defense in the form of sovereign immunity.

---

    exception is applicable only when the recoupment counterclaim arises out of the "same transaction or occurrence" as the underlying claim. *Jicarilla Apache Tribe v. Andrus* at 1344.

Tribal employers have utilized immunity in a variety of disputes. Immunity bars employee actions for wrongful termination suits against tribal businesses operated on and off the reservation,[310] but not successful in other matters alleging off-reservation conduct.[311] On a motion invoking sovereign immunity to dismiss for lack of jurisdiction, the Plaintiff bears the burden of proving by a preponderance of the evidence that jurisdiction exists.[312] An action against a tribal entity is an action against the tribe; therefore, immunity protects the tribal entity.[313]

The assertion of immunity generates scrutiny by courts evaluating the entity raising the defense. In *Runyon v. Association of Village Council Presidents*,[314] the court reasoned that immunity applies if the tribe is a real party in interest. To determine real party status the tribe's financial relationship to the entity is of paramount importance. If a judgment reaches the tribe's assets immunity can apply but if a judgment will not reach the tribe's assets, immunity will not apply.

Whether the tribe is the employer, or a contractor standing in the tribe's shoes as employer, can be a factor in whether a lawsuit circumvents the defense of sovereign immunity. Harrah's, a private nontribal corporation, contracted with a tribe to manage the tribal gaming enterprise.[315] When a dispute over leave emerged, the court reasoned that for sovereign immunity to apply, Harrah's had to be a subordinate economic entity to the tribe. In ruling whether Harrah's was a subordinate economic entity of the tribe, the court evaluated numerous factors:

---

[310] *Baker v. Menominee Nation Casino*, 897 F.Supp. 389, 394 (E.D. Wis. 1995) (tribal casino immune from employee wrongful termination suit); *Gavle v. Little Six, Inc.*, 555 N.W.2d 284, 296 (Minn. 1996) (Tribal business operating a casino immune from sexual harassment claim); *Pink v. Modoc Indian Health Project, Inc.*, 157 F.3d 1185, 1187 (1998)(off reservation tribal business immune from employee's racial discrimination, wrongful discharge and retaliatory discharge claims); *Tenney v. Iowa Tribe of Kansas*, 243 F.Supp.2d 1196, 1199 (D.Kan. 2003).

[311] *Wright v. Colville Tribal Enterprise Corporation*, 111 P.3d 1244 (Wash. App. 2005).

[312] *Garcia v. Akwesasne Housing Authority*, 268 F.3d 76, 84 (2nd Cir. 2001).

[313] *Local Woodworkers Union v. Menominee Tribal Enterprise*, 595 F.Supp. 859, 862 (E.D.Wis. 1984).

[314] 84 P.3d 437 (Alaska 2004)

[315] *Johnson v. Harrah's Kansas Casino Corp.* 2006 WL 463138 (D.Kan. 2006)

1. the announced purpose for which the entity was formed;
2. whether the entity was managed to form or exploit specific tribal resources;
3. whether federal policy designed to protect Indian assets and tribal cultural autonomy is furthered by the extension of sovereign immunity to the entity;
4. whether the entity is organized under the tribe's laws or constitution rather than federal law;
5. whether the entity's governing body is comprised mainly of tribal officials;
6. whether the tribe has legal title or ownership of the property used by the entity;
7. whether tribal officials exercise control over the administration or accounting activities of the organization;
8. whether the tribe's governing body has power to dismiss members of the organization's governing body;
9. whether the entity generates its own revenue;
10. whether a suit against the entity would impact the tribe's fiscal resources, and whether it may bind or obligate tribal funds;

The court placed paramount importance on the tenth factor. In evaluating all of the factors, the Court found against Harrah's ability to assert the defense of sovereign immunity.

If a tribe creates a separate entity and that entity is the employer, courts evaluate the organic documents creating these entities to determine the extent of tribal influence and protection. Section 17 corporations are separate legal entities created by Congress under a charter which defines the owner of the entity as the tribe, how the corporation is operated through the delegation of authority to a board and officers of the corporation, whether the corporation can sue or be sued, and under what circumstances can the corporation waive sovereign immunity.[316] When tribes separately organize a housing authority[317] or corporation,[318] it

---

[316] 25 U.S.C. § 477.
[317] *Dillon v. Yangton Sioux Tribal Housing Authority*, 144 F.3d 581 (8th Cir. 1998).
[318] *Namakagon Development Company v. Bois Forte Residential Housing Authority*, 517 F.2d 508 (8th Cir. 1975).

does not necessarily waive its immunity. In some cases, the inclusion of a "sue or be sued" clause does not waive immunity[319] but other cases have reached the opposite conclusion.

Can an employee, official, or agent of the tribe assert the defense of sovereign immunity if sued in an employment related dispute?

The cloak of immunity, which protects the tribe from suit if raised, can also protect the agents, officials, and employees of the tribe. Extension of the immunity defense to agents, officials, and employees makes sense since the tribe acts through its individual representatives. The doctrine of tribal immunity extends to individual tribal officials acting in their representative capacity and within the scope of their authority.[320] The doctrine does not extend to tribal officials when acting outside their authority in violation of state law.[321] Tribal immunity also extends to all tribal employees acting within their representative capacity and within the scope of their official authority.[322] Tribes are immune from suit in state and federal court.[323] The immunity protection extends to businesses owned by the tribe if it functions as an arm of the tribe.[324] If a sovereign did not have the power to make the law, a tribal official enforcing the law is acting outside the scope of authority.[325] Some courts permit the assertion of immunity for all employees

---

[319] *Hagen v. Sisseton-Wahpeton Community College*, 205 F.3d 1040 (8th Cir. 2000).

[320] *Puyallup Tribe, Inc. v. Dept. of Game of Washington*, 433 U.S. 165, 171-72, (1977); *Davis v. Littell*, 398 F.2d 83 (9th Cir. 1968); *Ferguson v. SMSC Gaming Enterprise*, 475 F.Supp.2d 929 (D.Minn. 2007) (no individual liability under Title VII even if it applied).

[321] Id., Also see, *Santa Clara Pueblo v. Martinez*, 436 U.S. 49, 59 (1978); *Kizis v. Morse Diesel International, Inc.*, 260 Conn. 46, 51 n. 7, 794 A.2d 498 (2002)

[322] *Bassett v. Mashantucket Pequot Museum & Research Center, Inc.*, 221 F. Sup.2d 271, 278 (D.Conn.2002).

[323] *Kiowa Tribe of Oklahoma v. Mfg. Tech.*, 523 U.S. 751 (1998).

[324] *Marceau v. Blackfeet Housing Authority*, 455 F.3d 974 (9th Cir. 2006).

[325] *Northern States Power Company v. Prairie Island Mdewakanton Sioux Indian Community*, 991 F.2d 458, 460 (8th Cir. 1993); See, Ex Parte Young, 209 U.S. 123, 159 (1908); *Pennhurst State Sch. & Hosp. v. Halderman*, 465 U.S. 89 (1984).

of the tribe,[326] but others save immunity for employees at the top of the organizational chart.[327]

Terminated employees cannot avoid the tribe's defense of sovereign immunity by suing tribal officials in their individual capacity. In *Sabiron v. Gregory*,[328] plaintiff sued the tribal casino employer for wrongful termination alleging that he was terminated because he exposed illegal gaming. The employee sued seventeen members of the present and former tribal council and the defendants raised the defense of sovereign immunity. The employee alleged that his employer violated federal law.[329] The court rejected the employee's claim finding that immunity precluded suit reasoning that the employee-plaintiff could not evade immunity by suing tribal officials instead of the tribe and even if the federal law applied to the tribe does not mean that Congress abrogated the immunity defense in enacting the law. The cloak of immunity which protects the tribe also protects its officials when those officials are acting within the course and scope of their duties for the tribe. Moreover, the court found that immunity protects tribal officials when making discretionary managerial acts like personnel decisions.

In *Van Etten v. Mashantucket Pequot Gaming Enterprise*,[330] plaintiff was seriously injured in an automobile accident after a holiday celebration which was held for the benefit of tribal gaming employees. The injured person sued the tribe and

---

[326] *Bassett v. Mashuntucket Pequot Museum and Research Center, Inc.* 221 F.Supp.2d 271, 278 (D.Conn. 2002)

[327] *Baugus v. Brunson*, 890 F.Supp. 908, 911 (E.D. Cal. 1995)(security officer not a tribal official).

[328] 2005 WL 1274984 (Cal. Ct. App. 2005)

[329] Federal Financial Institution Act, 31 U.S.C. 5328.

[330] 2005 WL 3112753 (Conn. 2005); Also see, *Cook v. Avi Casino Enterprise, Inc.* 2006 WL 3694859 (D.Ariz. 2006); *Filer v. Tohono O'Odham Nation Gaming Enterprise*, 129 P.3d 78, 85 (Ariz.App. 2006)(court found that employees of tribal casino who allegedly served alcohol to an intoxicated patron who subsequently caused a fatal auto accident protected by sovereign immunity); *Basset v. Massachusetts Pequot Museum & Research Center, Inc.*, 221 F.Supp.2d 271, 277 (D.Conn. 2002). But see, *Baugus v. Brunson*, 890 F.Supp. 908, 911 (E.D. Cal. 1995) (immunity extends to tribal official and security guard not a tribal official).

individual employees of the gaming enterprise who organized the holiday party. At least some of the costs of the party were satisfied from contributions from the employees. In dismissing the complaint, the court found that the defendant employees acted within the scope of employment which is determined by evaluating whether the employee acted, at least in part, to serve the employer. Another way of asking the same question is whether the employees conduct was disobedient or unfaithful to the employer's business.

Does a tribal employer waive its immunity relating to off-reservation activity?

In a world without nuance, the answer is tribes do not waive their immunity from suit when engaged in activity off the reservation.[331] When nuance is an ingredient of the response, the answer is layered with additional analysis. A hypothetical provides insight on the question.

The ABC tribe has twenty thousand acres of land, which is outlined by reservation boundaries. The tribe operates a government and enterprises on the reservation. The ABC tribe also owns and operates a hotel one hundred miles away from the reservation where the ABC tribe has implemented a policy where every thirteenth guest is tossed into the hotel's pool just after check-in. After toweling off, guests 13, 26, and 39 commence a lawsuit raising claims of battery, intentional infliction of emotional distress, and negligence naming the ABC tribe as the defendant. Is the tribe immune?

There are two practical answers. First, guests 13, 26, and 39 can argue that the ABC tribe's ownership of the off-reservation hotel exposes the assets of the hotel to suit and available for satisfaction of a judgment. On the other hand, the existence of a commercial venture off the reservation does not dilute the sovereignty of the ABC tribe within the reservation. Courts recognize that tribes, like corporations, act as unincorporated legal persons when engaging in off reservation business enterprises involving non-Indians and in those situations the tribe is subject to generally applicable laws.[332]

---

[331] *Kiowa Tribe of Oklahoma v. Manufacturing Technologies, Inc.*, 523 U.S. 751 (1998).

[332] *San Manuel Indian Bingo and Casino v. NLRB*, 475 F.3d 1306 (D.C. Cir. 2007).

In *Kiowa Tribe of Oklahoma v. Manufacturing Technologies, Inc.*,[333] the Supreme Court addressed whether a tribe's off-reservation execution of a contract waived the tribe's immunity from suit in state court when a dispute arose under the contract. Also at stake in the suit was whether the commercial, rather than the governmental, nature of the transaction was determinative in the analysis. The Supreme Court preserved the tribe's defense of immunity and rejected the commercial government distinction.

Can the federal government be responsible for the acts of tribal employees when the employees work in programs funded by the federal government?

Yes. Congress extended the liability of the United States under the Federal Tort Claims Act (FTCA) through Public Law 101-512,[334] which imposes liability on the United States for the acts of tribal organizations and their employees administering a grant under the Tribally Controlled School Act of 1988 (TCSA).[335] Employees of a school operated under a TCSA grant are considered employees of the Bureau of Indian Affairs and can be sued under the FTCA. In *Adams v. Tunmore*,[336] a volunteer employee receiving a stipend from the tribe's general fund worked in a school funded by the TCSA. The court addressed whether the manner of payment and the source of funds impacted whether the FTCA applied, and the court said no. The court focused on the employee's work and the mission of the program, which was financed by the federal government in concluding that federal protection extended to these facts.

Congress has also consented to suit under the FTCA for certain claims arising out of the performance of Indian Self-Determination and Education

---

[333] 523 U.S. 751 (1998).
[334] 25 U.S.C. § 450(f).
[335] 25 U.S.C. § 2501-2511.
[336] 2006 WL 2591272 (E.D. Wash. 2006); Also see, *Mentz v. United States*, 359 F.Supp.2d 856 (DND, 2005)(employees of school operating under TCSA grant are employees of the Bureau of Indian Affairs and can be sued under FTCA); *Big Owl v. United States*, 961 F.Supp. 1304 (DSD, 1997)(school board members of school operated under TCSA grant and therefore employees of Bureau of Indian Affairs and can be sued under FTCA).

Assistance Act of 1975.[337] Tort claims against tribes, tribal organizations, or their employees, which arise out of the tribe or tribal organization carrying out a self-determination contract, are considered claims against the United States and are covered to the full extent of the FTCA.[338]

What sovereign has the power to prosecute a crime committed by a tribal employee?

Employees stealing (or committing other crimes) from tribal employers can be prosecuted for their criminal act. Whether the prosecutor charging the crime is an agent of the tribal, state, or federal governments depends on the location and type of crime, whether the alleged criminal is Indian or non-Indian, and whether the victim is Indian or non-Indian. A specific hypothetical assists with application of the rules. There is a theft of $800 from a tribal gaming enterprise by tribal member employee Chuck and by non-Indian employee Shirley. Chuck and Shirley have turned themselves over to the authorities. Of the "authorities" who can prosecute Chuck and Shirley?

When does the tribe possess criminal jurisdiction?

Tribes can exercise criminal jurisdiction (authority), and if exercised, a tribe has the power to enforce its criminal laws on tribal members,[339] nonmember Indians,[340] but not non-Indians.[341] The tribe can therefore prosecute Chuck for the crime but cannot prosecute non-Indian Shirley.

When does the federal government possess criminal jurisdiction?

The United States has criminal jurisdiction in Indian Country. In 1834, under the Indian Country Crimes Act, the federal government had criminal

---

[337] *FGS Constructors, Inc. v. Carlow*, 64 F.3d 1230, 1234 (8th Cir.1995)
[338] See, *Department of the Interior and Related Agencies Appropriations*, 25 U.S.C. § 450f notes); see also 25 U.S.C. § 450f(d); 28 U.S.C. §§ 1346(b), 2671-2680; *FGS Constructors, Inc.*, 64 F.3d at 1234. See generally BIA Federal Tort Claims Act Coverage General Provisions, 25 C.F.R. §§ 900.180-188 (2007);
[339] *ExParte Crow Dog*, 109 U.S. 556 (1883).
[340] 25 U.S.C. § 1301(2),(4).
[341] *Oliphant v. Suquamish Indian Tribe*, 435 U.S. 191 (1978).

jurisdiction in many circumstances, but not when an Indian committed a crime against an Indian. That gap in the law was exposed in the *Crow Dog* case,[342] which precipitated application of the Major Crimes Act.

In 1885, the federal government through the Major Crimes Act granted to itself criminal jurisdiction authorizing federal officials to prosecute Indians who committed some crimes on the reservation.[343] The federal government acted in 1885 because an Indian man named Crow Dog was prosecuted by the federal government for killing Chief Spotted Tail on Indian lands. The Supreme Court agreed with Crow Dog's argument on appeal that the federal government lacked jurisdiction to address on-reservation crimes committed by an Indian perpetrator upon an Indian victim.[344] The Major Crimes Act grants criminal jurisdiction to the federal government for crimes of murder, manslaughter, kidnapping, rape, robbery, incest, sexual abuse, and assault with a dangerous weapon. Gaming-related crimes can be separately punished under 18 U.S.C. § 1167 and 1168. Because the federal government can prosecute Indians and non-Indians, the federal government could prosecute both Chuck and Shirley for theft of $800 from the tribe's gaming enterprise under Section 1167.

When do states possess criminal jurisdiction?

There are two instances where a state can prosecute Indian Country crimes. For instance, where two non-Indian employees commit a crime in the workplace the state has the authority to prosecute.[345] However, when Indians are involved in the crime as victim or perpetrator, the states lack the power to prosecute on-reservation crimes except where that authority was granted to certain states under Public Law 280. In Public Law 280[346] states, the rules which apply to non-280 states apply with the additional threat of state criminal prosecution of Indians and non-Indians regardless of the victim's status. Public Law 280 states include almost all of California, Oregon, Wisconsin, Minnesota, Alaska, Nebraska.[347]

---

[342] *ExParte Crow Dog*, 109 U.S. 556 (1883).
[343] The Major Crimes Act is located at 18 U.S.C. § 1153 (1885).
[344] *Ex Parte Crow Dog*, 109 U.S. 556 (1883).
[345] *U.S. v. McBratney*, 104 U.S. 621 (1881).
[346] 18 U.S.C. §1162, 28 U.S.C. §1360 as amended by 25 U.S.C. §1321 et seq.
[347] The State of Washington applies a complicated mix of Public Law 280 jurisdiction.

In a Public Law 280 state, the state could prosecute both Chuck and Shirley for the $800 theft. In a non-Public Law 280 state, the state could not prosecute Chuck but could prosecute Shirley.

The following chart summarizes criminal jurisdiction when major crimes are committed by employees on the reservation in a non-Public Law 280 state.

Non-Public Law 280 State	**Prosecuted by:**
Indian employee stealing $1,500[348] from the tribal casino	Tribe,[349] Federal[350]
Non-Indian employee stealing $1,500 from the tribal casino	Federal[351]
Indian employee assaulting (gun) an Indian employee	Tribe,[352] Federal[353]
Indian employee assaulting (gun) non-Indian employee	Tribe,[354] Federal[355]
Non-Indian employee assaulting (gun) an Indian employee	Federal[356]
Non-Indian employee assaulting (gun) a non-Indian employee	Federal,[357] State[358]

---

[348] 18 U.S.C. §1168; Theft by an employee of a gaming establishment carries a maximum twenty-year prison sentence and $1,000,000 fine.
[349] *U.S. v. Wheeler*, 435 U.S. 313, 328 (1978).
[350] 18 U.S.C. §1168;
[351] 18 U.S.C. §1168
[352] *U.S. v. Wheeler*, 435 U.S. 313, 328 (1978).
[353] 18 U.S.C. §1153.
[354] U.S. v. Wheeler, 435 U.S. 313, 328 (1978).
[355] 18 U.S.C. §1153.
[356] 18 U.S.C. §1153.
[357] 18 U.S.C. §1153.
[358] *United States v. McBratney*, 104 U.S. 621 (1881).

Note, the crimes referenced trigger federal jurisdiction under federal laws and therefore, close scrutiny of the nature of the crime is a prerequisite in determining whether the federal government may prosecute. For example, an employee which assaults another employee without the aid of a deadly weapon may not trigger federal law[359] and therefore, the federal government may not possess the requisite jurisdiction to prosecute.

Where more than one sovereign has authority (jurisdiction) to act in response to a crime, the criminal defendant can be prosecuted by some or all of the sovereigns possessing jurisdiction without the defense of double jeopardy precluding prosecution.[360] The Double Jeopardy Clause of the United States Constitution only applies to successive prosecutions by the same sovereign.[361]

What governments assert jurisdiction over off-reservation crimes?

An Indian who commits a crime off the reservation is subject to state or federal criminal jurisdiction. Therefore, theft committed by an Indian while visiting the local off reservation town is subject to the same state laws and due process protections as anyone else. The caveat to that general rule is an Indian leaving the reservation to engage in a federally protected right like hunting or fishing.[362]

Are there civil remedies available to tribal employers for those employees who violate the law but cannot be prosecuted by the tribe?

Yes. If there is either a consensual commercial relationship (employer-employee) or if the matter affects the political integrity of the tribe, a tribe can commence suit or other dispute mechanism to recover the monies stolen by an employee or other person regardless of whether the employee is Indian or non-Indian, member or nonmember. Therefore, an employee who steals

---

[359] Outside of gaming two federal criminal laws impact the criminal jurisdiction question. The Indian Country Crimes Act (18 U.S.C. § 1152) and Major Crimes Act (18 U.S.C. § 1153) provide federal prosecutors with the authority to prosecute crimes in Indian Country.
[360] *U.S. v. Lara*, 541 U.S. 193 (2004).
[361] *Heath v. Alabama*, 474 U.S. 82, 88 (1985).
[362] *Antoine v. Washington*, 420 U.S. 194 (1975).

money from the tribe could concurrently be faced with prosecutors from more than one sovereign, the gaming commission in a license revocation hearing, the loss of a job with whatever grievance rights are available, and a civil proceeding started by the tribe to recover the stolen money.

CHAPTER 5

How does gaming impact tribal employers?

With the overwhelming success of tribal gaming the dominant eye-level shelf in the business section of book stores should be reserved for tribal leaders sharing insightful management tips regarding the operation of tribal gaming enterprises and the other businesses run by tribes. In a short time, tribal gaming has grown significantly to a billion dollar business.[363] These business ventures have, in some instances, created a gap between hiring the workers necessary to perform the myriad tasks generated by the moving parts on the casino floor and back of house, and the employment practices, which create and enhance best employment practices. In response to this gap created by significant growth over a short time, tribes are bringing considerable resources to define the terms and conditions of the employment relationship through employment laws, updated policies, job descriptions, organizational charts, and other employment documents.

Tribal gaming has existed for years as an exercise of inherent tribal sovereignty. In 1987, California challenged tribal bingo by asserting that tribal officials committed criminal acts when tribal gaming was operated in violation of California law. California used a federal law called PL 280 which delegated authority to California wherein state civil and criminal jurisdiction applied to on-reservation activities. Two tribes operating bingo halls, the Cabazon and Morongo tribes, filed a lawsuit challenging California's assertion of authority.

---

[363] The National Indian Gaming Association estimates tribal gaming revenues in 2006 were $25.6 billion.

The case is *California v. Cabazon Band of Mission Indians*[364] wherein the United States Supreme Court disagreed finding that California could not interfere with tribal gaming since PL 280 did delegate criminal jurisdiction to certain states but despite California's "criminal" label outlawing certain aspects of gaming, California could not call something criminal when so many people and the state itself were engaged in gaming. The *Cabazon* Court confirmed tribes' inherent right to exercise their sovereignty which included providing gaming. A year after *Cabazon* Congress promulgated the Indian Gaming Regulatory Act (IGRA) which affirmed tribal gaming but imposed federal regulation and compelled the tribes and states to work together regarding Las Vegas-style gaming.

IGRA does not define the terms and conditions of the employment relationship as it does not impose federal or state employment rules on tribes engaged in gaming, however as will be discussed, IGRA does present an opportunity to negotiate the terms of that relationship. IGRA impacts employees most significantly by requiring gaming employees called primary management officials and key employees to apply for and receive a gaming license as a prerequisite to employment for the gaming enterprise. This prerequisite to employment has been expanded by many tribes and states to include most employees receiving a paycheck from tribal casinos. For those employees required to acquire a gaming license, the impact on tribal employers was oftentimes a delay in the employee's first day and sometimes the loss of what appeared to be a good employee because of information revealed by the regulator's due diligence.

On the face of IGRA, tribal employment law is not redefined, however because of the significant influx of employees working for gaming tribes, employee disputes increased and these disputes oftentimes pitched nonmember employees against tribal employers. Courts and agencies which enforce employment laws dealt with more claims involving tribal casinos and nonmember employees which at times nurtured increased scrutiny of tribal employers.

An example which amply illustrates an increased scrutiny of tribal employers is the National Labor Relations Board (NLRB) which for decades took the position that the National Labor Relations Act (NLRA) did not apply to tribal

---

[364] 480 US 202 (1987).

employers. Without a change in the law, the NLRB changed its stance arguing the NLRA applied to tribal employers. An aspect of the NLRB's change of view, and some courts' subsequent consent to the new NLRB position, is attributable to the significant number of nonmember employees working for tribal casinos and the revenues generated by tribal enterprises.

It is true that IGRA did not impose employment rules on tribal employers, however it is equally true, that as a consequence of IGRA's requirement that tribes negotiate with states the terms of offering Las Vegas gaming, in some instances states used these negotiations to leverage tribal concessions regarding inclusion of state employment laws.[365] These agreements regarding Las Vegas-style gaming are referred to as compacts.

These compacts, which sometimes impose state employment laws on tribes, undermine tribal sovereignty. The state's imposition of state employment laws is underwritten by the assumption that state law is necessary to protect casino workers. The state's paternalism asserts that without the protection of state law casino workers cannot get a fair deal, but that assumption neglects the deal struck by consenting adults seeking the wages and benefits provided by tribal employers. States complain vigorously when the federal government imposes its rules on states and fails to abide by federalism's dictate to respect state sovereignty. The sting of federal paternalism to the states should condition the states to think twice before imposing similar dictates on the tribes, but unfortunately this logic is lost when opportunity is presented.

Tribal gaming has had a significant impact on tribal employment. This chapter explores gaming fundamentals and thereafter employment issues which are encountered by these enterprises.

In defining the terms and conditions of the relationship between the tribal casino and its employees, analysis of the following is necessary:

>Role of the tribal regulator issuing employee licenses
>Identification of the casino employees

---

[365] As one example, Michigan compacted with tribes located in Michigan to provide the equivalence of state worker's compensation and unemployment compensation benefits.

Federal law impact on casino employee.

Tribal state compact impact on casino employee

Thereafter, the book explores best practices for tribal casino employers.

What are the roles of the tribe as employer and as regulator of the tribe's gaming enterprise?

Gaming has significantly increased the number of people working for tribal enterprises. Some estimate that tribal casinos employ more than six hundred thousand people 75 percent of whom are non-Indian.[366] Tribal gaming enterprises range from a couple hundred slot machines with a handful of table games to the largest casino in the world.[367] By any measure, tribal gaming collectively is big business presenting many opportunities for tribes as employers, to get it right and wrong.

Tribal gaming involves unique internal and external relationships. The unique internal relationships focus on the tribe as owner and regulator of the tribal gaming enterprise whereas the unique externality is the intersection of three sovereigns (tribal, state and federal) each having a role in tribal gaming. These internal and external relationships have an impact on the terms and conditions of the employment relationship.

Internal relationships

In tribal gaming, the tribe is both regulator and owner of the enterprise.

Regulating tribal casinos employs a different model than those used by the states for privately owned gaming enterprises. In Las Vegas, New Jersey, and other places, casinos are owned by private entities and regulated by state governments. Under the model used by the states, there is a clear distinction

---

[366] National Indian Gaming Association at *www.indiangaming.org*. The six hundred thousand estimate includes employees employed by other employers which serve the tribal gaming industry.

[367] The Mashantucket Tribe owns Foxwoods Resort which includes 340,000 square feet of gaming space. The Tribe claims it is the largest casino in the world.

between privately owned and operated casino and the government regulator charged with oversight.

Under the blueprint created by the Indian Gaming Regulatory Act, tribal gaming established a different model where the tribe is both the regulator and owner of the casino. From an outsider's perspective, tribe as owner and regulator presents a distinction without a difference since a single entity cannot adequately and independently serve both functions of owner and regulator. Tribes overcome this challenge through promulgating a gaming ordinance, which segregates ownership of the casino from regulation. Not only have the tribes achieved independent regulation of their enterprises, tribal regulators concentrate their efforts oftentimes on a single enterprise, which therefore is more heavily scrutinized than those casinos on the Strip in Las Vegas or near the boardwalk in Atlantic City.

The lines of regulation and management can blur. There are numerous examples of the blurred line between regulator and casino operator, but a good example focuses on employer due diligence of prospective employees. Since the tribal regulator is spending significant time and tribal resources conducting background investigations of employee licensees; some tribal casinos perform little if no due diligence on prospective casino employees. That is a mistake. The bold line separating regulators and operators exists when both perform their respective duties and those duties are crystallized as regulators perform due diligence in evaluating prospective licensees while employers perform due diligence in evaluating prospective employees.

A failure by a tribal casino to perform independent due diligence in evaluating prospective employees can lull the employer to overlook its duties to constantly monitor employees. If lulled to inaction, tribal employers are exposed to potential liability and legitimate claims of malfeasance when employees break the rules by, for example, stealing money from their employer. If the tribal gaming commission does not revoke the licensee's license for theft, the tribal casino may choose not to investigate, and the employee continues to steal. That is a mistake. Because the line between regulation and management is sometimes blurred between regulator and management, the roles and responsibilities of the respective groups can be confusing and unfulfilled. This chapter sets forth a series of recommendations, which are generated, in part, by focusing on the separate roles of regulation and operation of tribal casinos.

External relationships

Tribal gaming brings the three sovereigns together in a confluence of power over the games offered, the means and manner of regulation and the relationship between employer and employee. A review of federal gaming law reveals a focus on the games, the means and manner of regulation, but not on the employer-employee relationship. However, federal law does contemplate an agreement between the tribes and states as to a slice of the games offered, and through those agreements some states address the employment question. The first step in the analysis is a review of the requirements of federal gaming law.

Has the federal government promulgated law in the tribal gaming arena?

The federal government promulgated the Indian Gaming Regulatory Act (IGRA)[368] in 1988 to construct a three sovereign cooperative, which regulates tribal gaming. Under the auspices of IGRA, tribes which are engaged in gaming must comply with the minimum standards imposed by IGRA and demonstrate compliance through the adoption of a comprehensive tribal law approved by the Chairman of the National Indian Gaming Commission (NIGC). The NIGC is a federal regulator created by, and charged with enforcement of, IGRA.[369]

The comprehensive tribal law contemplated by IGRA is a tribal gaming ordinance.[370] Specifically, meeting IGRA's standards are achieved through its operational section 2710 which (1) enumerates the minimum standards for tribal gaming and (2) requires the tribe to submit its comprehensive gaming law to the Chairman of the NIGC for approval.[371] Those standards include the use of gaming revenues, audits of the gaming operation, regulation of the casino, licensing of at least a portion of the casino employees, adherence to

---

[368] 25 U.S.C. §2501 et seq.
[369] 25 U.S.C. §2506.
[370] 25 U.S.C. §2710 refers to ordinance or resolution however a significant majority of tribes use ordinance to memorialize its comprehensive gaming law. The NIGC maintains, on its Web site, a copy of the approved tribal gaming ordinances.
[371] 25 U.S.C. §2705 (a)(3); 25 U.S.C. §2710.

health and safety standards, and the necessity of working with the state to offer certain games. Once these standards are met, tribes are free to shape the law to their individual needs, customs, and traditions. As a result, tribal gaming law is uniform across all gaming tribes as to minimum standards while at the same time unique as to those aspects of the law, which exceed IGRA minimums.

In the integration of tribal, state, and federal sovereigns, IGRA does not simply layer three sovereigns on top of each other in the regulatory landscape. Instead, IGRA delegates the primary responsibility of ownership and oversight of the gaming enterprise to the tribes, a portion of regulatory oversight is reserved to the federal regulator, and the final segment of control is intended to be shared between the tribes and the states. More specifically, this segmentation of control from the three sovereigns is dependent in part on the games offered by the tribal casino. IGRA defined three classes of gaming by describing traditional games as class I, bingo, and some other games as class II, and what is considered Las Vegas-style gaming (slot machines and black jack) as class III.[372] Class I gaming is regulated by the tribes, class II by the tribes and the federal government (NIGC), and class III gaming contemplates and requires good faith negotiation between states and tribes before the tribe can engage in Las Vegas-style gaming.[373] The role of the federal government's regulator as to class III gaming is an open question, which may or may not receive a legislative modification.[374] For these sovereigns the primary tools of regulation are

Tribe	**Federal**	**State**
Gaming Ordinance	Indian Gaming Reg. Act	Compact
Tribal Gaming Agency	NIGC	State Regulator
Tribal Regulations	Federal Regulations	State Regulations

---

[372] 25 U.S.C. §2703

[373] 25 U.S.C. §2710

[374] There is a debate regarding the role of the federal government when tribes offer Las Vegas-style gaming. In *Colorado River Indian Tribes v. National Indian Gaming Commission*, 466 F.3d 134 (DC Cir. 2006) the tribe successfully challenged the NIGC's authority to regulate its Las Vegas or class III games.

There are myriad other tribal, federal, and state laws which may impact the tribal gaming rules. For example, tribes promulgate gaming revenue allocation ordinances to codify the expenditure of gaming revenues, the federal government's disclosure requirements regarding large expenditures of funds by patrons apply to tribes and state safety law may apply to the gaming operation as a requirement of the tribal-state compact.

From this convergence of tribal, federal, and state laws tribal gaming employers ask the following relevant questions:

Does federal gaming law define the terms and conditions of the employment relationship?

Does federal nongaming law define the terms and conditions of the employment relationship?

Do tribal-state compacts require the application of state employment laws which define the terms and conditions of the employment relationship?

In the absence of federal law or tribal-state compact language defining the terms and conditions of the employment relationship, has the tribe defined the relationship and through what document, law or other mechanism?

These questions deserve attention and will be addressed in this chapter. However, before these relevant questions are answered, a couple fundamental questions deserve a more complete overview. Understanding the role of a tribal gaming employer demands a more complete understanding of the regulator.

Who is in charge of regulating tribal gaming?

Most of the regulatory oversight of tribal casinos falls to the tribes. The federal government, through the NICC, and the states, through their regulatory bodies, serve a regulatory role, but despite those contributions, the tribes serve the role of primary regulator. IGRA's 2710 imposes upon the tribes the sole proprietary interest in the tribal gaming enterprise as well as the primary responsibility for regulating the gaming. Accordingly, the tribes are both owners of the casinos and regulator of the gaming operations. Tribes have, through tribal gaming ordinances, created a balance and separation between the ownership and regulatory functions of the gaming enterprise. The goal is to separate management from regulation of the casino.

To meet the regulatory requirements the tribe's gaming ordinance will create a gaming commission or Tribal Gaming Agency (TGA) and delegate regulatory oversight to the commission. Oftentimes, the gaming commission is comprised of part-time or full-time appointed or elected officials who manage a full-time staff of employees which handle compliance, licensing, surveillance, and the due process afforded licensees.

An aspect of the minimum standards imposed by IGRA is the obligation to perform necessary due diligence in evaluating prospective and current employee-licensees. To that end, IGRA requires that tribes have an adequate system to ensure that background investigations are conducted on key employees and primary management officials.[375] The background investigation must adhere to

> a standard whereby any person whose prior activities, criminal record, if any, or reputation, habits, and associations pose a threat to the public interest or to the effective regulation of gaming, or create or enhance the dangers of unsuitable, unfair, or illegal practices and methods; and activities in the conduct of gaming shall not be eligible for employment.[376]

This extremely broad standard is referred to as the licensing standard. The licensing standard specifically requires the tribe to continuously evaluate gaming enterprise employees to ensure that the privilege of a gaming license is deserved.

Enumerated in gaming ordinances, tribal gaming commission regulations, federal regulations, and tribal state compacts, tribes fulfill their obligation to evaluate licensees against the measuring stick of the licensing standard by delegating authority to the tribal gaming commission which gathers significant information from prospective and present employee-licensees through a lengthy application, serious due diligence, and procedural safeguards which provide due process in the issuance and removal of employee licenses. The licensing standard permits substantial discretion in the gathering of information from the licensee and others and thereafter in the decision regarding issuance of the license.

---

[375] 25 U.S.C. §2710(b)(2)(F)(i).
[376] 25 U.S.C. §2710(b)(2)(F)(ii)(II).

In addition to licensure of the employee-licensee, gaming ordinances vest in gaming commissions the broad authority to regulate tribal gaming operations, to investigate any suspicion of wrongdoing associated with any gaming activity, and to conduct internal audits of the gaming operation. Tribal law layers on top of those duties the broadest of responsibilities to perform such other duties the GRC deems appropriate for the proper regulation of the gaming enterprise which may require the commission to oversee construction of the facility, the service of alcohol, and the safety of food in the ever-present buffet. The law provides significant depth and girth in imposing upon the tribal regulator a duty to regulate the tribe's gaming enterprise, and its licensees (employees and vendors).

Tribal gaming commissions almost always restrict the disclosure of information developed through its exercise of due diligence in evaluating prospective licensees. This restriction against disclosure includes, but is not limited to, the gaming enterprise. Accordingly, when the gaming commission performs a background check and suitability determination of a licensee, the information generated by the commission is not shared with casino human resources. Whether the tribal casino, as employer, is exercising its duty of evaluating prospective and current employees is a question, which is independent from whether the gaming commission is performing a background investigation as part of the commission's license analysis. Gaming employers, therefore, have an independent duty to evaluate prospective and present employees to protect employees, patrons, and members; and to protect themselves from claims of negligent hiring and retention.

Recognition of the division of responsibility imposed by the law between employer and regulator is necessary to protect the tribe from employment-related claims. As part of that analysis, tribes recognize that the gaming commission is not the employer, and therefore the work performed by the gaming commission to evaluate its licensees is not credited to the tribal employer in making employment-related decisions to hire, fire, and retain its employees. This licensee-employee distinction is critical in understanding the independent and oftentimes overlapping duties of a regulator and employer.

Who is the employer in tribal gaming?

IGRA requires the tribe to own the tribal casino.[377] The tribal government's organizational chart therefore is the best tool in identifying the gaming entity employer. The typical organizational chart includes either the tribe's elected officials, or an enterprise board appointed by those elected officials, serving as the casino's board of directors. The elected officials will be members of the tribe elected by tribal membership. Enterprise boards could be comprised of elected officials, but more likely will be appointed by the tribal council. These appointed officials will more than likely be tribal members, but they can also be nonmembers who can contribute to the enterprise board's collective wisdom and experience. Understanding the composition of tribal council requires insight on the tribe's constitution and if there is no constitution, an understanding of how the tribe elects its officials. Enterprise boards are frequently a product of tribal law wherein the board is formed as a governmental subdivision, a chartered entity, or a corporation organized under a corporation's ordinance.

As a board of directors, the council or enterprise board supervises casino management on a range of issues including, but not limited to, revenue, marketing, human resources, expansion, game selection, maintenance, compliance, and guest service. In its supervisory capacity, the board or council may meet frequently or infrequently or involve itself a little or a lot in operations. Depending on the role served, the tribal council and enterprise board may be employees of the tribe and oftentimes are licensed by the tribe's gaming commission.

Since federal law requires the tribe to have the sole proprietary interest (financial interest) in the gaming enterprise, workers at a tribal casino are ultimately working for the tribe. Tribes organize numerous systems to define the chain of command; however, the chain of command is inevitably a combination of

---

[377] 25 U.S.C. § 2710.

Tribal Members

Tribal Council

Enterprise Board (sometimes)

General Manager of the Casino

Directors of Marketing, Food and Beverage, Table Games, Slots, Maintenance, Human Resources, Accounting

Workers of the Casino

In defining employer two answers emerge. If the gaming enterprise is a subdivision of the tribal government, the employer is the tribe. The tribe is represented by its elected officials which is oftentimes, but not always, the tribal council. As a subdivision of tribal government, the tribal council is the employer. The organic document creating the casino is the tribe's gaming ordinance which will implicitly define the tribe as employer.

Under the second scenario, if the tribe organizes the casino as a corporation the corporation is the employer and the organic document creating the corporation is the articles of incorporation. The tribe is the owner of the gaming operation under this organizational alternative since it will either own all of the corporation's shares, or simply own the gaming enterprise, and delegate management responsibility to its corporate entity.[378] If the casino is organized as a corporation, it is likely that the tribal council has appointed a board of directors.

Under either model, where the casino is owned as a subdivision of the government or as a corporate entity created and owned by the tribe, the employer, and regulator duties are the same. Because casino personnel are both employees of the enterprise and licensees of the commission, there are at least two tribal entities measuring performance or compliance.

---

[378] Under Section 2710 of the Indian Gaming Regulatory Act a management contractor can operate the tribe's casino, but the contractor cannot own the enterprise.

On the regulatory side of this analysis, federal law imposes specific minimums the tribal regulator must meet in evaluating employee-licensees. Sometimes the tribal-state compact sets additional or concurrent minimal standards for consideration by the tribal regulator in evaluating an employee-licensee. On the other hand, federal gaming law does not set standards for tribal employers.

Does federal gaming law define the terms and conditions of the employment relationship?

No. Federal gaming law does not require the application of federal employment laws. Therefore, from the perspective of the Indian Gaming Regulatory Act, federal employment law is not imposed on tribal gaming enterprises. The employment relationship between tribal casinos and employees, however, is impacted in at least two ways by IGRA.

First, certain employees must acquire a gaming license before they are eligible for employment. Second, when tribes engage in Las Vegas-style gaming, the tribes and the state must negotiate a compact which addresses numerous aspects of the relationship and sometimes includes explicit employment standards and practices.

IGRA defines minimum licensing standards, which the tribal gaming commission utilizes in issuing, denying, suspending, or revoking gaming licenses. Even though IGRA does not require the application of specific employment laws to tribal gaming, indirectly a by-product of IGRA has allowed states to impose state and federal employment laws through compacting. Some states have seized that opportunity. For example, some compacts require tribes to participate in state workers' compensation and unemployment compensation programs. The California compacts take the additional step of requiring tribes to comply with aspects of the state's human rights laws. The Arizona compact requires compliance with federal employment law at tribal casinos.

Does federal nongaming law define the terms and conditions of the employment relationship?

Maybe. The United States Supreme Court asserts that the federal government can dilute tribal sovereignty through the imposition of federal law. Congress has not explicitly applied FLSA, NLRA, ERISA, and OSHA (to name just a few) to tribal employers. Moreover, in a couple instances,[379] Congress has excepted tribal employers from application of federal employment law. Despite the opportunity to explicitly apply federal law to tribes, Congress is silent; and in this silence, the Supreme Court and other federal courts have interpreted silence to mean that federal law applies, but other courts have concluded the opposite—the federal employment law does not apply.

The law does not provide an answer at this time, but rather a series of arguments. The law and the judges, who interpret the law, invite a case-by-case and fact-by-fact analysis of the question. Chapter 2 provides a more complete discussion of the question.

When the federal courts evaluate whether federal employment laws apply to tribal gaming enterprises, two oppositional themes emerge which argue in favor of applying federal law because tribal gaming enterprises are not government and the contrarian view which asserts that tribal enterprise, whether involved in gaming or the manufacture of widgets, is government in action. In this case-by-case analysis the courts are evaluating numerous factors which are susceptible to the summary of a single question:

> *Are tribal casinos big business and not government, or are tribal casinos government in action with a veneer which looks like big business?*

Both points of view are briefly discussed.

a. *Tribal casinos are big business*

Proponents of the imposition of federal employment (and other) laws into tribal casino employment relations argue that tribal casinos are engaged in commerce with vendors, patrons, and employees which hail from beyond the tribe's jurisdiction. This argument asserts that since tribes benefit from commerce originating beyond the tribe's borders, the tribes likewise should assume the responsibility of following the laws from beyond their borders. Accordingly, when the tribes invite outside patrons and vendors, the tribes also invite application of the laws where these patrons live.

---

[379] Title VII of the Civil Rights Act of 1964 and the Americans with Disabilities Act.

The argument continues by using per capita distributions as leverage for its pitch. Even if the tribes are using a portion of the gaming revenues to provide governmental benefits like roads, education, and health care, some tribes are sending checks to tribal members, which in some cases creates millionaires out of lucky individuals which happen to be members of tribes located near urban populations a portion of which patronizes the casino. The argument asserts that the creation of millionaire members, even if rare, is not the intended consequence of a government engaging in business.

b. *Tribal casinos represent government in action*

The revenues and jobs generated by tribal casinos benefit tribes, tribal government, and members of the tribe in many ways.[380] A dollar generated by a tribal gaming enterprise flows to employees in wages, the other sovereigns (federal and state) in income taxes, the local vendors in contracts, and to the tribe for the welfare of its members. Just as the states' sale of a lottery ticket creates revenues which are used to increase the effectiveness of government, the tribes use gaming revenues to preserve and enhance the welfare of tribal members. This use of gaming resources by states and tribes is government in action. Whether the action of government is the product of states or tribes, there is an argument that the use of the revenues should be the strongest variable in determining whether government action forecloses the application of law from sovereigns from outside the tribe's jurisdiction. In other words, if the tribe uses the gaming revenues for education, health, and welfare (government), there is no business excuse for the application of federal employment law.

To carry the argument another step, the revenues created by tribal gaming are not part of a zero sum game. A dollar for a tribe is not a dollar less for the state. Importantly, a dollar for the tribe may also be, under some circumstances a dollar for the state. When a tribe located in Minnesota generates a dollar and uses that dollar to reduce state welfare roles by providing services to its member, the state spends a dollar less because the welfare recipient is a beneficiary of the tribe's work. Because of the governmental work performed by tribes using

---

[380] The National Indian Gaming Commission publishes a comprehensive report detailing these benefits. The latest report is titled "The Economic Impact of Indian Gaming in 2006."

gaming revenues, nontribal governments like states and counties can use their finite resources elsewhere to benefit local nonmembers.

There is also a parallel between the expansion of revenue for public good through the increase in economic activity by private business within a state and the economic activity generated by tribal gaming enterprises. Local and state governments recognize the benefits from allocating significant public resources to attract business which generate jobs and boost tax roles. The purpose for tribal gaming is to generate jobs for that portion of the population with the highest unemployment rate and create revenues (quasi tax) which are intended for the welfare of tribal communities. When states enrich their citizens by attracting business, the states do not compromise their sovereignty; and likewise, tribes assert the success of gaming is not adequate reason for the federal government and its regulators to expand the law's reach.

Do tribal-state compacts define the terms and conditions of the employment relationship?

Sometimes. Most tribal-state compacts are silent on the terms and conditions between the tribal gaming employer and its employees. Sometimes, as in the case of California, the compacts require tribal gaming employers to adopt the equivalent of state employment laws. For a more detailed analysis of this question, please see chapter 3. Because of the compacting process, state employment law may, because of the compact's limited reach, apply to the casino employee, but may not extend to the employee working for tribal government operations, which is not part of the casino.

What best practices do tribal employers follow because of the unique regulatory and legal environment created by tribal gaming?

Since tribes uniquely are both owner and regulator of tribal gaming enterprises, separation between the entities is a critical factor in the success and integrity of both. The unique regulatory and legal environment of tribal gaming has generated best practices which tribal employers adopt. Since a portion of the employer best practices are a reaction to the role of the tribal gaming regulator, a prerequisite to understanding the employer's role is understanding the role of the regulator.

Tribes create independent regulators intending to serve the distinct purpose of regulation, leaving casino management to the casino.[381] The regulator licenses the gaming facility, employees, and vendors. While tribal regulators are performing these duties, the tribal council or its enterprise board is operating the casino, hiring employees, and contracting with vendors. Tribal law defines the role of regulator and operator in a manner, which draws clear distinctions between them; however, in reality there is overlap in the roles which leads to a healthy debate regarding scope of authority. Understanding the role of the regulator helps define scope of duty and authority for the tribal employer.

What is an independent regulator and how does it impact tribal gaming employers?

By clearly defining the role of the regulator in the gaming ordinance, tribal councils can increase the chance that regulators will avoid the mission creep which moves regulators beyond the sweep spot of regulation to second guessing casino management business decisions. Casino management need and deserve an opportunity to make *business* decisions, which are frequently, but not always, successful. By clearly delegating regulatory authority to the regulator and concurrently limiting the exercise of power beyond clearly delegated authority will tribal leadership mitigate the overzealous exercise of regulatory jurisdiction into the purview of enterprise management. Tribal councils can achieve this necessary goal by clearly delegating to a gaming commission via the gaming ordinance those duties, which are regulatory in nature.

Whether a gaming commission is independent is determined by multiple factors including

---

[381] Casino personnel reading this statement will cry foul as there is an ongoing debate within many tribes, which addresses the role of the casino regulator. On paper, the regulator focuses on regulatory issues while the casino focuses on business. The clean distinction between regulation and management, which exists on paper, does not exist in reality. This distinction generates a healthy debate between regulators, casino management, elected officials, and others regarding the proper role of the gaming commission. Gaming commissions have a very difficult role in performing the regulatory function, restricting themselves from mission creep while frequently responding to membership that the commission's mandate is not to correct all perceived ills at the casino.

Is the commission adequately funded?
Does the commission have experienced personnel?
Do commission personnel take their jobs seriously?
Do commission personnel have access to education and training?
Does the clear delegation of authority create a true separation of powers between the gaming commission and the tribal government?
Do the gaming commissioners serve staggered terms?
Is for cause removal the standard for terminating a gaming commissioner?
Are the appointed officials in the gaming commission hired on a full-time basis?
Since most gaming commissions and their employees are organizationally under the tribal government, does the commission hire, fire, and discipline its employees?
Are the regulations promulgated and other decisions made by the commission viewed by the Tribal Court with deference?
Does anyone serving on tribal council also serve on the commission?
Is the commission able to seek support and cooperation from other regulators?
Does the surveillance department report to the commission?
Does the commission have an adequate talent pool knowledgeable in investigations, audits, legal, technology, advantage play and surveillance?
Is there a restriction precluding the commission from gaming at a casino it regulates?

The responses to these questions will assist in defining whether the gaming commission has received a clear delegation of regulatory authority.

Is there a clear delegation of authority to the commission in the gaming ordinance?

A clear delegation of authority granting and limiting regulator power increases the likelihood that the regulator will exercise its regulatory authority without crossing the line between regulation and management of the gaming enterprise. With this clarity, the regulator and those regulated understand their roles. The law therefore promotes employee understanding of the regulator's role increasing employee compliance with the rules, decreasing noncompliance which therefore minimizes the risk of an adverse licensing decision (revocation). This process increases the likelihood of the reasoned exercise of regulatory authority thereby minimizing the potential for arbitrary and capricious regulator decisions. When regulators exercise their regulatory authority in a reasonable way the pool of prospective employees increases since the risk of an arbitrary loss of a license is mitigated. Tribal casinos therefore attract better workers.

Do tribal members and tribal leadership understand the gaming commission's limited role as a regulator?

Regulators are primarily created to protect the assets of the tribe. This purpose of asset protection however can create the basis for regulator intrusion upon all action and inaction by casino management. When tribal members, tribal leadership, and licensees understand that regulators have a limited regulatory role defined through the delegated authority granted by the gaming ordinance, it is less likely that membership and leadership will ask the regulator to exercise authority which is not granted by the gaming ordinance. This is important as there are times when tribal membership and leadership hold the gaming commission accountable for casino decisions which are not regulatory in nature. When gaming employees make good choices and profits increase the gaming commission does not interfere and likewise when casino employees make decisions which do not produce good results, those decisions should be judged by the business judgment rule not through regulatory scrutiny. A simple example is illustrative:

> *After the exercise of reasonable due diligence, the casino general manager approves the purchase of ten blue slot machines and ten green slot machines. After a couple months of performance, the blue machines are yielding excellent return on investment, but unfortunately the green machines are offsetting those profits through dismal performance.*

Praise for the purchase of the blue machines and scrutiny related to the green machines should come from the tribal council or board of directors supervising the general manager. Scrutiny for the purchase of the green machines should not come from the gaming commission, which uses the *protection of tribal assets* as the lever for exercising authority beyond the specific delegation of powers granted by the gaming ordinance. Regulators frequently do not want the pressure of exercising authority which exceeds their regulatory role, and those regulators which possess a view of their role which is based on the law, better serve the tribe through the exercise of limited regulatory authority.

Tribal members and leadership need to understand the limited regulatory role of the gaming commission as a misunderstanding of the gaming commission's limited role can generate significant efforts by members and leaders to push the gaming commission into a managerial role. If a casino general manager is hired but is not liked by the members, there is a natural reflex to seek gaming commission assistance in quashing the employment. The gaming commission, however, only decides whether the prospective general manager is eligible for license; and therefore, the employment question is left to the board of directors. Gaming commissions, which impose their regulatory muscle beyond the licensing decision, are exceeding their authority. Prudence requires members, leaders, and gaming commissions to follow these practices.

Is due process clearly defined for the issuance, denial, suspension, and revocation of gaming licenses?

Gaming commissions' due process in the issuance, denial, suspension, and revocation of a gaming license will have the most significant impact on the employee-licensee. There is a substantial impact on the retention of a gaming license when the gaming commission, through its regulations, clearly defines (1) when licensees are disqualified to receive or keep a license, and (2) the neutrality of the hearings granted to the prospective or active licensee. Clear regulations, which define the qualifying criteria used by the regulator in the issuance or denial of a license, are an element of due process. These regulations are an element of due process since they define expectations and use those expectations to judge whether the license is issued. Likewise, the allegiance to fair hearing procedures, which govern licensing hearings conducted by the gaming commission, can contribute to the meaningful due process tribal gaming employees deserve. The retention of a gaming license is a prerequirement to employment, therefore, these principles of employment and regulatory due process are intertwined.

The absence of a clear delegation of authority to the regulator opens the door to regulatory creep, which is a regulators assumption of more and more power. This failure to grant clear and limited authority can lead some regulators to seize on ambiguity and maximize their regulatory reach. The maxim that power corrupts and absolute power corrupts absolutely can be applied to some unchecked regulators. Unchecked regulators sometimes find themselves reaching over the regulatory line to engage in casino management decisions, which sometimes involve critical employment related issues. Therefore segregating the regulatory and employment functions to regulator and employer respectively is dependent in part on the forethought exercised in delegating authority to the regulator. The tribal gaming ordinance is a critical juncture in determining the delegated nature and scope of the regulator's role.

What is the role of casino employer in performing due diligence in evaluating prospective employees?

Where a clear and limited delegation of authority is granted to the gaming commission, the employment function is the exclusive province of the tribal casino. Accordingly, tribal casinos have a duty to perform the full range of employment functions, which include hiring, firing, disciplining, and coaching employees.

The role of the gaming commission in the employment process is issuance of a license for some or all of the employees. The *some or all qualifier* limits the licensing obligation under federal law only to primary management officials and key employees, which therefore applies to only a portion of the casino workforce.[382] Whether a license is a prerequisite for all employees is determined by the tribe or its regulator through the gaming ordinance or the regulations promulgated by the gaming commission. Some tribal gaming ordinances meet the minimum threshold required by federal law and therefore require the licensure of primary management officials and key employees. On the other hand, some tribes require the licensure of all employees receiving a paycheck from the gaming enterprise. Whether licensed or not, gaming employers have a duty to perform the full range of employer duties.

Because gaming commissions are performing substantial due diligence in making licensing decisions as a prerequisite to the hiring of some or all of the casino's employees, some tribal casinos assert redundancy as the reason for neglecting the employer's duty of performing due diligence on prospective employees. Under this logic, due diligence in the form of a reference check,

---

[382] 25 U.S.C. § 2710 (b)(2)(F)(i).

background investigation, and thorough interview is abandoned by the tribal casino employer under the mistaken belief that the regulator's licensing work is sufficient. The flaw in this analysis is the tribal gaming employer never sees the licensee application or the commission's work in evaluating the licensee. Since the casino employer never sees the results of the gaming commission's licensing work, reliance on work not seen is not reasonable for an employer. From a liability perspective the safety of employees and the avoidance of a claim for negligent hiring is mitigated by the reasonable exercise of due diligence by *employers*. Reliance on the due diligence of another entity, like a gaming commission making licensing decisions, is not reasonable.

Are there times when employer and regulator duties overlap?

Just as employers perform due diligence in evaluating a prospective employee at the same time regulators exercise due diligence in evaluating a prospective licensee, employers and regulators have similar ongoing duties to evaluate their employees and licensees respectively.

When Sam, the marketing director, steals $800 from the tribal casino, it triggers numerous independent mechanisms. Sam's employer will investigate and the facts generated by the investigation will present the casino with an employment related decision. The gaming commission will also investigate the theft; and if the facts reveal Sam's theft, Sam will lose his license, and if not already lost, will lose his job. Sam will also face criminal and civil sanctions stemming from the theft.

In response to the theft, these parallel proceedings carry different labels with the same goal-due process. The employer's grievance procedure is the employee's opportunity to contest his termination. The gaming commission's license revocation hearing is the licensee's chance to convince the commission that he deserves to retain his gaming license. Finally, a court of law will provide due process in evaluating whether criminal or civil sanctions are appropriate. Which court has jurisdiction to hear these matters is addressed in chapter 4.

Regulators and employers have different functions which oftentimes look the same and cover the same territory. For tribal casinos and gaming commissions, the roles and responsibilities of the regulator and employer can be more confusing since the tribe is owner, operator, and regulator.

Are there limits to the access demanded by the gaming commission to employment-related documents?

Gaming ordinances grant the gaming commission access to every inch of space and every piece of paper maintained by the gaming enterprise. Casino employers must understand that the delegation of authority to regulators includes access to personnel records. The human resources director who maintains those personnel records is a licensee and has a duty to cooperate with the regulator and she has a duty to cooperate on the casino's behalf, which is also licensed by the regulator. Human resources directors often struggle with the inconsistent messages of confidentiality to employees versus disclosure of confidential data to the regulator. Review of the law increases understanding of the basis for this tension.

Casino employers may have a duty of affirmative disclosure to the gaming commission. The gaming enterprise and its agents and employees are licensees, and as licensees have duties to the licensor or gaming commission. Oftentimes the gaming commission's authority is defined by the tribe's gaming ordinance.[383] Gaming ordinances frequently grant broad powers to gaming commissions. For example, the Confederated Tribes of Coos, Lower Umpqua, and Siuslaw Indian's gaming ordinance grants the following broad powers to its gaming commission:

> The Commission shall exercise all powers necessary to regulate Class II and Class III gaming on Confederated Tribes' Indian Land.[384]

Following this broad delegation of authority, the Tribal Council delegates to the gaming commission the power to license, promulgate regulations, review contracts, inspect books and records, impose penalties, and exclude individuals from the gaming facility. Under this broad delegation of authority, the gaming commission oftentimes requires the gaming facility and its employee-licensees, under the auspices of the gaming ordinance language, or through regulations promulgated under the ordinance, to disclose violations of the law, regulations, and internal controls. Since the casino or gaming enterprise is a licensee, it

---

[383] Sometimes, the gaming commission is created under an ordinance, which is separate from the gaming ordinance.

[384] Confederated Tribes of Coos, Lower Umpqua, and Siuslaw Indian's Gaming Ordinance, 5-2-7.

has an affirmative duty to disclose violations, which are attributable to it as well as violations attributable to individual employee-licensees. Compounding this challenge is the reality that a failure to disclose a violation can be an independent violation of the licensing requirements.

Under the broad delegation of authority to gaming commissions, tribal casino employers must address access of the gaming commission to essentially all aspects of the gaming operation including personnel records. Gaming commissions assert a regulatory interest in the information gathered by tribal employers in the application and due diligence of tribal employees as well as the employers ongoing monitoring of casino employees.

For example, when employees complete an employment application the prospective employee is engaged with its future employer. That same employee also completes a gaming license which engages the licensee to her future regulator. On the surface, these are complete and separate acts—one in the employment realm and the other in the regulatory arena. However, the gaming commission argues that the employees' representations to its future employer are a good source for comparing answers to similar questions on the gaming application and therefore, access to the employment application should be given to the diligent gaming commission.

Another example illustrates the gaming commission's desire for unlimited access to employee records. An allegation is leveled that the employee licensee has engaged in welfare fraud. The criminal complaint alleges that while the employee-licensee collected paychecks from the employer for the last eight months, the employee was collecting welfare checks from the state where he resides. Gaming commissions argue that an allegation of criminal activity leveled at its licensees is certainly relevant to whether the licensee should continue holding the license. Given the relevance of the behavior to both employment and licensing, the gaming commission asserts it should have access to the employee's personnel records.

If the gaming commission revokes a gaming license, which disqualifies the licensee from employment in a regulated position, can the employee seek unemployment benefits?

The licensing and employment relationships are separate, but they overlap again when an employee-licensee loses their license, which prohibits the continuation of the employment relationship. In these instances, casino employers must educate state officials who administer state unemployment compensation proceedings. Tribal gaming enterprises face unemployment compensation proceedings where the gaming commission revokes a gaming license causing the casino employer to terminate the employee since in many positions a license from the gaming commission is a prerequisite to continued employment. When the employee is subsequently terminated and seeks unemployment benefits, the employer may not be able to justify the state's requirement of elevated cause for termination. Sometimes the casino employer needs to educate the unemployment compensation official in understanding that without a license, issued and revoked by a separate regulator, the employer cannot hire or keep the unlicensed employee. Some tribes have asked commission personnel to testify at unemployment compensation hearing to reinforce the separation between employer and regulator.

How are tribal casino employer best practices summarized?

Tribal gaming employers understand that tribal gaming presents unique managerial and regulatory roles, which impact best practices. A partial list of those best practices follows

> *The duties of the tribal gaming employer first require clear delegation of authority to the gaming regulator.*
>
> *Federal gaming law does not impose federal employment standards on tribal employers.*
>
> *Federal employment law may impose federal employment standard on tribal employers (see chapter 2).*
>
> *Casino employers have a duty to evaluate prospective employees.*
>
> *Casino employers have a duty to make independent decisions regarding employee misconduct.*
>
> *Casino employers must reconcile employee confidentiality with unlimited regulatory access to employee information.*

CHAPTER 6

Can tribes promulgate their own employment laws and policies?

Yes. Tribes can make the rules which define the relationship between tribal employer and employee. When tribes make the rules, mental calisthenics are required because leaders choosing to establish a tribal minimum wage or define unlawful discrimination must simultaneously hold a collection of consistent and inconsistent principles in mind, weigh some principles as more worthy or more consistent with the tribe's values and make a choice which cannot guaranty the avoidance of probable risk. Unless the tribe meets or exceeds all federal employment laws and practices, and therefore exercises less tribal sovereignty, the tribe is engaged in some degree of risk. Where the tribe is on the spectrum of risk is directly dependent on its choices in either complying with federal law or departing from those principles.

An inspection of a tribal leader's brain simultaneously holding a collection of principles reveals the following competing thoughts:

> Does federal minimum wage law apply? To the government? To the gaming enterprise? To this employee hired with grant dollars? Does the gaming compact influence this decision? How about that funding agreement the chairman signed last year? Could the tribe get sued, audited or spend the next year responding to DOL record requests? How will this impact those employees agitating for a union? That legal opinion discussing intentional violations of federal law, statute of limitations, attorneys' fees, penalties, and the rest seems like a doomsday scenario. Where's the coffee?

All of these variables, influences, and concerns form the confluence of relevant thoughts and considerations raised by the complicated question of whether tribes can define their own employment rules. This confluence of thoughts and considerations create risk for tribes acting or failing to act on this important question.

There is a legislative fantasy where a tribal leader is presented with two policy alternatives, the leader listens to her colleagues or legal counsel regarding which option best reflects the tribe's values and the members' priorities, and council unanimously votes to support one policy over another. This fantasy is emasculated by the reality of relevant legal principles, which must impact an informed decision.

Consider the following principles, discussed earlier in the book, in attempting to define and enforce tribal employment rules:

Inconsistent	*Rules Source*
State laws do not apply	Worcester[385]
State laws may apply	Hicks[386]
State laws apply if the tribe consents	Compact[387]
Federal laws apply only when Congress says	Bryan[388]
Assume federal laws apply	Tuscarora[389]
Federal laws do not apply if the writing is confusing	Canons of construction[390]
Federal government is obligated to act in the tribes' best interests	Trust responsibility[391]

---

[385] *Worcester v. Georgia*, 31 U.S. 515 (1832).
[386] *Nevada v. Hicks*, 121 S.Ct. 2304 (2001).
[387] The compacts entered into frequently by tribes and states, which govern Las Vegas-style gaming within tribal casinos may contain state law requirements.
[388] *Bryan v. Itasca County*, 426 U.S. 373, 392-93 (1976) wherein the United States Supreme Court limited the application of Public Law 280. Also in *Ramah Navajo Chapter v. Lujan*, 112 F.3d 1455 (10th Cir. 1997) the court ruled that the rule of sympathetic construction could overcome the deference shown to agency regulations.
[389] *Federal Power Commission v. Tuscarora Indian Nation*, 362 U.S. 99 (1960).
[390] *Bryan v. Itasca County*, 426 U.S. 373, 392-93 (1976)
[391] *Cherokee Nation v. Georgia*, 30 U.S. 1 (1831).

Federal laws may not apply if the tribe is performing essential government	Donovan,[392] Snyder[393]
Title VII and the ADA do not apply	Title VII[394] and ADA[395]
Title VII and the ADA apply if the Tribe consents	Compact/funding
Tribal law applies if the employee is a member	Montana[396]
Tribal law applies if the act occurs in Indian Country	Williams[397]
Tribal law applies to nonmembers with consent of the nonmember	Montana[398]
Federal courts may have power to hear a tribal dispute after the tribal court gets a turn	Tribal court exhaustion[399]
The tribe which does not consent to suit cannot be sued	Immunity[400]
The tribe which does not consent to suit cannot be sued unless the federal government is the plaintiff	Immunity limitation[401]
Tribal leaders and employees cannot be sued if the act is lawful and part of official duties	Immunity extension[402]
Congress can change the rules	Plenary power[403]

---

[392] *Donovan v. Coeur d'Alene Tribal Farm*, 751 F.2d 1113 (9th Cir. 1985).
[393] *Snyder v. Navajo Nation*, 2004 WL 1277031 (9th Cir. 2004).
[394] 42 U.S.C. § 2000 et seq.
[395] 42 U.S.C. § 1211(5)(B)(i).
[396] *Montana v. United States*, 450 U.S. 544 (1981).
[397] *Williams v. Lee*, 358 U.S. 217 (1959).
[398] *Montana v. United States*, 450 U.S. 544 (1981).
[399] *National Farmers Union Insurance Companies v. Crow Tribe*, 471 U.S. 845 (1985).
[400] *Santa Clara Pueblo v. Martinez*, 436 U.S. 49, 58 (1978).
[401] *United States v. Yakima Tribal Court*, 806 F.2d 853, 861 (9th Cir. 1986), cert. denied 481 U.S. 1069 (1987).
[402] *Fletcher v. United States*, 116 F.3d 1315, 1324 (10th Cir. 1997).
[403] *United States v. Kagama*, 118 U.S. 375, 384-85 (1886).

Tribal leaders face a significant challenge in maintaining all these frequently incongruent rules in mind while directing tribal lawyers and human resource directors to draft laws and policies, which reflect the traditions, customs, and goals of the tribe while at the same time responding to the needs of tribal members who cast the ballots placing them in office. Compared to the tribal leader, the lawyer has an easier task as she reviews the law, concedes it is confusing, and dispenses advice, which starts with "on the one hand" and later in the same paragraph shifts gears with "on the other hand." Like the lawyer, the human resources director has, by all accounts a very difficult job, but not as difficult as leadership's role in providing clear rules through promulgating strong and unambiguous laws.

None of this difficulty relieves the tribal leader of her responsibility to make policy choices based upon inconsistent rules thereby generating uncertain liabilities for the tribe. Tribal leaders frequently possess clarity of purpose in promulgating laws, which benefit the tribe and its members, but unfortunately the tribal leader is less comfortable with the available options after the tribal attorney describes the range of potential liability and unintended consequences of any action or inaction. For example, tribal leaders universally assert the benefits of reducing reservation unemployment through the preferential hiring of members but that clear dictate is blurred when viewed through the lens of liability. The liability analysis depends on the instability of common law, which can change with a single court decision, congressional act or agency rule change. The risks are significant for tribes, which read the rules inconsistently with what a judge, legislator, or agency director may decide in the future.

This collection of inconsistent rules places tribal leaders in the logrolling competition where two contestants wearing spiked shoes stand, walk, and run on a spinning log, floating in a dark pool of cold water. Getting and staying on the log represents the unpredictable nature of the law. Your opponent on the log trying to knock you off represents federal, state, and private interests which want your casino revenues or to dilute your sovereignty. Falling into the cold water represents the harsh risk of guessing incorrectly which direction the log (law) might spin. This metaphor comparing leadership decision-making with rolling logs reveals the struggle, which confront tribal leaders everyday. For tribal leaders, staying on the log and dry is a full time job the complexity of which is not fully appreciated by tribal members, employees, and officials from other sovereigns.

Tribal leaders are not a collection of passive officials waiting for another sovereign to define the rules. Instead, tribal leaders wear their sharp spikes and push the log in the direction which preserves and enhances their tribe's sovereignty and resists the forces on the log, which contradict those goals. If tribal leaders are passive about the tribe's sovereignty, the other sovereigns may use that passivity to expand the reach of federal and state law. This is a luxury tribes cannot afford.

The common practices, which reduce the uncertainty of leadership decisions in the employment arena, fall into the following themes:

1. *Write sound tribal employment ordinances.*

    Reasoning: Strong policy is not enough if there is a debate between application of federal law or application of tribal law. Clear rules defined through the law are elevated in importance by courts, exercise the tribe's sovereignty, and provide due process to employees by defining employer (tribal) expectations. In promulgating the law, there is not a single option but rather a range of options along the risk and sovereignty spectrums. After understanding the full range of viable options, promulgating a tribal employment code accomplishes numerous goals. A failure to codify tribal law in the employment arena presents an opportunity for states and the federal government to argue tribal policy should not apply. One of the issues discussed in a Wisconsin state case was whether the state court could assert state law where the tribe did not have a tradition of acting.[404]

2. *Update the Tribal Employment Rights Ordinance (TERO) to reflect hiring, training, and retention goals for outside contractors, tribal government, and its enterprises, and fund a tribal agency to enforce TERO.*

    Reasoning: The TERO, at a minimum, defines the tribe's preference policies for outsiders providing services on the reservation. The TERO's role can be significantly expanded to define preference

---

[404] *County of Villas v. Chapman*, 361 N.W.2d 699, 703 (Wis. 1985).

for outsiders and insiders. Those insiders are the tribal government and enterprises. TERO needs a regulator with adequate funding and personnel dedicated to its mission.[405]

Further, TERO can be charged with enforcement of the tribe's employment laws protecting employee guarantees of due process and from unlawful discrimination as defined by the tribe. Tribes are using regulators to provide uniform due process to governmental and enterprise employees. The Ho-Chunk Nation's Personnel, Employment and Labor Code is a good example of a tribal regulator providing due process for employees hired by tribal enterprises and those working for its government.[406] Sovereignty is dependent upon the enforcement of active laws and regulations.

3. *Clearly communicate the rules to employees through orientation, employee handbooks, and other employment documents*

Reasoning: Leadership sets tribal employer rules by promulgating an employment code while the employee handbook applies those rules to the employee. Due process is enhanced through the handbook by defining the employer-employee relationship since clear rules reveal the path to success and hazards of failure. When employers define success and the implications of failure due process is strengthened.

4. *Obtain written consent to the rules*

Reasoning: Sovereignty is strengthened when tribal employment rules apply to members and nonmembers alike. As discussed in chapter 2, tribes possess less authority over nonmembers unless those nonmembers consent to tribal rules.

---

[405] The Navajo Nation has a model, which enforces its preference rules on all employers within its jurisdiction and is enforced by its Office of Navajo Labor Relations. 15 N.T.C. 7.

[406] In appendix A, see the Ho-Chunk Nation's Personnel, Employment and Labor Code, chapter 1, section 4.

5. *Define the jurisdiction of the tribal court for employment-related disputes.*

   Reasoning: Tribal court jurisdiction is delegated three ways. The court's authority is delegated by the tribe's constitution, statutory law,[407] or consented to by regulation or policy. The third method of delegation, regulation, or policy, may not be sufficient if the court lacks the authority from constitutional or statutory delegation. Judicial oversight can be defined by defining the court's scope of review.[408] From the employer's perspective, defining employee rights to judicial oversight is a way to shape the application of the rules.

6. *Consider a limited waiver of immunity permitting the tribal court to award declaratory relief and back pay when hearing employment-related disputes.*

   Reasoning: Most tribal employers provide grievance opportunities to employees, which is prudent due process, educational for the employer and an opportunity to resolve real disputes. Tribal court oversight with defined scope of review increases due process; limits the arguments for unions, state, and federal court review; and permits the tribe to develop employment common law.[409]

7. *Make employment-related decisions and execute employment documents while on reservation lands.*

   Reasoning: Tribes can exert more authority when the employer is located on the reservation. Even if the employee works sixty miles

---

[407] The Ho-Chunk Nation grants employees a right to appeal to the tribal court after the employee exhausts the grievance process. Tribal law defines this as the exclusive remedy for the employee. Ho-Chunk Nation Personnel, Employment and Labor Code, chapter 5, section 35 (appendix A).

[408] The Ho-Chunk Nation defines judicial review in a narrow manner by permitting its courts to reverse a grievance board decision if the decision is arbitrary or capricious. Ho-Chunk Nation Personnel, Employment and Labor Code, chapter 5, section 35 (e) (appendix A).

[409] The nation grants a limited waiver of immunity permitting the Nation's court to award monetary damages not exceeding $10,000 and equitable relief, including reinstatement, correction of personnel information, and other remedies. Ho-Chunk Nation Personnel, Employment and Labor Code, chapter 5, section 35 (appendix A).

away from the reservation, reservation-based decisions *may* increase the likelihood of more deference to tribal rules.

8. *When engaged in for profit ventures memorialize the goal of generating revenue to serve the government's mission of serving members of the tribe.*

   Reasoning: Employees working for the on-reservation health clinic or gaming enterprise are employed in an essential government function so therefore an explanation of its benefits in the clinic's and casino's organic documents is important. An explanation in the gaming ordinance that casino revenues keep the clinic doors open and nurses employed is more important.

9. *Provide meaningful due process to employees through clearly defining the rules, the rewards for exceeding expectations, and the consequences of poor performance and a chance to present evidence if the tribe considers an adverse employment action.*

   Reasoning: Employee handbooks, job descriptions, annual reviews, and weekly employee meetings give employers an opportunity to explain how employees can succeed and turn temporary setbacks to success.

10. *Provide reasonable wages and benefits and tell employees why the wages and benefits are reasonable.*

    Reasoning: Tribal employers should spend more time explaining to employees why working for the tribe is important and rewarding. Included on this list is wages, benefits, time off, meaningful work, participation in a larger community, and an opportunity for employees to exercise their significant skills.

11. *Tell employees about the tribe, its people, its traditions, and customs*

    Reasoning: Employees can be an employer's best or worst advocate. Employee sense of the tribe's history, culture, and values increases understanding and understanding can bring advocacy.

12. *Engage in a cost-benefit analysis before executing compacts and funding agreements to ensure a balance between the tribe's sovereignty goals and the necessity of resources to operate tribal programs*

Reasoning: This cost-benefit analysis is already generating significant discussion among tribal leadership. With the development of tribal employment law, a limited waiver of immunity for employment claims and a reputation for due process, federal funding agreements with requirements including the adoption of federal law is a point of negotiation instead of automatic inclusion.

By acting on some or all of these suggestions, tribes can exert sovereignty where there is a real or perceived gap in the law. Coherent laws and policies increase employee understanding of the rules, and with this increased understanding, there is more certainty. With more certainty, risk may be reduced but not eliminated. Outside the risk analysis defining the rules has the real benefit of limiting politics through meaningful due process giving employees every opportunity to find success.

Can tribes write and apply employment laws?

Yes. Inherent sovereignty appropriately assumes that the tribe has the right to exercise its authority by writing and applying employment law. Said another way, the tribe's sovereignty is exercised if the tribe defines the terms and conditions of the employment relationship. Conversely, tribal sovereignty is diluted if another sovereign defines the employment rules.

Defining the rules through the law is a better choice than merely promulgating policy in an employee handbook. Tribes recognize that writing policy defines the relationship between employer and employee, but in a dispute where a court is asked to apply a federal employment law to protect an employee, the tribal employer is disadvantaged if it is arguing against application of the federal law in favor of a tribal policy since law trumps policy. To level the playing field, the tribal employer may more effectively argue for application of its law instead of application of the federal law, if the tribe has taken the practical step of memorializing its employment laws.

Numerous tribes have promulgated employment laws. The Ho-Chunk Nation[410] promulgated a comprehensive employment code in 2004 as the Personnel, Employment and Labor Code which is part of the Nation's Employment Relations Act of 2004. The law is reproduced in appendix A of this book.

Review of the nation's employment law reveals a comprehensive approach in defining the terms and conditions of the employment relationship between the nation and its employees. Among many other matters, the employment law allocates authority to a regulator to enforce the provisions of nation employment law, it defines equal employment opportunity by prohibiting discrimination based upon sex, race, religion, national origin, pregnancy, age, marital status, sexual orientation, or disability; and it defines preference in a comprehensive manner. Employment preference for tribal employers is a frequently debated topic, which deserves attention in tribal employment laws and herein.

Can tribal employers prefer tribal members and nonmember Indians in hiring and other employment-related decisions?

Yes. Tribal employers may prefer tribal members and nonmember Indians in hiring and other employment-related decisions. Therefore, a tribal government may prefer its members when hiring, promoting, training, and force reductions. Moreover, tribal employers may prefer its members, over members of another tribe, in these decisions.[411] This latter practice of preferring tribe specific individuals over Indians from other tribes has met with some resistance by federal regulators.

Preference is another aspect of determining whether a tribe defines the terms and conditions of the employment relationship, or is shaped by other sovereigns

---

[410] The author is grateful for significant cooperation from personnel within the Ho-Chunk Nation in permitting use of the Nation's laws.

[411] *Dawavendewa v. Salt River Project Agr. Imp. and Power Dist.*, 154 F.3d 1117 (9th Cir. 1998) held that tribe specific preference violates the law when utilized by private employers on or near the reservation.

and their representatives. The broader question is how does employment preference fit into tribal self-determination. Self-determination is comprised of many goals which when unified increase a tribe's opportunity to set and achieve its goals. One of the goals, which increase the likelihood of self-determination, is the increase of employment among tribal members. Increased employment certainly enhances the economic independence of the employee and it serves to increase the independence of the tribal employer. The Harvard Project on American Indian Economic Development argues that economic development and self-determination are both sides of the same coin:

> The most commonly self-reported goals of Native nations in the arena of development are not wealth and capitalistic riches for their own sake. Rather, Native nations are pursuing economic development in order to have the freedom to control their own political, cultural, and social destinies; and to have the ability to sustain communities where their citizens can and want to live.[412]

The viability of tribal communities where tribal members can and want to live is dependent, in part, on jobs. Tribal communities are not homogenous so therefore, economic vitality varies from community to community. As a group, however, Indians are the most disadvantaged group in the country.[413] Indians have the shortest life expectancy of any group, an unemployment rate of 45 percent, which is ten times the national average, and a poverty rate of almost 65 percent.[414] A tool enhancing the economic standard of living in tribal communities and cutting the unemployment rate, is granting employment advantage to members over others.

Productive workers hired from the pool of available tribal members' increases the tribe's self-sufficiency. The increase in self-sufficiency is evident from the productivity of the tribal employee, and it creates a pool of experienced workers from the tribe who, with increased employment experience, can be more productive in the future. An increase in employment generates

---

[412] The Harvard Project on American Indian Economic Development, *The State of the Native Nations* (Oxford University Press, 2008) at 112.
[413] Stephen L. Pevar, *The Rights of Indians and Tribes* (Southern Illinois Press, 2002) at 3.
[414] Id.

opportunities for other economic advantages like health care, education, and business development.

In a larger context, tribal preference is consistent with the preference exercised by national sovereigns. In America and Sweden, there is a preference for hiring citizens of those countries. America prefers Americans, and Sweden prefer the Swedish. When Navajos prefer Navajos in the hiring process, there is logic in that choice which is consistent with the accepted practices of America, Sweden, and other sovereigns.

Tribes universally agree that utilization of the skills available in tribal communities is important to the individual tribal members and to the tribe. To that end, tribes prefer hiring tribal members and Indians over hiring non-Indians.[415] Depending upon the tribe's law or policy this practice is called tribe specific or Indian preference. Priorities are defined by creating a hierarchy in the hiring process. For example if the tribe prioritizes the hiring of tribal members over others, tribal members are at the top of the hierarchy list followed by second, third, and fourth priorities. Following is that aspect of a preference policy, which addresses a tribe's hierarchy representing the tribe's first priority in hiring, followed by its second, third, and fourth choices:

Hiring Hierarchy

ABC tribal member

Spouse of a tribal member

Indian from a tribe other than ABC

Others

As seen from the policy, tribal members are given top priority or top preference in the hiring process followed by other categories of individuals. Different

---

[415] Ho-Chunk Nation Personnel, Employment and Labor Code, chapter 1, section 5(b) (appendix A). The nation applies Ho-Chunk preference when the employee will be funded with tribal, as opposed to, federal monies. The nation hierarchy is consistent with the sample provided.

tribes implement different hierarchies. This example illustrates a hierarchy of tribe specific preference over Indian preference. A review of many tribal policies on preference reveals unique hierarchies, which reflect the tribe's values on this issue.

Enumeration of a hierarchy is not enough when defining a preference law or policy. To properly execute a preference law or policy, the hierarchy must be joined to additional criteria, which are defined by leadership. The additional criteria necessary to properly execute preference is the use of a test for application to the hierarchy. At least three preference tests are used by tribes, which are enumerated in the following chart next to the existing hierarchy:

Hiring Hierarchy	*Tests*
ABC tribal member	Mandatory
Spouse of a tribal member	Break the tie
Indian from a tribe other than ABC	Minimum qualifications
Others	

These tests (list on the right above) are used to determine how the hierarchy (list on the left above) works in preferring one applicant over another applicant. The hierarchy by itself is not enough to exercise preference but combined with one of the tests preference is applied in a manner, which reflects the tribe's values. As defined below, the tests are enumerated from most assertive (mandatory) to least assertive (break the tie). Whether the tribe chooses the most or least assertive test, any combination of hierarchy can be joined to any test or combination of tests. A hypothetical describes the tests and reveals how they work.

The hypothetical

The tribe is interviewing prospective employees for an opening in the office of general counsel, the tribe's top lawyer. Chuck is a lawyer, has twenty-eight years of experience representing tribes, and his resume reveals strong references. Shirley is a lawyer, has a year of experience representing tribes, and her resume reveals strong references. Both Chuck and Shirley possess a license to practice law, which is required by the short job description. Chuck is not Indian, and Shirley is a member of the tribe.

In the hiring decision, if the hierarchy which prefers tribal members over all others is the only thing consulted regarding preference, Shirley is the tribe's new general counsel. However, the committee, which makes the hiring recommendation, will use the hierarchy as one factor of many in making its recommendation. The hiring committee will consider Chuck's overwhelming experience, his ability to make a contribution to the tribe's legal goals on day one and his seasoned judgment when close calls on the law are required. On the other hand, the committee will highlight Shirley's dedication to the tribe, the likelihood she will grow in her position and her intimate knowledge of the community, its culture, and people in performance of her job. All of those factors are relevant in making a sound decision.

Utilization of the three tests permits tribal leaders to identify and implement rules, which reflect the tribe's values in making specific decisions regarding preference. If leadership does not define a test, which reflects the tribe's values, the human resources director or those on the hiring committee, will use their own tests in determining whether Chuck or Shirley receives an offer of employment. The choice should be the prerogative of elected officials instead of the human resources director. Through leadership's declaration of a specific test, guidance is delegated to hiring committees and directors of human resources regarding the practical choice of Chuck or Shirley. Understanding the three tests is a prerequisite to an informed decision.

The *mandatory test* is the most assertive form of preference. Mandatory preference permits only the hiring of tribal members, so therefore, if the prospective employee is not a tribal member, he will not be considered for the position. The benefit of mandatory preference is the endorsement of hiring the maximum number of tribal members. By utilizing the mandatory test, Shirley as the tribal member, is hired as the tribe's general counsel. Chuck, as a nonmember, is not considered because the general counsel position is classified as a mandatory tribal member job.

The second test used by tribes in applying preference is the *minimum qualifications* test, which asks the hiring committee to evaluate the resumes of both applicants; and if both meet the minimum qualifications set forth in the position description, preference is used to choose between the two applicants.

Chuck's significant more experience is not relevant in the use of preference since both Chuck and Shirley meet the position's minimum qualification, and therefore Shirley as a member is hired as the new general counsel.

The third test is *break the tie* where preference only enters the conversation if due diligence of the prospective employees reveals a tie in their experience, skills and talents.[416] If due diligence does not uncover a tie preference does not play a role. In the hypothetical, Chuck's twenty-eight years of experience greatly exceeds Shirley's single year of practice, and therefore, under *break the tie* Chuck is hired as the new general counsel. On the other hand, if Chuck and Shirley's resumes were comparable in experience, there is a candidate tie which is broken by selecting Shirley via tribal preference.

These three tests are not an exhaustive list of possible alternatives. Using a test along with a hierarchy allows leadership to define how preference is implemented. Without the guidance of a test, leadership is allowing the hiring committee and human resources director to execute preference in a manner, which reflects their values. Sometimes the committee and director will make choices, which are consistent with the tribe's values, and sometimes they will circumvent the preference goal. In choosing a test, there is not just one right answer. The right answer is when delegating authority to hire people describe your hiring goals with sufficient specificity to remove the speculation regarding what leadership might want since it is not clearly defined. Increased communication through the law and policy will increase consistent application of the rules and yield results more efficiently.

Preference has been challenged by federal regulators and rejected job applicants. Examination of both Indian preference and tribe-specific preference permits a more complete analysis of the issue. Initially, Indian preference is examined, and thereafter, tribe-specific preference is evaluated.

The federal government allows,[417] and the Supreme Court permits, Indian preference. The United States Constitution forms a portion of the foundation

---

[416] Ho-Chunk Nation Personnel, Employment and Labor Code, chapter 1, section 5(b) (2) (appendix A). The nation's law states that "Preference is only afforded to distinguish between equally qualified candidates or applicants for positions. This test is discussed herein as "Break the Tie."

[417] 25 U.S.C. §472

for the federal policies treating Indians differently than non-Indians. The Constitution expressly authorizes the federal government to regulate commerce with the tribes.[418] Moreover, the federal government's trust responsibility to tribes certainly recognizes and enforces the idea of preference for tribes. Extension of these ideas to individual Indians was tested when a federal agency's policy for preferring Indian applicants over non-Indian applicants was challenged by a rejected prospective employee.[419]

The federal government's Bureau of Indian Affairs is part of the Department of Interior, which facilitates, to a large extent, the relationship between the federal agencies and the tribes. The BIA's hiring practice which preferred Indians over non-Indians was the issue in *Morton v. Mancari*. The policy was supported by the logic that Indian employees could better execute BIA objectives than non-Indian employees.

Non-Indian applicants who were not hired under the BIA's Indian preference policy sued the BIA claiming its policy violated the prohibition against race based decisions under federal law.[420] When the dispute reached the United States Supreme Court, the justices evaluated whether the BIA's hiring practice was inconsistent with federal law. The Supreme Court reasoned that the BIA was not making raced based decisions by preferring Indians over non-Indians but instead the BIA was making choices based upon political affiliation—the applicant's relationship to a federally recognized tribe, and therefore, the policy did not violate federal law. As the Court stated

> Contrary to the characterization made by appellees, this preference does not constitute "racial discrimination." Indeed, it is not even a "racial" preference. Rather, it is an employment criterion reasonably

---

[418] United States Constitution, Article 1, Section 8, Clause 3 (the Commerce Clause) provides that "Congress shall have the Power . . . to regulate Commerce with foreign Nations, and among the several States and with the Indian Tribes." Please note that the author does not believe in the use of roman numerals in the versions of this book published outside of Italy. Accordingly, the so-called preferred method for citing the Constitution lacks the use of roman numerals.

[419] *Morton v. Mancari*, 417 U.S. 535, 545 (1974).

[420] Equal Employment Opportunity Act of 1972 (42 U.S.C.§ 2000e-2000e1 and the Fifth Amendment to the United States Constitution.)

designed to further the cause of Indian self-government and to make the BIA more responsive to the needs of its constituent groups.[421]

Accordingly, if the BIA can prefer Indians over non-Indians in its hiring practices and not violate federal law, the ABC tribe can prefer Indians over non-Indians. The question is whether the ABC tribe can elevate its tribal members in the hiring hierarchy above Indians who do not belong to the ABC tribe.

Extension of the *Morton v. Mancari* logic asserts that since the BIA was not making race-based decisions by preferring Indians over non-Indians but rather making decisions based upon political affiliation, supporters of tribe specific preference assert that preferring tribal members over nonmember Indians is likewise not race based. Furthermore, supporters of tribe specific preference argue that the unemployment rates of tribal members create abundant incentives to promote tribal member employment through the tribe's hiring practices.

Moreover, supporters of tribe specific preference argue that tribal member employment oftentimes makes better employees since tribal members know their communities better, have increased insight into the community and its institutions, and a better understanding of historical context all of which increases their effectiveness.

To complicate the question further, there are tribes, which use preference to give a hiring advantage to a spouse of a tribal member who is frequently a non-Indian. Whether the tribe can prefer the spouse of a tribal member over others is a question which parallels the issue of tribe-specific preference. Recent litigation challenging tribe specific preference raises numerous interesting issues.

In *EEOC v. Peabody Western Coal Company* (*Peabody*),[422] a private company executes a lease with the Navajo Nation, which requires the company to prefer in its hiring practices members of the Navajo Nation over Indians

---

[421] *Morton* at 553.
[422] 2006 WL 2816603 (D.Ariz. 2006); Also see *Dawavendewa v. Salt River Project*, 276 F.3d 1150 (9th Cir. 2002). The *Dawavendewa* litigation made two separate trips from the Arizona District Court to the Ninth Circuit Court of Appeals.

from other tribes. The EEOC argues that tribe specific preference serves to victimize Indians who are not members of that tribe, or stated another way, the employer prefers a local Indian over an Indian from somewhere else; and in the parlance of federal employment law commits national origin discrimination.

Prior to *Peabody Coal,* in the *Dawavendewa* cases[423] the Ninth Circuit held, in the first case, that a claim of national origin discrimination arises when discriminatory practices are based on the place in which one's ancestor's lived rejecting the argument that discrimination against someone from another country was a prerequisite to triggering the law. Based on this conclusion the *Dawavendewa* court held that differential employment treatment based on tribal affiliation is actionable as "national origin" discrimination under Title VII.

Against the backdrop of *Dawavendewa,* the *Peabody* case has proceeded but instead of a private individual as plaintiff, the EEOC started the suit in *Peabody*. The parties have litigated the issue for years and as of this writing, it is pending before a federal appellate court. In support of tribe specific preference, the Navajo Nation has presented numerous arguments, which deserve some analysis.

The Navajo Nation argues that the law supports the idea that tribes can admit to their lands those individuals they choose and exclude others. From that premise, tribes can certainly place conditions on those individuals the tribes admit to tribal lands. For instance, patrons at tribal gaming enterprises play by the tribe's rules, adhere to the imposed speed limit on the road to the casino and smoke in designated areas consistent with the conditions imposed by the tribe. The same logic applies to the relationship between the tribe as

---

Dawavendewa focused on whether a private utility enforcing a lease provision, which required use of the Navajo tribe specific preference law violated the federal government's prohibition against national origin discrimination when the employer preferred Navajo's with lower pre-employment test scores over a candidate from another tribe.

[423] *Dawavendewa v. Salt River Project,* 154 F.3d 1117 (9th Cir. 1998) (*Dawavendewa1*); *Dawavendewa v. Salt River Project,* 276 F.3d 1150 (9th Cir. 2002) (*Dawavendewa 2*).

employer and its employees. If the tribe can condition admittance of people to tribal lands, tribes can place conditions on the method for selecting the employee and the terms and conditions of a continuing relationship.

Furthermore, the Navajo Nation is a federally recognized tribe and its relationship with the United States is partially defined by two treaties. Under those treaties, the Navajo Nation argues that it possesses the power to exclude nonmembers from Navajo lands and the correlative power to condition the entry of nonmembers seeking to do business within the Navajo territory. As to preference, the nation has codified these principles in its employment preference provisions in the Navajo Preference in Employment Act.[424]

The nation bolsters its argument by asserting a federal law which was a reaction to poverty on the Navajo reservation and in that law (the Rehabilitation Act) the federal government required tribe specific employment preference.[425] The Rehabilitation Act was amended before and after Congress promulgated Title VII of the Civil Rights Act.[426] The nation also argues that the Indian Mineral Leasing Act of 1938 has been construed as permitting tribal preference in hiring.[427] Moreover, 326 leases contain Navajo preference and all were approved by the federal government.

Additionally, tribal preference is exempt from the application of Title VII.[428] The exemptions reveal the clarity of congressional intent of the unique legal status of tribes.[429] The exemption in Title VII was included to benefit tribes and must be construed to favor the tribes.[430]

The United States Supreme Court states that the United States can commence a lawsuit against a tribe without the risk of an immunity defense asserted by the

---

[424] 15 N.N.C. § 601-19 (2005).
[425] 25 U.S.C. § 633.
[426] Act of August 23, 1958, Pub. L., 85-740, 72 Stat. 834; Act of June 11, 1960, Pub. L. 86-505, 74 Stat. 199; Act of Dec. 22, 1974, Pub. L. 93-531, 88 Stat. 1723; Act of Aug. 22, 1996, Pub. L. 104-193.
[427] 25 U.S.C. § 396a-396g.
[428] 42 U.S.C. § 2000e(b)(1), 2000e-2(i).
[429] *Morton v. Mancari*, 417 U.S. 535, 545 (1974).
[430] *Montana v. Blackfeet Tribe*, 471 U.S. 759, 767 (1985).

defendant tribe. Tribes argue the EEOC does not have the authority on behalf of the federal government to commence an action against a tribal defendant. When controversies under Title VII involve a government, government agency, or political subdivision the EEOC is to yield to the United States attorney general to determine if suit shall be commenced.[431] Tribes are governments,[432] and therefore, the EEOC lacks authority to commence suit. Title VII is interpreted consistently with its plain language.[433] Furthermore, the canon of statutory construction informs the analysis by requiring an interpretation of statutory language to benefit the tribes if the language yields more than one interpretation.[434]

Also, when tribe specific preference is included in a lease or other agreement a failure to enforce the terms of the lease fails to provide due deference to the parties' financial relationship. When courts reject the terms in a contract between parties in an arms-length transaction, uncertainty is the natural by-product which undermines current and future contracts.

Tribes assert that Supreme Court endorsement of Indian preference is beneficial but not necessary. Under the auspices of inherent sovereignty, tribes define their unique rules unless the federal government has exercised its plenary power and diluted the tribe's inherent sovereignty. Therefore, whether preference is exercised and in what form is a tribal decision, which does not need the federal government's endorsement. The argument that the Supreme Court's endorsement of tribe specific preference is a prerequisite to its use misses the point. Tribes do not look to the federal government for permission to define preference. Instead, tribes look to themselves first in defining their rules and secondly determine whether the federal government has exercised its plenary power and prohibited the act under consideration. In other words, tribes exercise inherent sovereignty in determining whether tribe specific preference is its highest priority.

---

[431] 42 U.S.C. § 2000e-5(f)(1); *Occidental Life Insurance Co. v. EEOC*, 432 U.S. 355, 360 n.11 (1977).

[432] *Kerr-McGee Corp. v. Navajo Tribe of Indians*, 471 U.S. 195 (1985).

[433] *Amoco Prod. Co. v. Village of Gambell*, 480 U.S. 531 (1987).

[434] *Montana v. Blackfeet Tribe*, 471 U.S. 759, 767 (1985). Credit should be given to the Navajo Nation and its attorneys Louis Denetsosie, Paul Frye, and Lisa Enfield in their excellent Ninth Circuit Court of Appeals Brief.

Inherent sovereignty asserts that tribal sovereignty is not derivative from a delegation of authority from the federal or state governments. Rather inherent sovereignty recognizes that tribes preexisted the United States and the tribes derive their sovereignty from their members and the historical respect for their existence. Inherent sovereignty starts the analysis with the assumption that tribes can define their own rules unless that power has been limited or removed by the federal government or by the voluntary waiver of the right by the tribe.

Tribes assert that federal civil rights laws do not preclude preference.[435] Moreover, the receipt of federal monies pursuant to the Indian Self-Determination and Education Assistance Act should not undermine tribe specific preference when the tribe has adopted tribe specific laws.[436] Preference has been the focus of a couple other noteworthy cases. In a casino case,[437] an employee alleged that the management contractor operating the casino's use of tribal preference violated federal civil rights laws. The Court responded that

---

[435] See, Taylor v. Alabama Intertribal Council Title IV, 261 F.3d 1032, 1035 (11th Cir.2001), cert. denied, 535 U.S. 1066, 122 S.Ct. 1936, 152 L.Ed.2d 841 (2002) (plaintiffs cannot circumvent the Title VII bar against race discrimination claims based on a tribe's Indian employment preference programs simply by allowing a plaintiff to style his claim as § 1981 suit.); *NLRB v. Pueblo of San Juan*, 280 F.3d 1278, 1284 (10th Cir.2000) (recognizing that the specific provisions of Title VII, prohibiting discrimination in employment and excluding Indian tribes from its coverage, controlled over the general provisions of § 1981 and precluded any discrimination claim against the tribe); see also, *Wardle v. Ute Indian Tribe*, 623 F.2d 670, 673 (10th Cir.1980) (dismissing § 1981 claim against tribal employer based on Title VII provisions barring discrimination suits concerning the use of Indian hiring preferences); *Stroud v. Seminole Tribe of Florida*, 606 F.Supp. 678, 679 (S.D.Fla.1985). Further, the Fourth Circuit has continuously recognized that the same analysis should apply to disparate treatment claims under § 1981 as under Title VII. See e.g., *Bryant v. Aiken Reg'l Med. Cen. Inc., 333 F.3d 536, 545 (4th Cir.2003),* cert. denied, 540 U.S. 1106, 124 S.Ct. 1048, 157 L.Ed.2d 891 (2004); *Mallory v. Booth Refrigeration Supply Co. Inc.*, 882 F.2d 908, 910 (4th Cir.1989).

[436] 25 U.S.C. § 450e(c).

[437] *Yashenko v. Harrah's NC Casino Company LLC*, 352 F.Supp. 2d 653, 657 (W.D. N.Car. 2006).

Title VII of the Civil Rights Act does not apply to tribes, therefore, Indian tribal preference programs when implemented by a tribe cannot serve as the basis of a Title VII employment discrimination suit.

In *Willis v. Bashas Inc.*[438] Plaintiff, an African American sued an on-reservation grocery store which refused to hire him because he was not Navajo. Defendant grocery store followed Navajo preference as it was a requirement of the lease Defendant executed. Plaintiff proceeded in the suit under Title VII of the Civil Rights Act of 1964. In response to defendant's motion to dismiss, the Court refused deciding that it could proceed without the Navajo Nation as a party defendant but would tailor any judgment in the case respecting the Navajo Nation's immunity and noting that there may be little left to litigate.

What is a Tribal Employment Rights Ordinance (TERO)?

At their core, Tribal Employment Rights Ordinances (TERO) are tribal laws requiring non-Indian vendors entering the reservation to build a school or pave a highway to hire tribal members as workers on the project and pay a competitive wage. The laws promote employment of, and seek to counteract discrimination against Indian people. These laws also provide a mechanism for favoring and certifying Indian-owned business in the contracting process leading up to construction of a project. The law also defines competitive wages required for the workers on these projects.[439] This view of TERO is accurate as it recognizes the important work performed by those persons operating the tribal employment rights office, which regulates compliance with the law. Outside vendors have an obligation to utilize the pool of talent and skill found on the reservation, pay competitive wages, which benefits both the vendor and the worker.

TERO's important work as traditionally viewed, however, is not enough to contribute to the preservation of a tribe's ability to exercise its inherent right

---

[438] 2006 WL 1328833 (D.Ariz. May 15, 2006).

[439] TERO's use federal standards to define competitive wages on federal projects but tribes can define a competitive wage which reflects its standards in housing projects under NAHASDA (25 U.S.C. § 4114[b] [3]) and under ISDA contracts (25 U.S.C.§ 450e[c]).

to define the employment relationship between the tribe and its employees. Therefore, the traditional view of TERO, as only applying to outsiders entering the reservation to perform a specific task, should be expanded to include application of its hiring, training, and promotion edicts to include the tribe, tribal subsidiaries, and enterprises controlled by the tribe.

Application of TERO to all aspects of hiring within the reach of the tribe's jurisdiction is compelling since the preference principles are defined by tribal law, enforced by regulators with an understanding of their importance, clearly defining leadership's view, and filling the vacuum created by the ambiguity of whether federal law applies to tribal employers. Accordingly, TERO should apply to outside vendors and as importantly, it should apply to the tribal government's workers, employees at the casino, all three shifts at the convenience store, and the other enterprises owned by the tribe.

The Navajo Nation is assertive in codifying and enforcing its laws which promote the hiring of Navajos over other applicants. All employers within the territorial jurisdiction of the Navajo Nation shall give preference in employment to Navajos.[440] The enforcement mandate lies with the Office of Navajo Labor Relations with oversight by the Navajo Nation Labor Commission. Navajo law's excellence flows from its specificity:

> Irrespective of the qualifications of any non-Navajo applicant or candidate, any Navajo applicant or candidate who demonstrates the necessary qualifications for an employment position shall be selected.[441]

TERO can provide education and insight on application of the tribe's preference policies (laws), and TERO can provide meaningful due process for employees, and prospective employees, who are aggrieved by employers failing to follow tribal law. Furthermore, TERO can, in addition to its core duties, provide a one-stop shop providing due process for preference, wrongful termination, disputes regarding wages, safety concerns, allocation of leave, and other violations of tribal law and policy.

---

[440] Navajo Preference in Employment Act, 15 N.T.C. § 601 et seq.
[441] Navajo Preference in Employment Act, 15 N.T.C. § 604 (C)(1).

Enforcement of the preference and other employment laws is a critical aspect of complying with tribal law. Tribes delegate enforcement authority to regulators in the Tribal Employment Rights Office. Acronym confusion is a risk when the law and the regulator share the same four letters which comprise both acronyms—TERO. Nevertheless, TERO describes both the ordinance and the office, which enforces the ordinance.

As a regulator, the Tribal Employment Rights Office is faced with significant responsibilities whether its mandate is to enforce preference and wage requirements on outside vendors, or is expanded to enforce the law for all employment matters within the tribe's jurisdiction. Adequate funding is always an issue for regulatory agencies and should a tribe foist these additional duties on the tribal employment rights office commensurate funding and resources in the form of skilled personnel should follow.

Are there best practices in implementing a tribal preference policy?

Yes. Drafting a sound preference policy starts with an understanding of and allegiance to the laws shaping preference within the tribal jurisdiction. Accordingly, an understanding of the tribe's preference laws is necessary.

If the law does not define both the hierarchy of hiring (described above) and adopts a test for applying the hierarchy, policy should fill that void. To ensure the right test is implemented, consultation with leadership to determine the tribe's values is a necessary prerequisite.

Preference should be the subject of orientation and training. Frequently, employees do not understand the purpose of preference, its interaction with the law, and how it is utilized by the employer. Employees who do not benefit from preference may resent those employees who do benefit from the policy, and therefore, additional information regarding preference may address those concerns.

Preference policy can be used to advantage members in hiring, lay offs, promotion, training, and other aspects of employment. Clear policy should encompass the full extent of preference's reach as defined by the tribe.

In addition to defining employment rules through tribal law, how does policy address specific rules in the tribal workplace?

In a representative democracy, elected officials are the conduit through which member values are defined in the law. The average tribal employee does not read tribal employment codes, so therefore, the gap from the law to the workplace is covered by workplace policies. Tribal council defines the law through tribal ordinances and from these ordinances, tribal employers speak to employees by drafting policies to reflect the rules defined by tribal law. For example, tribal law permits severance payments and a tribal enterprise believes that employees deserve an extra paycheck when discharged to bridge the employee's finances from the present employer to the next job. As a result, severance policies are created to reflect this employer's values, which are consistent with this tribe's law. Workplace policies are compiled in what is frequently labeled an *employee handbook*.

What is an employee handbook?

Employee handbooks are used by employers to define the terms and conditions of the relationship between employer and employee. Employee handbooks welcome employees, define sexual harassment, set work hours, and orient employees to the employer's general practices. A handbook used by tribal employers will bear many similarities to a handbook used by nontribal employers and some policies not shared with nontribal employers.

Employee handbooks define a portion of the terms and conditions of the employment relationship. In addition to employee handbooks, employers use procedure manuals, personnel action forms, organizational charts, pay scales, training, coaching, discipline, and a variety of other tools to promote and reinforce good employee practices.

The employee handbook is an important piece in the fabric of rules and other ingredients, which define the terms and conditions of the employment relationship, but it may not be the most important piece. There is evidence, which argues that once the fundamentals of an employment relationship are in place the strongest factor in whether the employer will succeed is the manager.⁴⁴² Most people do not work for the employee handbook, tribal council, the general manager of the casino, or the tribal administrator. Instead, employees work for their supervisors and employee performance or nonperformance can turn on their answers to the following questions:

1. Do I know what is expected of me at work?
2. Do I have the materials and equipment I need to do my work right?
3. At work, do I have the opportunity to do what I do best every day?
4. In the last seven days, have I received recognition or praise for good work?
5. Does my supervisor, or someone at work, seem to care about me as a person?
6. Is there someone at work who encourages my development?
7. At work, do my opinions count?
8. Does the mission/purpose of my company make me feel like my work is important?
9. Are my coworkers committed to doing quality work?
10. Do I have a best friend at work?
11. In the last twelve months, have I talked with someone about my progress?
12. At work, have I had opportunities to learn and grow?

These twelve questions have been characterized as the "simplest and most accurate way to measure the strength of a workplace."⁴⁴³ In defining the terms and conditions of the employment relationship, tribal employers' attention to employee feedback to the questions enumerated above can assist in refining policies and processes which reinforce productive work environments. A

---

[442] M. Buckingham, C. Coffman, *First, Break All the Rules* (Simon & Schuster, 1999) at twenty-one. The book is a response to the investigation of twenty-four different companies, representing twelve distinct industries, which scored four business goals: productivity, profitability, employee retention, and customer satisfaction. After investigating the business information provided the authors and their organization interviewed 105,000 employees.

[443] Id.

failure to pay attention to employee feedback will reduce productivity, employee retention, profitability, and customer satisfaction. Handbooks are an important ingredient in creating a workplace culture but cannot supplant the value of training a good management team.

Are tribal employee handbooks different from those handbooks used by nontribal employers?

An employee having never visited the ABC tribe will open the tribe's employee handbook to find many similarities between the tribe's handbook and the employee's former nontribal employer. In reading further, the new employee will also find many policies, which are slightly different or a complete departure from those provisions found in handbooks used by nontribal employers. This section provides an overview of those policies, which are different in Indian Country.

The new employee will also recognize that working for a government employer, there are places where the rules are memorialized and some rules which are not written anywhere. Many, but not all, tribal governments have constitutions, which delegate authority from tribal members to elected officials. Many tribes operate with tribal councils, which serve both the legislative and executive functions. Other tribes utilize different entities to serve the legislative and executive functions using a tribal council to serve the legislative function and a governor or Ogema[444] to serve the executive function. How the tribal government is organized will impact how and who defines the rules.

In the private sector, a benevolent dictator oftentimes is the owner of the business and makes most important decisions. This management style is also found with some tribal employers, but frequently working for a tribal government presents an opportunity to serve tribal membership through their elected officials. Instead of one person at the top of the organizational chart, there are governmental departments lead by elected officials which make and enforce the law, delegate authority to draft policy, and may have a significant role in important employment decisions like hiring and firing employees. Working for a tribal government therefore requires an understanding of the system and its written and unwritten rules.

---

[444] The Little River Band of Odawa Indians utilizes an elected executive called an Ogema.

If employee handbooks define the rules between employer and employee, where do the rules come from?

Tribal governments of all forms create laws and codify the law in constitutions, codes, and ordinances. Through these laws and delegated authority, tribal employers implement policies, which define the terms and conditions of the relationship between employer and employee. Often the terms and conditions of the employment relationship are defined through an employee handbook.

Tribal law and employee handbooks are two of several writings, which create a fabric of rules and expectations. Documents, which memorialize employment rules, are part of a system where some writings govern other writings. As there is a chain of command for employees where the director manages the manager and the manager supervises the other workers, there is also a document chain of command where documents at the top of the chain can define documents lower in command.

For example, if the tribe adopts a legal standard through an ordinance or employment code for separation of employees, the employee handbook must follow that standard as it is the law. Likewise, if the tribe adopts the federal government's Fair Labor Standards Act through an ordinance, the handbook must address the FLSA minimum wage, overtime, and other standards. Understanding the fabric of the rules is a necessary prerequisite when drafting or modifying employee handbooks. Therefore, the typical hierarchy is summarized by the following documents:

Tribal Constitution

Statutes and Ordinances

Resolutions

Regulation

Employee Handbooks, Policies, and Procedure

> *Where is tradition and custom?*

Note, all tribes do not have constitutions and the labels of ordinance, code, or statute used to codify the law is not important. The important task is to have clarity regarding the system used and create mechanisms, which clearly define what office holder, body, council, board, or committee, has authority to create and modify these documents, and the nature and extent of that authority. Accordingly, the hierarchy referenced above is a generic approximation and not intended to describe the documents utilized by all tribal governments. Since it fails to address tribal traditions and customs, the hierarchy is deficient in at least one respect. Within some tribes, traditions and customs can overrule the written rules, but in others, tradition and custom provide context for the rules but cannot override a written rule. Therefore understanding the particular tribe's use of tradition and custom is a prerequisite to understanding its impact.

What does the hierarchy show?

The hierarchy shows that (1) policy must be consistent with the law; (2) there are numerous documents, which influence employer rules; (3) unintended consequences must be accounted for from document to document; and (4) employer decisions are influenced by factors outside the hierarchy.

First, the hierarchy shows that law defines policy and policy must be consistent with the law.[445] For example, if the tribe has an ordinance which grants to its employees tribal court review of the government's termination of employment, the handbook cannot remove the right granted by the law. The law controls policy, and therefore policy follows law. To extend the chain of command comparison, the law is the director of finance and policy is the payroll clerk. The director controls the clerk as the law controls policy.

Second, the hierarchy demonstrates that the terms and conditions of the employment relationship are not defined by just the handbook or other employment manual. Instead, the employment relationship is impacted by a variety of sources. Those sources are employment codes, constitutional delegations of authority to a court, implementation of a tribal employment rights office, traditions and customs of the tribe, and common law defined

---

[445] Ho-Chunk Nation Personnel, Employment and Labor Code, chapter 1, section 3(a) (appendix A). The law supersedes the policy manual.

by court decisions. Accordingly, when modifying the handbook isolating the drafting team in a room without access to tribal council, the legal department, and others may yield a product, which is inconsistent with other tribal rules.

Third, the hierarchy can also create unintended consequences for tribal employers. Two examples illustrate separate challenges. A narrow focus on just a handbook policy, which limits the employee's due process to the exclusive grievance procedure, may be inconsistent with the tribal ordinance granting to the tribal court jurisdiction over all employment-related disputes or all disputes within the court's jurisdiction.

The second example views unintended consequences from another perspective. A tribal employer may utilize the employment at-will standard and later in the handbook unintentionally dilute at-will by instituting an inflexible progressive discipline policy. With proper drafting, some unintentional consequences can be mitigated.

Fourth, a cursory review of the hierarchy reveals numerous documents which color the landscape between employee and employer but are missing from the list. Documents, which delegate and define authority, are job descriptions and organizational charts. Moreover, the personnel action form and other procedural employer documents shape process. Oftentimes, employee handbooks incorporate by reference other substantive documents like travel policies and preference regulations. A definitive understanding of the relationship between employer and employee necessarily includes analysis of these other important documents. How these documents fit into the fabric of the employer-employee relationship is an employer obligation, which requires analysis.

Finally with tribal employers a complete understanding of the hierarchy, its rules, and the documents memorializing the rules may not provide a complete picture. The missing ingredient in the above list is the role of tradition and custom. The traditions and customs of the tribe may have no impact on employees but in other places, tradition and custom are an important aspect of an employee's day. Frequently, tradition and custom are memorialized in policies of due process, definition of the expanded Indian family (bereavement policies), and in tribal preference. Sometimes tradition and custom are not written but will nevertheless have an impact on an employee. The impact of written and unwritten tradition and custom is as varied as the 560 federally recognized tribes.

If employee handbooks define the rules, is it necessary for employees to agree to those rules?

Employers define the terms and conditions over the employment relationship through the handbook, and employees either accept the rules or work elsewhere. Employers could negotiate specific agreements with each employee; however, for efficiency, uniformity, fairness, and other reasons, employers define a set of rules for all employees and present to employees a take-it or leave-it proposition. The take-it proposition is the employee's acceptance of the job offer, and therefore the rules set forth in the handbook are accepted as a consequence of accepting the job. The leave-it proposition is the rejection of the job offer by the prospective employee.

Some employers argue that by working for the employer, workers accept the employer's terms and conditions. Courts can be critical of *work-as-acceptance* provisions, finding that better evidence of employee consent is necessary to bind the worker to the employer's rules. One court addresses the issue through a cultural icon:

> **Homer Simpson talking to God:**
>
> "Here's the deal: you freeze everything as it is, and I won't ask for anything more. If that is OK, please give me absolutely no sign."
>
> [No response]
>
> "OK, deal. In gratitude, I present you this offering of cookies and milk. If you want me to eat them for you, please give me no sign."
>
> [No response]
>
> "Thy will be done."[446]

---

[446] *Seawright v. American General Financial Services, Inc.* 2007 WL 3341692 (6th Cir. 2007) citing *The Simpsons: And Maggie Makes Three* (Fox Television Broadcast, January 22, 1995).

Arriving on the first day and starting work together with a lack of employee objection to handbook rules assumes employee consent just as God's choice not to react to Homer Simpson's offers provided adequate consent for Homer to eat the cookies.[447] Whether this silent acceptance of employer work rules is adequate is questioned by the courts.

Whether the employer seeks consent through a signed acknowledgement, work-as-acceptance provision, or other method, the relationship between employer and employee is a contract. Employers frequently include language in handbooks, which inform employees that the handbook does not create a contract between the employer and employee; but in reality, employers have contracts with all employees. Those contracts may not be written, but at a minimum, all of those contracts trade employee time for employer money. Instead, when employers include anticontract language in handbooks, the employer is actually saying that the handbook is not intended to make enforceable promises from employer to employee beyond the trade of time for money.

As compared to nontribal employers, is the explicit employee consent to the terms and conditions of the employment relationship imposed by tribal employers more important?

Yes.

Tribes hire tribal members and nonmembers, and courts view the categories differently when deciding whether a tribe's rules apply to persons within each category. Tribes assert their rules, or jurisdiction, over tribal members with greater certainty than tribes are able to assert their jurisdiction over nonmembers. Because of inherent sovereignty and the consensual nature of employment, tribes certainly exercise jurisdiction over nonmembers. Since there is an arc of power, which rises and falls depending on the category of employee, consent from all employees is arguably more important for tribal employers. This arc of jurisdiction is not prevalent for employees working for states, a private business, or for most other employers; so therefore outside of Indian Country, this issue of consent is not as important.

---

[447] Unfortunately, this is the only Homer Simpson reference in the book.

The United States Supreme Court addressed this issue outside of the employer context when the court evaluated a tribe's power to regulate the fishing rights of nonmembers on tribal lands.[448] The court reasoned that tribes could regulate nonmembers if the conduct threatens or has some direct effect on the political integrity, the economic security, or the health or welfare of the tribe. Also, the court found that the tribe could define the rules for nonmembers which enter consensual relationships with the tribe. In the employment context, a consensual relationship is trading green dollars for employee time. Accordingly, getting employees to consent to a tribal employer's rules reinforces the law's endorsement of a tribe exercising jurisdiction (writing the rules or defining the terms and conditions) over the employer-employee relationship regardless of whether the employee is a tribal member, nonmember Indian, or non-Indian.

Moreover, since there is an open question regarding the applicability of federal employment laws to tribal employers, a state or federal court may consider an employee's consent to tribal law and remedies as a factor in deciding whether tribal or other law applies and which court has the power to decide the merits over the employment-related dispute. For all of these reasons, tribal employers should clearly define the rules, obtain employee consent before application of the rules, train employees to understand the rules, and enforce the rules through fair processes. The following language is written from the first-person perspective and therefore intended to be executed as a separate consent:

> As an employee of the ABC tribe (the "tribe"), I consent to the exclusive jurisdiction of the tribe, these handbook rules and the tribal court for any and all disputes in connection with my employment with the tribe. I also consent to the application of tribe's law, both substantive and procedural, regarding any and all proceedings, matters, and things relating to my employment relationship with the tribe.

Employee consent to the tribe's exercise of jurisdiction enhances the tribe's likelihood of successfully defining the employment relationship for members and nonmembers and for Indians and non-Indians. The tribe's inherent sovereignty favors the tribe defining the terms and conditions of

---

[448] *Montana v. U.S.*, 450 U.S. 544, 101 S.Ct. 1245 (1981).

the employment relationship. Moreover, federal law accounts for the exercise of sovereignty for all employees including non-Indians. Written consent to those rules and to the exercise of sovereignty enhances the tribal employer's argument that its rules apply and the rules of other sovereigns—federal and state—do not apply.

What are the limits to employee consent?

Consent overcomes significant hurdles under the law, and therefore consent can be the magic necessary to reduce liability, define the rules, and who interprets the rules. When adult employees knowingly consent to the application of an employer's rules and those rules conflict with federal laws, which may protect the employee from certain employer decisions, is consent enough to relieve the employer from liability? Said another way, does consent trump the law? Is there a limit to the magic of consent?

There are limitations to consent. The federal government's Equal Employment Opportunity Commission may not possess jurisdiction over tribal employers, but its position regarding the use of consent appeals to some courts. The EEOC asserts that some employers are overzealous in limiting employee in contracts requiring Alternative Dispute Resolution (ADR), employee handbooks, employee benefit plans, and noncompete agreements. If those efforts include promises, which foreclose employees from filing a charge or from participating as a witness in regulatory investigations, the agreements are not valid. The EEOC further asserts that these pledges may create separate and additional violations of the antiretaliation aspect of the law. The EEOC position was endorsed by the United States Supreme Court, which found that any agreement which materially interferes with communication between an employee and the EEOC "sows the seeds of harm to the public interest" protected by the EEOC.[449]

Since Title VII does not apply to tribal employers,[450] the EEOC does not possess authority to enforce the law as to tribal employers within tribal

---

[449] *General Telephone Co. v. EEOC*, 446 U.S. 318, 326 (1980).
[450] Title VII does not apply but the tribal employer could agree to follow the law in a funding agreement, compact, or other process. Even in those instances where a tribal employer consents to the law, the EEOC still may not possess jurisdiction.

jurisdictions. Accordingly, the EEOC argument does not directly control, however, the logic of the EEOC's position and these cases reinforcing it may appeal to a tribal court or regulator interpreting an employee handbook, which attempts to limit an employee's rights, steer the employee to arbitration, or foreclose court review of employer grievance decisions.

A purpose of employment law is the preservation of civil rights in the workplace. For regulators like the Office of Navajo Labor Relations, the primary purpose of a charge of discrimination is to inform the regulator of possible discrimination and secondarily to give individuals a path to a remedy. Therefore, a charge filed with the regulator carries two potential claims for relief—the charging party's claim for individual relief and the regulator's claim to vindicate the public's interest in preventing employment discrimination.[451]

Furthermore, if the Fair Labor Standards Act applies to tribal employers, through consent employees *cannot* relieve their employers from paying overtime compensation.[452] Accordingly, if FLSA applies, a nonexempt employee working more than forty hours in a workweek is entitled to overtime compensation even if the employee consents, rejects, waives, or says no thanks to overtime compensation. Therefore, before a tribal employer can determine the effectiveness of a waiver of certain perceived employee rights, an assessment of what rights exist is necessary. For tribal employers, this assessment is complicated since an analysis of federal law, state law, tribal law, tribal policy, contracts and grants, compacts, and myriad other elements are necessary before conclusions are drawn. Even with a complete analysis of all the variables, tribal employers, unfortunately, must make judgment calls because even the best analysis brings an element of uncertainty.

Consent is meaningful regarding the waiver of discretionary employer benefits but less meaningful when seeking the eradication of certain rights. Tribal

---

[451] *General Telephone Co. v. EEOC*, 446 U.S. 318, 326 (1980); Also see, *Gilmer v. Interstate-Johnson Lane Corp.*, 500 U.S. 20, 28 (1991)(individual who signs an agreement to submit an employment discrimination claim to arbitration remains free to file a charge with EEOC).

[452] See, *Allen v. SunTrust Banks, Inc.*, 2008 WL 1925082 (N.D. Ga. 2008)(Court found unlawful retaliation when employer attempted to obtain a release from members in a pending class action suit)

employers can more confidently rely on the consent of employees regarding an employer's selection of at-will versus for-cause, zero-tolerance drug and alcohol testing, limiting the employee's expectation of privacy, arbitration as the method for dispute resolution, and myriad other matters. Simply put, if the law creates an employee right, waiver may not be effective; but when an employee benefit is not guaranteed under the law, consent to their exclusion is meaningful. Accordingly, outside Indian Country, a determination of "rights" is easier since federal law explicitly defines to whom it applies. Inside Indian Country, whether federal employment law applies is an open question, so therefore in the absence of explicit language applying federal employment law to tribal employers, tribes have a stronger argument that consent is meaningful as to the waiver of federal law.

Employers go to significant lengths in obtaining consent from employees. An Oklahoma state court[453] was asked to determine whether an employee waived their right to pursue a retaliatory discharge claim in court after signing an acknowledgement, which appears to be thorough and comprehensive. The consent is stated in its entirety here as an example of one employer's effort to impose its handbook provisions on employees.

> As conditions of my employment with Bar-S foods Co., I hereby consent (1) to provide samples of my blood and/or urine for analysis when reasonably requested during the course of my employment and to comply with the Bar-S Foods Co. Drug and Alcohol Testing Policy; (2) to utilize the Bar-S Foods Co. Problem Resolution Process to resolve any and all grievances, claims, and disputes which are in any way related to my employment or termination of my employment; (3) to submit unresolved legal claims or disputes which are in any way related to my employment or termination of my employment to exclusive, final, and binding arbitration as provided in the Bar-S Foods Co. Problem Resolution Process; (4) to abide by the terms and conditions of all current Bar-S rules, guidelines, policies, procedures, and employee handbook provisions, as those terms and conditions may be modified by Bar-S Foods Co. from time to time.

---

[453] *Thomson v. Bar-S Foods Co.*, 147 P.3d 567 (Okla. 2007).

> I understand and agree that my employment by Bar-S Foods is conditioned upon my consent to submit any legal claim or dispute which in any way relates to my employment or termination of my employment to exclusive, final, and binding arbitration in accordance with the current Bar-S Foods Co. Problem Resolution Process, a copy of which has been made available for my review. I understand that this requirement of exclusive, final and binding arbitration applies to any claim of unlawful harassment or discrimination arising under Title VII of the Civil Rights Act of 1964, as amended; under the Age Discrimination in Employment Act, as amended; or under any similar state anti-discrimination statutes, as well as to any other legal claims or disputes arising from my employment or termination of my employment. As a condition of my employment by Bar-S Foods Co., I expressly waive any right I might otherwise have had to a jury trial of claims arising from my employment or termination of my employment.

Employee's consent to the rules imposed by the tribal employer in exchange for the opportunity to engage in meaningful work and collect a paycheck is a bargain, which can be accepted or rejected. If accepted, employee complaints targeted to tribal rules, which are different from the federal rules smacks of whining without any equitable foundation. On the other hand, if tribal employers make material promises to employees which are not kept, the benefit of the bargain justifying consent to tribal rules is not realized, which when serious should trigger meaningful repercussions.

Do tribal employers include unique policies in employee handbooks?

Yes. Tribal employers include in employee handbooks many policies, which nontribal employers utilize. Significant portions of the employee handbook used by a tribal employer share the same language utilized by nontribal employers. Unlike their nontribal counterparts, there are policies implemented by tribal employers, which you will not find as an employee for Wal-Mart or General Motors. Good reason exists for these differences since in some aspects, tribal traditions and customs percolate into the workplace.

Before an overview of specific policies is addressed, a brief summary of the role and purpose of employee handbooks is necessary. Many employers use the terms policy, procedure, and handbook interchangeably. Many employers draw a distinction between the employee handbook and standard operating procedures wherein the employee handbook is a compilation of the universal policies, which outline the terms and conditions of the relationship between employer and employee. If the employee handbook is a compilation of the universal policies, which define the employment relationship for all employees, the standard operating procedures are specific to employer departments. Accordingly, the employer handbook defines the employee, and the standard operating procedures tell the employee how to perform their job. By drawing this distinction between employee handbook and standard operating procedures, the handbook is a document which does not grow to an unmanageable length, failing to serve the employer's need of clear rules. Moreover, by creating standard operating procedures, which are department specific, the procedures are more effective at targeting the workers who will use the specific procedures.

How employers utilize labels of policy, procedure, or handbook are not as important as crafting a document that memorializes the rules, standards, expectations, and conduct of both the employer and employees. There are numerous reasons to draft sound policy and procedure.

First, the process of drafting policy and procedure forces tribal leadership to anticipate and formulate answers to important questions. Will the tribe exercise tribal or Indian preference in its hiring decisions? Is the casino an at-will or for-cause employer? Does the tribe pay overtime compensation? These questions and many more need informed analysis.

Second, the receipt of federal money requires tribes to utilize those dollars effectively. The employee or employees that are responsible for achieving the objective outlined in the grant award, which generated the receipt of the federal funds, need guidance in accomplishing their assigned tasks. Frequently, the grant award will not provide the employee guidance necessary, so therefore developing the policy and procedure, which ensures success, will help fulfill the tribe's duty under the terms of the grant.

Third, *any* destination is satisfactory when an objective is not chosen before the trip is started. Likewise, employers without a map describing the employer's choice for accomplishing specific goals will inevitably fail to relieve employees of their confusion regarding mission. Telling employees what their expectations are and the best practices for exceeding those expectations will certainly increase the efficiency of accomplishing the tribe's goals.

Fourth, a failure to clearly tell employees that certain conduct will not be tolerated in the workplace significantly increases the employer's exposure to liability if presented with a claim. For example, in the sexual harassment arena, a failure to articulate, train, and enforce sound policy can significantly increase an employer's exposure to a large verdict in favor of the former employee.

Fifth, writing the rules through well-drafted policy and procedure and using those rules to make decisions regarding employee conduct will increase an employer's objectivity in employment-related matters. When supervisors utilize written policy and procedure to praise or criticize employee conduct, the decision is based upon a standard that was disclosed to employees, and therefore the employer's expectations are easily measured. On the other hand, when supervisors depart from the written policies and procedures, it is more difficult to measure the outcome by an objective standard. Clearly, policy and procedure can never anticipate and address every situation, and therefore supervisor discretion will always be necessary in many situations, but striving to memorialize sound policy and procedure is a practice that will increase impartiality and the appearance of impartiality. Said another way, sound policy may reduce tribal politics and its influence in the workplace.

Sixth, promulgating good policy and procedure will help decrease the employee's plea of ignorance regarding employer expectations. Accountability is a motivator and a teacher; and in organizations of more than one employee, policy and procedure can help all parties understand when they have met, exceeded, or failed to reach employer expectations.

What are the unique policies?

There are numerous policies discussed below which are either unique to tribal employers or tribal employers place a unique twist on a widely used policy. Above, one of the most important tribal policies, consent to tribal jurisdiction policy, was discussed. Below policies which address sovereignty, immunity, tribal history, tradition, and custom, how the government works, meaning of the tribe's logo, the benefits of working for the tribe, modification of the handbook, employment at-will, nepotism, bereavement, preference, personnel files, and due process. Employee handbooks include many more policies than the unique policies referenced herein.

The Sovereignty Policy

Many tribes tell employees that employee handbooks do not modify or waive tribal sovereign immunity. There is an opportunity to say more on this topic to give employees a better understanding of sovereignty and increase the level of informed consent. A sample policy might read

> The ABC tribe is a sovereign nation, which exists within the borders of the United States. One aspect of the tribe's sovereign status is its immunity to private lawsuits. This means that no private action can be taken against the tribe unless the tribe consents to the action. Nothing in this handbook constitutes a waiver of the tribe's sovereign immunity.

Most tribes say something about sovereignty in employee handbooks, but not all take the opportunity to provide some information regarding the principle. The proposed policy language addresses waiver and provides employees with more information.

Consent

Tribal employers should clearly define the rules, obtain employee consent before application of the rules, train employees to understand the rules, and enforce the rules through fair processes. The following language is written from the first-person perspective and therefore intended to be executed as a separate consent:

> As an employee of the ABC tribe (the "tribe"), I consent to the exclusive jurisdiction of the tribe, these handbook rules and the tribal court for any and all disputes in connection with my employment with the tribe. I also consent to the application of tribe's law, both substantive and procedural, regarding any and all proceedings, matters, and things relating to my employment relationship with the tribe.

Employee consent to the tribe's exercise of jurisdiction enhances the tribe's likelihood of successfully defining the employment relationship for members and nonmembers and for Indians and non-Indians.

Tribal history and culture

Your employees will be more effective if they understand and appreciate their employer. By providing employees a better understanding of the tribe through the inclusion of information in the employee handbook, the tribe is better preparing its employees to serve their employers effectively. Moreover, oftentimes employees can be the tribe's best advocates to the surrounding community. These employee advocates will be more effective if they possess some insight on the tribe's history and culture. The Little Traverse Bay Band of Odawa Indians[454] provides an excellent example:

> The Little Traverse Bay Bands of Odawa Indians or Ottawa people have been in this geographical area of Michigan long before the Europeans arrived here on Turtle Island, known as Canada, North, and South America. The Odawa were a migratory people, traveling from the Upper Peninsula and the northern area tip of Michigan in the fall, to the southern part of Michigan, where the climate was more hospitable during the winter months.
>
> In the spring, the Odawa people returned to their homelands to collect maple syrup, fish, and plant crops. When they weren't tending their gardens or doing their day-to-day chores, they gathered fruits, herbs, medicines, as well as any other food products they could dry and put away to be used during the long winter months.
>
> After the Europeans came and settled in what is known as Escanaba, NocBay, Mackinac, Cross Village, Good Hart, Middle Village, Harbor Springs, Petoskey and the Bay Shore Area, the Odawa ceased to migrate to the southern areas of the state. This

---

[454] The Little Traverse Bay Band of Odawa Indians provides an abundance of information regarding its culture, history, laws, and enterprises at *www.ltbbodawa-nsn.gov*. The tribe is a model for other sovereigns in its pursuit of excellence in governance and business.

was due to the new immigrants or early settlers, who brought with them new food staples and work, which the tribal people took advantage of. Permanent housing, schools and churches were then established and the Native people went to work for the settlers or began their own businesses to make their living.

After the 1836 and 1855 Treaties were signed, the benefits the U.S. Government promised the Tribes, did not materialize. The Ottawa's from this area began to organize to sue the US Government to try and recover monies agreed upon from the government.

There were three (3) main groups who worked together to unite the Ottawa people politically, to make the US Government aware of their treaty agreements. They were: the Michigan Indian Defense Association of 1933, The Michigan Indian Foundation 1947 and the Northern Michigan Ottawa Association in 1948. The Northern Michigan Ottawa Association was the "Parent" to all of the Federally recognized tribes because they were an organization.

The Little Traverse Bay Bands was originally known at the NMOA, Unit 1. Unit 1 began to file for Ottawa fishing rights (1980's) in the Federal courts. The Federal Courts would not recognize NMOA Unit 1, because they were an organization.

The tribe reorganized and took the name Little Traverse Bay Bands (Nov. 29, 1982). Again the Federal Court would not allow the tribe their rights, this time because they were not a Federally recognized tribe. The Little Traverse Bay Bands did not want to be Federally recognized under the Bureau of Indian Affairs, instead, they went for Reaffirmation by the Federal Government because of the treaties. On Sep. 21, 1994, President Clinton signed the bill that gave the Little Traverse Bay Bands of Odawa Indians, Federal recognition through Reaffirmation.

Role of tradition and custom

Since employee handbooks memorialize the rules between employers and employees, if the tribal employer utilizes tradition and custom in its decision making regarding hiring, firing, promoting, and retaining employees, the role of tradition and custom should be defined. It will be difficult to define how tradition and custom will impact every decision, however, at a minimum, it is a good practice to provide employees with notice that tradition and custom has and will play a role in the employer's decision making.

> The ABC tribe has written numerous policies for the benefit of employees of the tribe. This handbook is a compilation of those policies. Please also understand that the ABC tribe has rich traditions and customs, which impact the views of tribal members, tribal leadership, and the employment practices of the ABC tribe. For example, the tribe honors the individual voices of its employees because that is consistent with the teachings of tribal elders. Therefore some decisions, which impact the workplace, will be made after the affected employees have an opportunity to express their views. Furthermore, the tribe recognizes the need for time away from work to participate in religious ceremonies and rituals.

How the government works

Working for a government is different from other employers. By working for tribal governments, you are working for the tribal members whom are the beneficiaries of tribal programs and services. Including information in the employee handbook regarding governmental processes will provide a greater understanding of government operations to tribal employees. That greater understanding may increase employee effectiveness. Furthermore, included in the policy is context for the purpose behind the laws promulgated by the tribe as a direct benefit to the tribe's members and the political integrity of the tribe.

> The ABC tribe is a sovereign government, which has defined powers and responsibilities under its Constitution. The state and federal governments are similar to the ABC tribe since all sovereigns create rules for the benefit of citizens and members of the community. Under the ABC tribe's Constitution, the adult members elect a five member Tribal Council which serves a term of two years. Subgroups of the Tribal Council assist the ABC tribe with its decisions. Some of those subgroups are the Elders Committee, Housing Committee, Economic Development Committee, and Constitution Revision Community. The rules, terms, and conditions set forth in this handbook have a direct impact on the economic vitality and political stability of the ABC tribe.

The meaning of the tribe's logo

The tribe's history can be memorialized a number of ways including the logo used by the tribe. Describing the logo and its importance may assist employees in better understanding the tribe's history.

> On the face of this handbook, the ABC tribe has included the tribe's logo which was created by a tribal member to depict the tribe's history, values, traditions, and customs. [Insert description]

Working for a tribe is a fantastic opportunity

Tribes can do a better job of communicating the significant wages and benefits generated by tribal employers. An employee's understanding of the significant benefits afforded employees is important. Moreover, the employee's family, friends, and prospective employees will be impacted by the tribe's present workforce. Prudence reinforces reminding employees of the tribe's health and dental coverage, life insurance, short term and long term disability, retirement plans, incredible working environment, state of the art technology, and many other benefits.

Modification of the Handbook

A provision implementing the tribe's policy regarding modification of the handbook is certainly not unique to tribal employers, but nevertheless an important policy. Employers change policy from time to time, and therefore a good practice is telling your employees that changes will be encountered. Consider telling your employees that the handbook may be changed at any time:

> The tribe reserves the right to revise, supplement, modify, and rescind any policies or portion of the handbook from time to time as it deems appropriate in its sole discretion.

Employment at will

At-will employment is not unique to tribal employment, however, there is some confusion regarding its applicability. There are some claims that at-will employment is not permitted for tribal employers. To the extent that a grant limits use of the at-will doctrine, or the tribal court rules at-will is inconsistent with tribal law, at-will is not permitted. At many tribes, however, at-will is used as the legal standard for separating employees from the employment relationship.

Some tribes have drawn the conclusion that at-will employment aids politics in contributing to an unstable employment environment. The argument asserts that if at-will makes it easier to terminate employees, opportunities to shed less politically advantageous employees will be presented. In other words, at-will permits leadership to terminate those members who voted for the other candidate and replace them with voters aligned with the leader. Conversely, some tribal employers recognize that the at-will policy describes a legal standard relating to employee retention but it does not describe the moral obligation, which requires tribal employers to grant every employee an opportunity to succeed based upon objective criteria like performance reviews and job descriptions.

If the tribe is an at-will employer, consider memorializing the tribe's at-will policy:

> Employment with the tribe is voluntary and, therefore, employees are free to resign at-will at any time with or without cause or reason. Likewise, the tribe ay terminate the employment relationship at-will at any time with or without notice and for cause or for any reason deemed appropriate by the tribe. This policy is commonly referred to as employment at-will.

Just cause

The alternative to an at-will employment relationship is a just cause or for cause relationship. Employees, unless subject to an employment agreement with a promise to provide services for a fixed period of time, are always free to separate themselves from their employers for no reason and without notice, accordingly the employee's decision to separate themselves is at-will. Employers in a just cause employment relationship need a reason to terminate the employee and those reasons can be defined by the employer. The Ho-Chunk Nation provides a detailed list of reasons which generate employee discipline.[455] Once discipline is directed,[456] the employee has significant due process rights including mediation,[457] a formal grievance,[458] and judicial review.[459] Due process is enhanced by formal hearing procedures.[460]

Nepotism

When employers show favoritism or patronage granted by officeholders to their relatives, there is a cry of nepotism. The French and Italian used similar words to describe the favoring of nephews. In tribes where the expanded definition of "family" can multiply the number of an employee's nephews and nieces, sound policy helps employers make good choices.

Tribal employers deal with nepotism by addressing political patronage through the postelection termination of a portion of the tribe's work force followed by hiring friends and relatives to fill those vacant positions. The second

---

[455] Ho-Chunk Nation Personnel, Employment and Labor Code, chapter 5, section 30 (appendix A).

[456] Ho-Chunk Nation Personnel, Employment and Labor Code, chapter 5, section 31 (appendix A). The Nation has an intelligent progressive discipline policy:

> Depending on the nature of the circumstances of an incident, discipline will normally be progressive and should bear a reasonable relationship to the violation. Based on the severity of the employee conduct, progressive discipline may not be applicable.

[457] Ho-Chunk Nation Personnel, Employment and Labor Code, chapter 5, section 32 (appendix A).

[458] Ho-Chunk Nation Personnel, Employment and Labor Code, chapter 5, section 33 (appendix A).

[459] Ho-Chunk Nation Personnel, Employment and Labor Code, chapter 5, section 34(a) (appendix A).

[460] Ho-Chunk Nation Personnel, Employment and Labor Code, chapter 5, section 34(b-f) (appendix A). Another tribe has found a property right in employment once the employee emerges from the ninety-day probationary period. *Barnes v. Mashantucket Pequot Tribal Nation*, 34 ILR 6072 (Mash.Tr.Ct. 2007).

aspect of nepotism for tribal employers is structuring the organizational chart or chain-of-command to prevent relatives from directly supervising other relatives. Tribal employers implement nepotism policies to address both issues. An example:

> The employment of tribal members is an important goal for the economic security and political integrity of the tribe. Moreover, with the employment of tribal members and nontribal members from the same family may cause concerns with favoritism and employee morale. This policy addresses the hiring and retention of immediate family members. Immediate family member is defined as the spouse, parent, sibling, or child of an employee or a person involved in a dating relationship with the employee. Immediate family members of current employees may not occupy a position where they will be the immediate supervisor or immediate subordinate of their relative. Immediate supervisor is defined as the first level over an employee.
>
> The tribe does not permit hiring, firing, or retention decisions to be based upon political patronage.

The Ho-Chunk Nation provides an example of a nepotism policy by prohibiting supervision of a relative.[461]

Bereavement

The death of family can be devastating for employees. Tribes oftentimes use an expanded definition of family in determining whether employees may be absent from work and, therefore, a policy should be implemented to address this unique issue.

> In case of a death in your immediate family, you may receive up to three working days' paid leave; in the event of the death of a member of your immediate family that is more than five hundred miles from the workplace, you may receive up to five working

---

[461] Ho-Chunk Nation Personnel, Employment and Labor Code, chapter 3, section 15(i) (appendix A).

days' paid leave. This time off is intended to be used to attend memorial services as well as to attend to associate family matters. Immediate family includes your parents, grandparents, siblings, spouse, children, grandchildren, and any person who has been ceremoniously adopted into the employee's family as any of the relations listed above.

The tribe's language is important

Tribal leaders inform that we are born with a language which is revealed to us as we grow. Therefore, language inherently defines who we are as individuals and as tribal organizations. Some tribal employers address this through policy.

> The ABC tribe has a rich language that has been preserved by members of the tribe with assistance from the tribe's government. As part of the tribe's commitment to its language, many employment documents utilize the tribe's language as well as English.

The tribe's elders are revered

Tribal elders have traditionally served a valuable and respected role. Some tribal employers ask elders to serve on grievance committees, policy review boards, and other employer functions which enable those employers to benefit from the wisdom and insight provided by elders.

> Tribal members reaching their fifty-fifth birthday are elders of the tribe. Elders comprise a valuable and respected role for the tribe and its members. Elders serve Tribal employees by sitting on the grievance committee, which offers employees a fair opportunity to address concerns about employment-related decisions.

Progressive discipline is important

Part of the due process provided by employers to employees is giving employees multiple opportunities for success. Progressive discipline is designed to shape employees to the employer's rules.

> The best disciplinary measure is the one that is not necessary. The tribe prefers to utilize good management and fair supervision to

support its employees. When discipline is necessary, the tribe uses discipline of a progressive nature. Therefore, the tribe uses verbal warning, written warning, suspensions, and terminations in a manner that fits the tribe's needs. The tribe, at its sole discretion, is entitled to utilize discipline that is appropriate for the circumstances presented. This policy does not modify or change the at-will relationship.

The Ho-Chunk Nation has an intelligent progressive discipline policy:[462]

> Depending on the nature of the circumstances of an incident, discipline will normally be progressive and should bear a reasonable relationship to the violation. Based on the severity of the employee conduct, progressive discipline may not be applicable.

Equal Opportunity Defined

Unless modified through a compact, agreement, or waiver, federal antidiscrimination law does not apply to on-reservation tribal employment practices. Additionally, in most circumstances, state human rights laws do not apply to tribal employers. Accordingly, tribes and their employers need to define those criteria, which will not be used in making employment-related decisions. Those groups included on the list are protected classes under the law or policy, and those groups not included are not protected. The length of the tribe's list of protected classes depends in part on the tribe's values, its competitiveness for the best employees, the source of funds used to employ the worker, and whether the tribe intends to accept or reject federal minimum standards. This list is illustrative of a policy used by a tribe.

> The tribe grants equal opportunity to all qualified persons without regard to race, religion, color, gender, national origin, disability or age, sexual orientation, pregnancy, financial assistance, or political affiliation.[463]

---

[462] Ho-Chunk Nation Personnel, Employment and Labor Code, chapter 5, section 31 (appendix A).

[463] Ho-Chunk Nation Personnel, Employment and Labor Code, chapter 1, section 5(a) (appendix A). The Nation defines equal employment opportunity by declaring discrimination unlawful if based upon sex, race, religion, national origin, pregnancy, age, marital status, sexual orientation, or disability.

When a tribe defines and enforces this list, it gives substance to the tribal handbook claim that the tribe is an employer giving equal opportunity. For example, the Ho-Chunk Nation codified its sexual harassment policy in its employment code.[464]

Response to collection proceedings from other sovereigns

This is a policy which addresses whether the tribal employer will respond to judgments, garnishments, child support orders, and other legal mechanisms which execute upon employee wages in satisfaction of a directive from a court. The ABC tribe is located within the state of Minnesota and a Minnesota court has directed the tribe's administrative assistant to pay $500 a month in child support. Many tribes implement a policy which requires the directive from a court outside the tribe to be filed in the tribe's court, and recognized by the tribe's court before the tribal employer withholds and remits the $500 for support. The process is called full faith and credit or comity.

Preference Policies

The use of preference in tribal employment is a widespread practice, which incorporates many variations on these themes. A lengthy discussion of preference is included earlier in this chapter. There are two elements to a preference policy. The first element addresses what category of people is preferred and the second element directs when preference is used. The earlier discussion set forth the *hierarchy of hiring,* and the three tests used by tribes to apply the *hierarchy.*

There are at least three alternatives for the tests used by tribes in executing on preference. Below, there are a couple sample policies, which incorporate these tests. The first example describes the break-the-tie test, the second example describes the minimum qualifications test, and the third example is a hybrid of mandatory preference and minimum qualification. This section concludes with policy language, which incorporates the procedure for exercising preference.

---

[464] Ho-Chunk Nation Personnel, Employment and Labor Code, chapter 1, section 6(e) (appendix A).

The first element—Hierarchy of Hiring

The ABC tribe specifically sets forth the following preference:

1. Applicants or employees who are enrolled ABC tribal members,
2. Applicants or employees who are the spouses of ABC tribal members,
3. Applicants or employees who are enrolled members of other Indian tribes, and
4. All other applicants or employees.

The second element—Example 1, the Break-the-Tie test

Preference in hiring, job transfers, promotions, choice of shifts, and any reductions in the labor force is given in the order set forth above when applicants or employees are equally able to perform the duties and responsibilities.

The second element—Example 2, the Minimum Qualifications test

Preference in hiring, job transfers, promotions, choice of shifts, and any reductions in the labor force is given in the order set forth above when applicants or employees meet the minimum qualifications set forth in the job description.

Or irrespective of the qualifications of any non-Navajo applicant or candidate, any Navajo applicant or candidate who demonstrates the necessary qualifications for an employment position shall be selected.[465]

The second element—Example 3, the Hybrid test

Preference in hiring, job transfers, promotions, choice of shifts, and any reductions in the labor force is given to ABC tribal

---

[465] Navajo Preference in Employment Act, Section 4(C). The NPEA defines "necessary qualifications" as job-related qualifications, which are essential to the performance of the basic responsibilities . . . and defines "qualifications" to include the ability to speak Navajo and familiarity with Navajo culture, customs, and traditions.

members only if the open position is a supervisor, manager, director, or administrator. For nonsupervisory positions preference in hiring, job transfers, promotions, choice of shifts, and any reductions in the labor force is given in the order set forth above when applicants or employees meet the minimum qualification of the position.

Oftentimes, preference policies set forth specific requirements for employees which seek to utilize the policy.

To claim preference, an enrolled tribal member must be able to provide verifiable documentation. This can be in the form of a document bearing either:

1. the enrollment number issued by the Bureau of Indian Affairs, or
2. the enrollment number issued by the tribal government.

In the event that no documentation bearing the enrollment number is available, the applicant or employee must provide a notarized letter or resolution from the government of the enrolled tribal member's tribe attesting that the individual is a member of their tribe. This requirement must be complied with before an applicant or employee may receive preference in the human resources process. Providing proof of preference is the responsibility of the tribal member and must be received prior to the use of such preference.

Personnel Files

Employees deserve access to their personnel files.[466] Many tribes do not have laws, which define what is included and what is not included in an employee's personnel file. Tribal law should define personnel file and the rules regarding employee access.

---

[466] Ho-Chunk Nation Personnel, Employment and Labor Code, chapter 1, section 6(a) (appendix A). The nation declares access to personnel files a right and takes the additional step of protecting employee privacy. Ho-Chunk Nation Personnel, Employment and Labor Code, chapter 1, section 6(b) (appendix A).

For many employers personnel record means the following:

1. any application for employment
2. wage or salary history
3. notices of commendation
4. warning, discipline, or termination
5. authorization for a deduction or withholding of pay
6. fringe benefit information
7. leave records, and
8. employment history with the employer, job titles, dates of promotions, transfers, and other changes, attendance records, performance evaluations.

Employers also address through policy employee access to personnel files. Access rules define when, who is present, and whether making a copy of the file is permitted.

> You may review your personnel records at a mutually convenient time during regular business hours. If you wish to do so, please notify human resources so that a specific time may be scheduled when a representative will be available to answer your questions. Any concerns regarding the completeness or accuracy of the information contained in your files should be taken up with your immediate supervisor and/or human resources. If you disagree with an item in your file, you may appeal to human resources to have it corrected or removed. If your appeal is denied, you may place your own rebuttal or correction statement in the file.

Solicitation

As discussed in chapter 2 regarding union efforts to become the bargaining agents for tribal employees, a ground for charges of unfair labor practices is where employers permit some groups to solicit employees and deny the same right to unions. Therefore, employers implement uniform rules, which permit the Girl Scouts to sell cookies and employees to sell plastic food containers at the workplace recognizing that a union can ask for the same access to employees and the workplace. Alternatively, employers can implement and enforce the opposite provision ending all solicitations in the workplace.

The following policies are made for the safety and security of all employees and shall be strictly enforced. The purpose of this policy is to maintain an orderly workplace to avoid intrusion upon employees at their work and to preserve employee safety and security throughout the facility as to funds, supplies, records, and confidential information. Accordingly, all employees are to observe the following rules and report violations to their supervisors:

1. *Except for legitimate business purposes* and with prior authorization, individuals not employed by the ABC tribe may not, at any time, solicit, survey, petition, or distribute literature on any company property. This policy includes charity solicitors, salespersons, questionnaire surveyors, union organizers, or any other solicitor or distributor.
2. *Employees may not* solicit for any purpose during work time. Work time includes that time for which the employee is paid and expected to be performing services for the employer. Work time includes both the soliciting and/or the solicited employee's work time. Reasonable forms of solicitation are permitted during nonwork time, such as before or after work or during meal or break periods. Employees may not distribute literature for any purpose during work time or in work areas. The employee break room is a nonwork area.

Incorporation of traditional dispute resolution mechanisms.

Many employers give due process to their employees through grievance procedures, peer review, oversight committees, and a variety of other ways. Due process in employment is more than just the grievance procedure provided to employees complaining about an employer decision. Due process is comprised of communicating objective standards for employee success, presenting an opportunity to perform, providing feedback to employees in the course of performance, and a formal mechanism like a grievance if the employee is not satisfied with the employer's conduct.

Therefore, due process is delivered from employer to employee through the handbook, procedure manuals, standard operating procedures, coaching, performance reviews, discipline, incentive pay, safety rewards, grievance procedures, job descriptions, team meetings, and managers who believe in management by walking around. This expanded definition views due process as more than an opportunity for a grievance hearing. An expanded definition of due process also supports the legal argument that tribal employers deliver an abundance of due process even if the employer does not permit tribal court review or other alleged breach of the Indian Civil Rights Act.

Tribes have been resolving disputes for a long time and tribes have utilized traditional dispute resolution techniques that have been successful. However, in most tribal employee handbooks, those tribal traditional dispute resolution processes have not been utilized. Tribes should consider tailoring their dispute resolution techniques to their own circumstances. Whether the tribe utilizes talking circles, peacemakers, family group counseling, elder guidance, or another technique with roots in tribal history and custom is a question for the tribe.

As part of due process in the workplace, tribes implement statutes of limitation for a variety of causes of action. The Ho-Chunk Nation implemented a law limiting employment lawsuits to thirty days measured from the end of the grievance process and two or three years for contracts, torts, and warranty claims.[467]

---

[467] Ho-Chunk Nation Code, 2 HCC §14 (2005).

APPENDIX

Ho-Chunk Nation Code, Personnel, Employment and Labor Code, 6 HCC § 5 et seq.

HO-CHUNK NATION CODE (HCC)
TITLE 6 – PERSONNEL, EMPLOYMENT AND LABOR CODE
SECTION 5 – EMPLOYMENT RELATIONS ACT OF 2004

ENACTED BY LEGISLATURE: DECEMBER 9, 2004
(Effective Date: January 31, 2005)

LAST AMENDED AND RESTATED: JUNE 7, 2006

CITE AS: 6 HCC § 5

This Act supersedes the Ho-Chunk Nation's Personnel Policies and Procedures Manual initially adopted on December 21, 1994 and last amended by Legislative Resolution 9/04/02C.

Chapter VI (Drug, Alcohol and Controlled Substance Policy) enacted by Legislative Resolution 10/16/01D and Amended and Restated by Legislative Resolution 10/23/02B.

Chapter VII (Worker's Compensation Plan) supersedes the Ho-Chunk Nation Worker's Compensation Plan dated October, 1998.

TABLE OF CONTENTS

Chapter I - General Provisions

1. Authority 3
2. Purpose 3
3. Declaration of Policy 3
4. Responsibilities 4
5. Employment Clause 4
6. Employee Rights 5

Chapter II - Definitions

7. Definitions 11

Chapter III - Employment Policies

8. Position Classification and Allocation 17
9. Probationary Period 17
10. Employee Separation Policy 18
11. Recall Policy 19
12. Rehire Policy 19
13. Compensation and Payroll Practices 19
14. Performance Evaluations 22

15. Other Workplace Policies 24

Chapter IV - Employee Benefits

16. General 26
17. Ho-Chunk Nation Holidays 27
18. Annual and Sick Leave 28
19. Funeral Leave 31
20. Cultural Leave 32
21. Waksik Wosga Leave Policy 32
22. Jury Duty and Witness Leave 35
23. Military Leave 35
24. Educational Leave 37
25. Administrative Leave 37
26. Medical Leave 37
27. Unpaid Leave of Absence 40
28. Employee Assistance Program (EAP) 41

Chapter V - Work Rules and Employee Conduct, Discipline, and Administrative Review

29. General Hours of Work and Attendance 42
30. Employee Conduct 42
31. Employee Discipline 45
32. Alternative Dispute Resolution 46
33. Grievances 46
34. Administrative Review Process 47
35. Judicial Review 50
36. Employee Rights 51

Chapter VI - Drug, Alcohol and Controlled Substance Policy

37. General 52
38. Purpose 52
39. Policy 52
40. Definitions 55
41. Pre-Employment Screening 58
42. Initial Drug Test 58
43. Random Drug Testing 59
44. Reasonable Suspicion Testing 59
45. Drug and Alcohol Testing for Employees Required to Possess a Commercial Drivers License (CDL) 60
46. Off-Duty Involvement with Drugs, Alcohol, and Substances 60
47. Part-time, Summer, and Contract Personnel 61
48. Searches 61

49. Disciplinary Action 61
50. Employee Assistance Program (EAP) 63
51. Rehiring Procedures for Drug Policy Violations 63
52. Testing Procedures 63
53. Reporting Procedures for Drug Policy Violations ... 64
54. Enforcement of the Zero Tolerance Policy for Elected and Appointed Officials 66

Chapter VII - Worker's Compensation Plan

55. Purpose and Scope 68
56. Definitions 68
57. Reporting Obligation 70
58. Medical Benefits 71
59. Return to Work 72
60. Disability Benefits 72
61. Dependent Benefits 74
62. Recurrence 75
63. Election of Remedies 75
64. Administrator 75
65. Appeals 76

CHAPTER I
GENERAL PROVISIONS

1. **Authority.**

   a. Article V, Section 2(a) of the Constitution grants the Legislature the power to make laws, including codes, ordinances, resolutions, and statutes.

   b. Article V, Section 2(f) of the Constitution grants the Legislature the power to set salaries, terms and conditions of employment for all governmental personnel.

   c. Article V, Section 2(h) of the Constitution grants the Legislature the power to enact all laws prohibiting and regulating conduct and imposing penalties upon all persons within the jurisdiction of the Nation.

   d. Article V, Section 2(r) of the Constitution grants the Legislature the power to protect and foster Ho-Chunk religious freedom, culture, language, and traditions.

2. **Purpose.** This Act establishes uniform employment practices throughout the Ho-Chunk Nation in the utilization of human resources in the achievement of the desired goals and objectives of the Nation.

3. **Declaration of Policy.**

Ho-Chunk Nation Legislature
Employment Relations Act

a. This Employment Relations Act is the official employment law of the Ho-Chunk Nation. It supersedes the Nation's Personnel Policies and Procedures Manual and all policies, rules, and regulations enacted by Legislative resolutions pertaining to the employment law of the Nation.

b. This Act is applicable to all employees (non-enterprise and enterprise) of the Ho-Chunk Nation.

4. **Responsibilities.**

a. Department of Personnel. The *Department of Personnel Establishment and Organization Act* (1 HCC § 10) delegates to the Executive Director of the Department of Personnel the functions and authority to implement, manage, enforce, and promulgate i.e. create, establish, publish, make known and carry out the policies within this Act.

b. Departments and Units.

(1) Each department, division, or unit of the Nation with the approval and consultation of the Executive Director of the Department of Personnel may develop, implement, and revise as necessary internal procedures and operating rules pertaining to the unique operational requirements of the work unit for efficient and effective performance. Advance notice of internal unit procedures and rules shall be provided to employees and must be posted in public places to serve as notice to all employees.

(2) Internal unit procedures and rules shall not conflict with this Act. Where conflicts may arise between internal rules and procedures, this Act will govern.

5. **Employment Clause.**

a. Equal Employment Opportunity. With the exception of Ho-Chunk Preference in Employment as set forth in paragraph (b), below, it will be a violation of this Act to discriminate based on an individual's sex, race, religion, national origin, pregnancy, age, marital status, sexual orientation, or disability.

b. Ho-Chunk Preference in Employment Clause. The Nation exercises Native American Preference in employment and may exercise Ho-Chunk Preference in employment under limited circumstances, which furthers a legitimate governmental purpose.

(1) The Nation will exercise Ho-Chunk Preference in Employment, prioritized as follows:

    (a) Hocak Wazijaci Tribal member.
    (b) Spouse or Parent of Hocak Wazijaci Tribal member.
    (c) Native American Tribal member.

(2) Ho-Chunk Preference may be used to recruit, hire, train, recall and lay off employees of the Nation. For hiring purposes, Ho-Chunk Preference shall be used for tribally funded positions and Native American Preference shall be used for all federally funded positions. Preference is only afforded to distinguish between equally qualified candidates or applicants for a position. The Department of Personnel is responsible for monitoring the Preference Policy. Disciplinary action will occur for supervisors who do not adhere to this policy.

(3) The Department of Personnel shall research and prepare a written response to all written inquires of possible misapplication of the Ho-Chunk Preference Policy and Native American Preference. Individuals have the right to submit a written inquiry to the Department of Personnel, regardless of whether such individual is an employee at the time of the application process. Should the Department of Personnel find a violation of preference policy, the Director of Personnel can require additional interviews of all eligible candidates or the Director can override the selection of candidate.

c. Veterans Preference. Veterans are given priority-hiring status over equally qualified individuals for tribally funded positions. To be eligible for preference, the veteran must have an honorable or general discharge. Applicants claiming preference should supply a copy of the DD Form 214, (Certificate of Release or Discharge from Active Duty).

d. Hiring Policy. Upon a written offer of employment, the Nation shall require a pre-employment medical screening. Subject to the results of the pre-employment medical screening, confirmation of employment shall be by the Department of Personnel or supervisor.

6. Employee Rights.

a. Access to Employee Information. All employees may review his/her personnel file by submitting a written request to the Department of Personnel.

b. Disclosure of Employee Records.

(1) The Nation shall not disclose, in replying to external inquiries, any personnel or related records or information on an applicant, employee, or former employee, except pursuant to a written request by, or with the prior written consent of, the individual to whom the record pertains, unless disclosure of the records would be, subject to the *Ho-Chunk Nation Discovery Act.*

(2) Limitation on Access. Nothing in this section shall allow an individual access to any information compiled in reasonable anticipation of an administrative or judicial action or proceeding.

c. Safe Work Place. The Nation shall endeavor to provide all employees a safe and clean working environment. The Nation's *Occupational Safety and Health Program Act* (6 HCC § 8) shall apply.

d. Harassment.

(1) Harassment (both overt and subtle) is a form of employee misconduct that both demeans another person and undermines the integrity of the employment relationship by creating an unreasonably intimidating, hostile, and objectively offensive working environment.

(2) No employee shall be subject to retaliation or retribution for reporting harassment. Retaliation or retribution is strictly prohibited.

e. Sexual Harassment.

(1) Purpose. The purpose of the Ho-Chunk Nation sexual harassment policy is to:

(a) Prohibit sexual harassment in the workplace.

(b) Encourage employees who are victims or witnesses of sexual harassment to report such instances.

(c) Establish an administrative procedure for the reporting of instances of sexual harassment.

(2) Policy. Sexual harassment by or of supervisors, employees, or non-employees is strictly prohibited and will be investigated for possible disciplinary action.

(a) No employee shall be subjected to unsolicited and/or unwelcome sexual overtures or conduct, either verbal or physical.

(b) Sexual harassment will be treated as misconduct with appropriate disciplinary sanctions, up to and including termination.

(c) No employee shall be subject to retaliation or retribution for reporting sexual harassment. Retaliation or retribution is strictly prohibited.

(d) The Department of Personnel, shall promulgate guidelines and procedures for the reporting and complaint handling procedures within the Nation.

(e) An employee who believes that he or she has been subjected to unwelcome sexual conduct or that there exists an objectively hostile work environment has a duty to report the situation. Such report shall be made directly to the Department of Personnel.

(f) All reports, including both formal and informal, of sexual and other unlawful harassment will be promptly, actively, and confidentially investigated by the Department of Personnel.

(3) Prohibited Conduct.

(a) Unwelcome sexual advances, requests for sexual favors, and other verbal or physical conduct of a sexual nature constitutes prohibited sexual harassment when at least one of the following criteria is met.

1 Submission to such conduct is made either explicitly or implicitly a term or condition of an individual's employment.

2 Submission to or rejection of such conduct by an individual is used as the basis for an employment decision.

3 Such conduct has the purpose or effect of reasonably interfering with an individual's work performance or creating an intimidating, hostile, or offensive work environment.

(b) Examples of prohibited conduct include, but are not limited to:

1 Unwelcome sexually suggestive comments or sounds.
2 Unwelcome sexual flirtation.
3 Unwelcome touching.
4 Unwelcome advances or propositions.
5 Unwelcome jokes of a sexual nature.
6 Unwelcome slurs and other verbal, graphic, or physical conduct relating to an individual's gender.
7 Any display of sexually explicit pictures, greeting cards, articles, books, magazines, photos, or cartoons.

(c) The authoring, forwarding, viewing, or sending of graphic nudity, obscene, or pornographic material and the use of obscenity or profanity is strictly prohibited by the Nation's *Internet and Intranet Usage Act* (6 HCC § 4).

(4) Penalties.

(a) Where an investigation concludes that an employee has committed an act of sexual harassment, that employee must attend Employee Assistance Program (EAP) counseling, disciplined by a minimum three (3) day suspension, and may be subject to further disciplinary action up to and including termination.

(b) Providing false information in the course of a sexual harassment investigation is grounds for disciplinary action, up to and including termination.

Ho-Chunk Nation Legislature
Employment Relations Act

(c) A supervisor's failure to adequately respond to a sexual harassment matter or failure to discipline an employee for sexual harassment will result in disciplinary action. That supervisor must attend Employee Assistance Program (EAP) counseling, disciplined by a minimum three (3) day suspension, and may be subject to further disciplinary action up to and including termination.

f. Right to Work Provision. No person shall be required, as a condition of employment within the jurisdiction of the Ho-Chunk Nation, to:

(1) Resign or refrain from voluntary membership in, voluntary affiliation with, or voluntary financial support of a labor organization.

(2) Become or remain a member of a labor organization.

(3) Pay dues, fees, assessments or other charges of any kind or amount to a labor organization.

(4) Pay to any charity or other third party, in lieu of such payments any amount equivalent to or a pro-rata portion of dues, fees, assessments or other charges regularly required of members of a labor organization.

g. Whistleblower Protection. Employees who make disclosures described in this section serve the Nation's interests by assisting in the elimination of fraud, waste, abuse, and unnecessary expenditures. Employees making such disclosure(s) shall be protected from reprisals and shall not suffer adverse consequences as a result of prohibited personnel practices. All employees have a duty to report to the Attorney General information which the employee reasonably believes is a violation of any law, rule, policy, or regulation that pertains to the elimination of fraud, waste, abuse and unnecessary expenditures.

Legislative History:

Employment Relations Act
10/16/01	Chapter VI (Drug, Alcohol and Controlled Substance Policy) enacted by Legislative Resolution 10/16/01D.
10/23/02	Chapter VI (Drug, Alcohol and Controlled Substance Policy) amended and restated by Legislative Resolution 10/23/02B.
2/5/04	Administration Committee refers draft Employment Relations Act to full Legislature.
2/17/04	Legislature places Employment Relations Act out for 45-Day Public Review.
8/31/04	Legislature and the Executive Director of the Department of Personnel review submitted comments at off-site meeting.
11/2/04	Legislature tables Employment Relations Act for a final review at an off-site meeting.
11/15/04	Legislature and the Executive Director of the Department of Personnel review final draft at off-site meeting.
12/9/04	Legislature enacts the Employment Relations Act as 6 HCC § 5 by Legislative Resolution 19/9/04A.
5/4/05	Amended and Restated by Legislative Resolution 5/4/05A amending paragraphs 5b, 5c, and 8b.

Ho-Chunk Nation Legislature
Employment Relations Act

6/10/05	Amended and Restated for technical correction. Legislative 5/4/05A did not amend paragraph 12b.
7/5/05	Amended and Restated by Legislative Resolution 7/5/05E amending paragraphs 9a, 20a, and 21b(1). Allows employees to take Waksik Wosga Leave during the Initial Probationary Period and that Cultural Leave is leave without pay unless the employee requests annual leave.
6/7/06	Amended and Restated by Legislative Resolution amending paragraphs 34b(1) and 34b(2) changing the composition of the Grievance Review Board.
6/7/06	Amended and Restated by Legislative Resolution 6/7/06D deleting paragraph 6g(2) and incorporating paragraph 6g(1) into paragraph 6g.

Personnel Policies and Procedures Manual

8/20/88	Garnishment of Employee Wages; Wisconsin Winnebago Business Committee Resolution 8/20/88B.
12/21/94	Responsibility for Employee Training; Legislative Resolution 12-21-94D.
12/21/94	Legislature Adopts Ho-Chunk Nation's Personnel Policies and Procedures Manual.
1/4/95	Legislature enacts Drug and Controlled Substance Policy and Procedures.
2/7/96	Weather Conditions; Education, Employment, (et al) Committee Approval.
2/13/96	Resignations and Reemployment; Legislative Resolution 2/13/96C.
3/26/96	Trial Court Review; Legislative Resolution 3/26/96A.
6/19/96	Approval of Job Descriptions; Legislative Resolution 6/19/96E.
2/25/97	Ho-Chunk Preference; Legislative Resolution 02/25/97A.
5/27/97	Wages Upon Transfer; Legislative Motion dated 5/27/97.
6/10/97	Ho-Chunk Preference; Legislative Motion dated 6/10/97.
2/17/98	Cultural Even Time Off; Legislative Resolution 02/17/98A.
2/10/98	Equivalent Annual Leave Credit; Legislative Resolution 02/10/98D.
2/10/98	Funeral Leave; Legislative Resolution 02/10/98E.
3/31/98	Layoffs; Legislative Resolution 3/31/98B.
4/28/98	Family Medical Leave; Legislative Resolution 4/28/98A.
6/9/98	Amendment to Chapter 12 (Employee Conduct, Discipline and Administrative Review) for the Administrative Review Process; Legislative Resolution 6-9-98A
6/10/98	Ho-Chunk Preference, Legislative Motion dated 6/10/98.
6/16/98	Funeral Leave; Legislative Resolution 6-16-98C.
6/16/98	Religious Leave; Legislative Resolution 6-16-98D.
10/28/98	Cap on 4% Merit Increase; Legislative Resolution 10/20/98C.
12/15/98	Compensation Upon Promotion/Demotion and Transfer/Reclassification; Legislative Resolution 12/15/98A.
12/29/98	Unclassified/Appointed Employees; Legislative Resolution 12-29-98C.
1/26/99	Transfer of Annual/Sick Leave Policy; Legislative Resolution 1/26/99B.
3/17/99	Promotion, Demotion, and Transfer Policy; Legislative Resolution 3/17/99A.
3/23/99	Lateral Transfer Policy; Legislative Resolution 3/23/99G.
4/27/99	Right to Deny Services; Legislative Resolution 4/27/99E.
4/27/99	Conflicts with Internal Controls; Legislative Resolution 4/27/99D.
5/11/99	Training During Probationary Period; Legislative Resolution 5-11-99B.
8/10/99	Comparable Wage; Legislative Resolution 8-10-99C.
10/14/99	Use of Sick Leave for Family Medical Leave; Legislative Resolution 10/14/99C.
10/19/99	Cultural Leave; Legislative Resolution 10-19-99D.
11/30/99	Bridge Service Credit; Legislative Resolution 11/30/99A.
1/18/00	Forty Hour Maximum on Paid Leave or Holiday Pay; Legislative Resolution 1/18/00D.
4/4/00	Waksik Wosga Leave Policy; Legislative Resolution 4/04/00B rescinding Legislative Resolution 6-16-98D.
4/4/00	Defined Events; Legislative Resolution 4-4-00B.
2/13/01	40 Hour Maximum Policy; Resolution 2/13/01A.
2/27/01	Waksik Wosga Leave; Resolution 2/27/01A.
3/6/01	Automatic Merit Increase; Resolution 3/6/01G.
3/7/01	Automatic Merit Increase; Resolution 3/7/01O.

Ho-Chunk Nation Legislature
Employment Relations Act

3/21/01	Supervision of Children; Resolution 3/21/01D.
5/22/01	Election Voting Leave; Resolution 5/22/01I.
6/5/01	Youth Leadership Conference; 6/5/01E.
6/26/01	Maternity Leave; Resolution 6/26/01A.
8/9/01	Two or More Part-time Positions equal Full-time Status; Resolution 8/9/01B.
9/18/01	Funeral Leave; Resolution 9/18/01E.
10/16/01	Military Leave; Resolution 10/16/01B.
6/5/02	Equal Employment Opportunity amendment; Resolution 6/5/02B.
9/4/02	Reporting Work Injuries, Chapter 8, amended by Legislative Resolution 9/04/02C.

Drug, Alcohol and Controlled Substance Policy

1/4/95	Legislature enacts Drug and Controlled Substance Policy.
10/16/01	Legislature amends Drug and Controlled Substance Policy by enacting the Drug, Alcohol and Controlled Substance Policy as Chapter VI to the draft Employment Relations Act (6 HCC § 5) by Legislative Resolution 10/16/01D.
10/11/02	Corrects the numbering of paragraph 15. Testing Procedures (renumbered from 17 to 15).
10/23/02	Amended and restated by Legislative Resolution 10/23/02B.
10/19/04	Restated with enactment of the Employment Relations Act (6 HCC § 5) by Legislative Resolution 12/9/04A.

Worker's Compensation Plan

1998	Worker's Compensation Plan adopted.
12/09/04	Legislature adopts the Employment Relations Act as 6 HCC § 5 by Legislative Resolution 12/9/04A which incorporates the Worker's Compensation Plan as Chapter VII.

CHAPTER II
DEFINITIONS

7. **Definitions.** Whenever the following terms are used in this Act, they shall have the meanings indicated.

   a. Abandonment. Absent without authorized leave for three (3) consecutive work days or five (5) work days in a twelve (12) month period.

   b. Agency. Any external organization or unit engaged in business, providing services, information, or goods within the jurisdiction of the Ho-Chunk Nation.

   c. Appointments.

   (1) Acting Appointment. The temporary assignment of a person to a vacant position in the absence of the employee who normally fills such position. Persons appointed to acting assignments must possess the minimum qualifications for that position. Such persons shall have limited responsibilities and authority of the position unless directed otherwise by the appointing authority.

   (2) Interim Appointment. Interim appointments apply to Department Executive Directors. See *Confirmation Process of Executive Directors of the Ho-Chunk Nation Act* (2 HCC § 9).

   d. Bridged Service Credit. The linking or connecting of a recalled or rehired employee where regular status was held for purposes of considering seniority, pay, and vacation accrual rates.

   e. Calendar Day. A twenty-four (24) hour period beginning at midnight and ending at midnight.

   f. Class. A group of positions sufficiently similar in respects to the duties and responsibilities may be used with clarity to designate each position allocation to the class; common requirements such as to education, experience, knowledge, ability and other qualifications exist for all incumbents; common tests of fitness may be used to choose qualified employees; and the same schedule of compensation can be made to apply with equity under the same or substantially the same employment conditions.

   g. Classification Plan. A listing of job titles and descriptions in regular service.

   h. Cohabit or Cohabitant. Two individuals living together, who are financially and intimately associated in a committed relationship, yet not legally married.

   i. Comparable Wage. A wage that is up to 15% of the current wage or previous wage, unless otherwise authorized in writing.

j. Compensation. The payment made to employees in consideration of the number of hours worked in accordance with payment schedules or a contract, including pay for overtime and other forms of payment in connection with the performance of job assignments. Total compensation refers to that amount of pay plus employment related benefits received by employees, including contributions to the employee's medical and dental programs, retirement, sick and annual leave and other similar benefits.

k. Continuous Employment. Employment without interruption, including authorized vacation, military leave, or other paid leaves, unpaid Family Medical Leave, and maternity leave of absence.

l. Dates.

(1) Annual Review Date. The date one (1) year from the Original Date of Hire and each subsequent year of continuous employment. The Annual Review Date is subject to change based on a change of employment status.

(2) Original Date of Hire. The initial date of hire to a regular position.

m. Demotion. A change in employment status resulting in movement from one position to another that has lower qualifications and/or lesser job responsibilities and assigned a lower pay range.

n. Dual Position. An additional temporary position assigned to an employee on an as needed basis.

o. Employee. Any individual employed by the Ho-Chunk Nation, regardless of the source of the funds by which the employee is paid. The term "employee" shall include any person elected or appointed. The Nation further classifies its employees as follows:

(1) Contract Employee. An employee who has entered into a contractual employment agreement with the Ho-Chunk Nation.

(2) Department of Labor Program Employee. An employee who is a Native American and is assigned a trainee position to gain on the job experience.

(3) Exempt Employee. An employee classified by the Nation as exempt is salaried. Such employees are those occupying executive, administrative, professional positions, appointed, and elected officials. Weekly salary is computed using the position's annual fixed salary.

(4) Full-time Employee. An employee who regularly works a minimum of 32 hours per week on a continuous basis following a probationary period.

(5) Limited Term Employee (LTE). An employee holding a job of limited or specified duration. Limited Term Employees are not regular employees eligible to use

Ho-Chunk Nation Legislature
Employment Relations Act

the Administrative Review Procedure to file formal grievances, except in matters pertaining to prohibited discrimination or harassment. Other complaints may be filed with the Grievance Review Board. Limitation of LTE status is 480 hours per fiscal year, unless a one-time 160 hour extension is approved by the Executive Director and the Director, Department of Personnel or his or her designee.

(6) <u>Nonexempt Employee</u>. An employee covered by overtime. Such employees are entitled to overtime pay for work required to be performed in excess of 40 hours per workweek. (See Chapter III, paragraph 13g, for restrictions on payment of overtime.)

(7) <u>Part-time Employee</u>. An employee who has completed a satisfactory probationary period and regularly works less than 32 hours per week on a continuous basis. Part-time employees shall not hold supervisory positions.

(8) <u>Regular Employee</u>. An employee hired through the interview process, excepting appointed and elective positions.

(9) <u>Seasonal Employee</u>. An employee whose work is normally less than one (1) year but longer than six months, and who is expected to return on an annual basis.

p. <u>Employer</u>. Employer as used in this Act means any person who hires or employs any other person to perform work or services and pays for such services or work by means of wages or a salary and includes any person acting directly or indirectly in the interest of an employee in relation to an employee.

q. <u>Enterprise</u>. Entities of the Ho-Chunk Nation that provide for-profit goods and services.

r. <u>Examination</u>. The process of measuring and evaluating the relative ability and fitness of applicants by job related testing procedures, which may include a medical examination performed by a qualified health care provider.

s. <u>Executive Director</u>. The head of a specific Department of the Executive Branch.

t. <u>Flex Classification</u>. A position classification where a new hire may be employed at a higher base pay rate, not to exceed 30% of the base rate, than stated for that position based on qualifications that exceed the minimum job requirements. Whereas, for a "No-Flex" position, the employee is hired at the starting base pay rate.

u. <u>Good Standing</u>. An employee, who provides two (2) weeks written notice of intent to resign and does not have any punitive or administrative action pending prior to the resignation, resigns in Good Standing.

v. <u>Grievance</u>. A claimed violation, misinterpretation, or inequitable application of the policies and procedures having a direct adverse effect on the grieving employee.

w. Indian Tribe. An Indian tribe, band, nation or other organized group or community recognized as such by the United States Government.

x. Lateral Transfer. A change in employee status from one position to another position having the same or substantially similar duties and pay range.

y. Leave Without Pay. Voluntary request by an employee for leave not exceeding 40 hours without pay.

z. Merit Increase. Advancement of eligible employee's current pay from one salary step to a higher salary step within the same salary range based on satisfactory demonstration of individual efficiency and performance.

aa. Minimum Wage. Minimum wage means the prevailing minimum wage as determined from time to time by the Legislature.

bb. Misconduct. A deliberate and substantial disregard of the employer's interests or violation of the law or those standards of behavior, which an employer has a right to expect of every employee.

cc. Modified Duty Assignment. The assignment of an employee, who has been injured on or off the job (except in connection with off-duty employment) and has been medically released to perform limited employment tasks, to a job in which the employee can perform tasks based on physical restrictions for a designated period of time.

dd. Native American or Indian. An enrolled member of the Ho-Chunk Nation or an enrolled Indian of a federally recognized Indian tribe.

ee. Negligence. An employee's failure to exercise safe and ordinary care in carrying out, applying, or complying with this Employment Relations Act or other laws of the Nation. An employee is not using ordinary care, and is therefore negligent, if the employee does something that a reasonable person knew or should have known was contrary to Tribal law or fails to do something that a reasonable person knew or should have known to be in compliance with Tribal law.

ff. Nepotism. Favoritism shown to direct supervision of or the exercise of power or influence over relatives in employment or other services. See paragraph 15i, Chapter III for Employment of Relatives.

gg. Non-Enterprise. Administrative entities of the Ho-Chunk Nation providing goods and services without a goal to make a profit.

hh. Off-Duty Employment. The simultaneous holding of a job (second job) outside of the Nation by an employee.

ii. Paraprofessionals. Occupations in which workers perform some of the duties of a professional or technician in a supportive role, which usually requires less formal training and/or experience normally required for professional or technical status, and which may require certification and continuing education.

jj. Pay Rates.

(1) Base Rate. The beginning pay for a job as stated on the job description (not to be confused with pay range).

(2) Prorate. The proportional calculation of equivalency to the whole or full amount; an equivalent level of benefit credits over a given period.

kk. Performance Evaluation. A formal system to evaluate performance factors related to an employee's job duties, responsibilities and related employment characteristics on a regular and systematic basis by supervisory personnel.

ll. Person. A natural person, Indian or non-Indian, partnership, association, corporation, business trust, legal representative, or any organized group of persons.

mm. Probationary Period.

(1) Initial Probationary Period. A period of ninety (90) days in which a new hire or a rehired employee serves under close supervision and his or her performance is evaluated in order to assess his or her ability and adaptation.

(2) Performance Probationary Period. A period of thirty (30) days in which an employee, who is promoted, demoted, laterally transferred, recalled to a different position, or a rehired employee with Bridge Service Credit, serves under close supervision and his or her performance is evaluated in order to assess his or her ability and adaptation.

nn. Professionals. Occupations which require specialized knowledge and licensing, which is usually acquired through college training or through work, experience and other training which provides comparable knowledge.

oo. Promotion. A change in employment status from one position to another position that requires higher minimum qualifications, is assigned more difficult duties and responsibilities, and is assigned a higher pay range.

pp. Reclassification. The modification of job title and/or duties due to material difference between the existing job description and the actual job duties required to perform functions of a position.

qq. Second Job. The simultaneous holding of two (2) part-time jobs within the Nation.

rr. <u>Seniority</u>. The length of service to the Nation, including applicable bridge service credit.

ss. <u>Separation</u>.

(1) <u>Layoff</u>. Involuntary separation in good standing from employment for non-disciplinary reasons including, but not limited to, lack of funds or work, abolishment of position, reorganization, or the reduction or elimination of services.

(2) <u>Resignation</u>. Voluntary separation from employment in either "good standing" or "not in good standing."

(3) <u>Termination</u>. Involuntary separation from employment not in good standing.

tt. <u>Status Change Form</u>. The mandatory form necessary for new hire, transfer, promotion, demotion, change in significant duties or salary rate, employment separation (e.g., FML, Military, Unpaid Leave of Absence), or any other temporary or other change in employment status reported to the Department of Personnel.

uu. <u>Suspension</u>. The temporary removal of an employee from service, without pay, for disciplinary or investigative reasons and for a specified period of time.

vv. <u>Temporary Reassignment</u>. A short term, not to exceed 90 days, placement in a different position of employment.

ww. <u>Unpaid Leave of Absence</u>. Voluntary request for leave without pay, which exceeds 40 hours.

CHAPTER III
EMPLOYMENT POLICIES

8. **Position Classification and Allocation.**

   a. Position Classification. The Nation shall maintain a job description on each separate class of employment. The continuation of the class of employment is contingent upon funding authorization.

   b. Vacancies.

   (1) Position vacancies will be filled based on job description standards after notification of the vacancy to the Personnel Department.

   (2) The Ho-Chunk Nation makes it a policy that:

   (a) All vacant positions shall be posted to the general public within five (5) days, unless that position is subject to be filled from the Recall List.

   (b) Continuous Posting. Revenue generating positions subject to high turn-over will be continuously posted to maintain a pool of immediately available applicants.

   (c) All interview panels for Nation jobs shall consist of at least two-thirds Ho-Chunk Tribal members.

   (d) Position applications shall be screened by the hiring supervisor, who will report to the Department of Personnel those applicants to be interviewed.

   c. Position Reclassification.

   (1) Reclassification requests may be initiated by individual employees or supervisory personnel, and all such requests must be substantiated in writing with such specific detail given to those duties and responsibilities being performed continuously for six (6) months that are different in scope from those contained in the applicable job description.

   (2) Reclassification of a position shall not be intentionally used for the purpose of discrimination, personal gain, discipline, or retaliation.

9. **Probationary Period.**

   a. Initial Probationary Period. New hire and rehired employees without Bridge Service Credit rights shall serve an Initial Probationary Period of 90 days. During an Initial Probationary Period, an employee is not eligible for annual leave, sick leave, and other benefits paid for or sponsored by the Nation, unless otherwise specified. An exception to this restriction is the taking of Waksik Wosga Leave by Tribal employees.

The probationary employee may not grieve, except in matters pertaining to prohibited discrimination or harassment.

   b. Performance Probationary Period. Promoted, demoted, laterally transferred into a different position, recalled into a different position, and rehired employees with Bridge Service Credit must serve a Performance Probationary Period of 30 days.

   c. No probationary employees shall be promoted, demoted, transferred, or be temporarily reassigned during a probationary period.

   d. Employee Performance Evaluation. At the completion of an Initial or Performance Probationary Period, an employee shall receive an Employee Performance Evaluation without a merit pay increase. See Section 14, this Chapter.

   e. New employees who have completed the initial 90-day Initial Probationary Period are eligible for all benefits enjoyed as a regular employee, unless prohibited by law.

10. **Employee Separation Policy**.

   a. Termination. An employee's involuntary separation from employment, save a layoff, ends the employment relationship between the employer and employee.

   b. Resignation. An employee voluntarily wishing to leave employment with the Ho-Chunk Nation in good standing must file a written resignation with the immediate supervisor at least two (2) weeks prior to the effective date, stating specific reason(s) for the resignation. The employee's resignation shall be promptly forwarded through the Executive Director to the Department of Personnel.

   c. Layoff.

      (1) An employee may be subject to layoff for reasons including, but not limited to; lack of funds or work, elimination of position, or reorganization.

      (2) Whenever it becomes necessary to reduce the work force through layoffs, the Nation will endeavor to provide affected employees with at least ten (10) working days notice. The Nation may provide two weeks severance pay in lieu of ten working days prior to notice of layoff.

      (3) Employees shall be afforded the opportunity to apply for a voluntary layoff, when a layoff plan is being instituted.

      (4) When a layoff is to be implemented, the Executive Director will prepare a layoff plan. The plan will identify the number of positions by classification and identify incumbents to be laid off through the consideration of both ability and/or seniority in the position.

(5) Each job within the layoff plan shall be coded as "essential" or "non-essential" relative to furthering the department's mission statement and services provided by that Department. Each layoff plan must evaluate which positions within the department affected by a layoff will benefit the Nation, the department and provide actual services and advance the mission and purpose of the department.

(6) The Department Director shall notify the Director of Personnel of the intended action at least fifteen (15) calendar days before the effective date and provide a statement whether or not the employee gave satisfactory service.

11. **Recall Policy.**

a. The names of employees who are laid off or continue employment in a lower position will be placed on a Recall List giving the position held at the time of layoff. The Recall List will be maintained for a period of six (6) months from the effective date of the layoff.

b. When a vacancy occurs in a position on the recall list, persons appearing on the list will be offered employment in inverse order of their layoff dates (earliest to most recent), prior to considering other persons for employment.

c. An employee that is recalled to the same position within six (6) months will be eligible for Bridge Service Credit rights and shall be assigned a new Annual Review Date.

12. **Rehire Policy.**

a. Resignation in Good Standing.

(1) Former employees of the Nation who resigned in good standing and are rehired within six (6) months into the same position in the same department will be assigned the same rate of pay and are eligible for Bridge Service Credit. A new Annual Review Date shall be established.

(2) Former employees that are rehired into any other position within six (6) months will be eligible for Bridge Service Credit, with the exception that they will be assigned a pay rate in the same manner as a new hire. A new Annual Review Date shall be established and the employee must complete a 90-day Initial Probationary Period without possibility of a merit pay increase.

b. Terminated employees or employees who resigned without good standing shall be treated as a new hire and shall not be eligible for Bridge Service Credit.

13. **Compensation and Payroll Practices.**

a. Minimum Wages. No employee shall be paid less than the federal minimum wage.

b. Salary/Wage.

(1) Nonexempt employees will be paid at an hourly rate, for purposes of payroll accounting.

(2) Elected officials, appointed officials, and exempt employees shall be paid a fixed salary.

c. No Compensation for Unauthorized Leave. Unauthorized leave or unexcused absence will not be compensated in any form.

d. Salary and Wage Merit Adjustments. The Nation may periodically revise pay rates or ranges resulting from studies of prevailing wages and other influential considerations. The Executive Director, Department of Personal shall promulgate a standardized schedule to determine benchmarks for merit wage increases.

(1) To be eligible for merit increases, nonexempt employees must not have any categorical rating of "unacceptable" or "need improvement" on their Annual Performance Evaluation.

(2) The percentage of a merit increase will be determined in accordance with the Nation's classification and compensation plan and the availability of funding.

(3) An employee who has not received a scheduled Annual Performance Evaluation may be eligible to receive a merit increase. See paragraph 14b(2).

e. Compensation upon Position Reclassification. If a position is reclassified to a class having the same pay rate as the previous class, and if the employee meets the requirements of the reclassified position, the employee's pay rate and Annual Review Date shall not change, otherwise:

(1) If the position is reclassified to a class with a higher pay rate than the previous class and if employee meets the requirements of the reclassified position, then the employee's pay rate shall change to equal the base rate of the new position. If his or her current rate of pay is higher than the reclassified position's rate of pay then his or her rate will remain the same. In either case, the employee's Annual Review Date will not change.

(2) If the position is reclassified to a lower pay rate class, and if the employee is retained to occupy the reclassified position, the employee's pay rate and Annual Review Date shall be unchanged. If the employee's pay rate in the former position is greater than the maximum rate established for the lower position, the employee's pay rate will be

frozen until such time as the rate or range of the reclassified position reaches the employee's frozen rate.

 f. Transfer of Benefits. Regular employees upon transfer or reclassification shall carry over their annual and sick leave, unless prohibited by law or federal/state program guidelines.

 g. Overtime Compensation. See paragraph 7o(6) for employees eligible for overtime compensation.

 (1) All overtime must be pre-approved by the supervisor. Overtime may be paid only within appropriated funding levels consistent with the *Budget and Appropriations Process Act* (2 HCC § 4).

 (2) Overtime compensation for a given pay period will not be paid if the employee has any paid (not including holiday leave pay) or unpaid leave during that pay period. An employee is limited to a maximum of forty (40) hours of paid compensation during a workweek in which an employee has taken any paid (not including holiday leave pay) or unpaid leave. This section shall be administered pursuant to paragraph 7o.

 (3) Overtime will be available to all non-exempt employees and offered based on employee seniority.

 h. Employer Required Educational/Meeting Activities. Employee attendance at seminars, lectures, conferences, business-related meetings, and training programs at the direction of a supervisor will be considered hours worked and compensable.

 i. Travel Time. Travel time in connection with approved travel will be considered compensable hours worked for employees. Employees will be compensated for actual hours worked, less usual meal and commute time.

 (1) One day travel out of town or as part of the day's work activities will be counted as hours worked, excluding the employee's usual meal period and normal travel time to and from the employee's residence and work location where the day's travel starts and/or ends at the employee's residence.

 (2) For overnight travel out of town, a nonexempt employee will be paid a minimum of eight (8) hours for each normally scheduled workday. Any work, including travel, that an employee is required to perform while traveling, other than on a normally scheduled workday, will be counted as hours worked.

 j. Employee Service on Tribal Boards/Commissions/Committees. Employees may serve on boards, commissions, and committees. Dual compensation is prohibited, unless:

 (1) An employee elects to receive his or her regular pay while serving on the board, commission, or committee during normally scheduled work hours; or

(2) The employee elects to receive a stipend. The employee then must be in annual leave or unpaid leave status.

k. <u>Compensation Upon Employment Separation</u>. Final compensation shall be inclusive, up to the hour and date of separation of hours worked and all forms of accrued but unused time deemed compensable. Deductions will be made against compensation such as any mandatory or voluntary deductions, including legally authorized offset against pay.

(1) Separated employees will receive their final paychecks on the day paychecks are normally distributed.

(2) In the event of an employee's death, the employee's beneficiary as shown in personnel records shall be entitled to receive the employee's final paycheck, except where the beneficiary is a minor, in which case the Nation may hold the employee's final paycheck until a legal recipient can be identified by the Nation.

(3) Any property issued to the employee by the Nation must be returned before or at the time the final paycheck is provided. Otherwise, the Nation will withhold the final paycheck and other reimbursements until the property is returned or replaced.

l. <u>Severance Pay</u>.

(1) A supervisor may request to provide two (2) week severance pay, in lieu of retaining the services of an employee for the two (2) week period upon receipt of advance notice of resignation or the Nation may provide two (2) weeks severance pay in lieu of a two (2) week dismissal notice, provided that;

    (a) The employee is not on probation,

    (b) The employee leaves in good standing, and

    (c) The Director of Personnel authorizes the Payroll Office to disburse.

(2) <u>Limitation on Severance Pay</u>. Employees who are terminated as a result of misconduct for violation of the law or work rules, or while on probation, are not eligible to receive severance pay.

14. **Performance Evaluations**.

a. The Executive Director, Department of Personnel shall promulgate the process and procedures for Performance Evaluations to ensure regular reports are made as to the competence, efficiency, adaptation, conduct, merit, and other job related performance conditions of the Nation's employees.

b. <u>Annual Performance Evaluation</u>.

(1) Supervisors shall be responsible for the completion of an annual evaluation up to ten (10) days prior to the employee's Annual Review Date.

(2) An employee who has not received an annual evaluation within thirty (30) days after his or her scheduled Annual Review Date may be eligible to receive a merit pay increase in a range of 0% to 4%, not to surpass the maximum rate of his or her pay range, if the following criteria have been met:

(a) The employee has had no disciplinary action placed in his or her personnel file since the previous evaluation date.

(b) The employee's previous evaluation met the criteria for a merit increase. If the employee has not received an evaluation since working with the Nation, assuming the employment has been continuous, it will automatically be assumed that the employee has met the evaluation criteria to receive a merit increase.

(c) The employee is not currently on a temporary reassignment, any type of leave of absence, layoff or other event that would affect the employee's Annual Review Date.

(d) The Nation has not imposed any temporary across-the-board payroll restrictions that would suspend merit increases for all employees.

(3) If the above criteria are met, the necessary documentation will be generated, signed and processed by the Department of Personnel granting the employee a pay increase effective the date that the employee's Annual Review Date was due.

c. Failure to Complete Performance Evaluations.

(1) Non-Elected Supervisors. For the first violation, the supervisor failing to complete a Performance Evaluation shall be placed on probation and, for procedural violation, shall be required to take corrective action within ten (10) calendar days of the violation and probation. If the violation has not been corrected within ten (10) calendar days or if there is a subsequent violation within thirty (30) calendar days, the supervisor shall be terminated from the position. If a second violation occurs after the 30 calendar days have lapsed, the supervisor may be demoted or, alternatively, be subject to the same terms as if it had been a first violation. If the supervisor continues to violate this policy, he or she shall be terminated.

(2) Elected and Appointed Supervisors. Should the supervisor be an elected or appointed official, for the first violation, the supervisor shall be subject to a notice of a procedural violation and shall be required to take corrective action within ten (10) calendar days with a penalty of a monetary fine of $50.00. If there is a subsequent violation within thirty (30) calendar days, the supervisor shall be subject to a monetary fine of $100.00.

15. **Other Workplace Policies.**

    a. <u>Second Job</u>.

    (1) Employees may hold a second part-time job within the Nation, provided that the total hours worked by the employee does not exceed the permissible 40 hours per week or the equivalent of a full-time position. The holding of a second job within or while employed by the government is subject to the following restrictions.

    (a) The second job must not adversely affect the employee's primary part-time job performance and responsibilities.

    (b) Notice to the supervisor of the second job must be provided in writing before the employee commencing work at the second job.

    (2) An employee who holds two or more part/quarter-time positions for the Nation, for which the combined total of both positions is at least 32 hours per week, shall be considered a full-time employee of the Nation. In this event, the Department of Personnel will duly note the employee's employment record to indicate full-time employment status.

    b. <u>Dual Position</u>. An employee may be temporarily assigned by his or her supervisor to a position that constitutes a temporary work assignment or dual position. See paragraph 7n, Chapter II.

    c. <u>Confidential Information</u>.

    (1) Confidential information obtained as a result of employment shall not be used by an employee for any private interest, or personal gain.

    (2) Employment-related records and information are confidential and proprietary documents of the Nation.

    (3) No confidential document or information shall be divulged to any person who does not possess the legal or operational right to know.

    (4) All employees shall be required to sign a Confidentiality Agreement as a condition of employment.

    (5) Use or disclosure of confidential information may result in civil or criminal penalties, or employee discipline, up to and including termination.

    d. <u>Operators Permit</u>. Certain job positions require employees to have the use of an insured, privately owned automobile and to hold a valid driver's license.

(1) Failure to produce proof of insurance or a driver's license may bar the potential employee from employment.

(2) An employee who is required to drive and loses his or her driver's license or automobile insurance may be terminated for failure to meet the condition of employment.

e. <u>Publicity/News Release</u>. No employee shall use his or her position to present himself or herself as a representative of the Nation, or communicate with the news media on behalf of the Ho-Chunk Nation unless authorized or directed in writing by the Ho-Chunk Nation or its delegated representative(s).

f. <u>Unlawful Conduct in Labor Controversies</u>. It shall be unlawful for anyone to picket, or induce others to picket the establishment, employees, supply or delivery vehicles, or customers of anyone engaged in business or to interfere with the person's business, or interfere with any person or persons desiring to transact or transacting business with the person when a labor dispute exists.

g. <u>Medical Release as a Condition to Return to Work</u>. Employees are not allowed to return to work after a disability absence of more than five (5) workdays, or where any absence is caused by a contagious condition of a threatening nature to others, without the written medical release of a qualified physician. The Nation reserves the right to have such employees examined by a paid physician of the Nation.

h. <u>Abuse of Disability Provision(s)</u>. Employees who are found to have abused or fraudulently used temporary disability provisions will be subject to disciplinary action, including, but not limited to, termination.

i. <u>Employment of Relatives</u>. Nepotism is strictly prohibited.

(1) No employee may hold a job over which a member of his/her immediate family exercises supervisory authority. Immediate family is defined as parent, grandparent, sibling, child, step relative, spouse, or cohabitant.

(2) Any violation of the nepotism provision, mandates that the supervisor or Executive Direct, Department of Personnel must cure the violation within three (3) work days or obtain the resignation of or terminate the person(s) violating the nepotism law.

CHAPTER IV
EMPLOYEE BENEFITS

16. **General**. The Nation reserves the right to add, eliminate, or in other ways modify any discretionary benefits based upon the Nation's capacity to fund for the benefits.

   a. Mandatory Benefits. The mandatory benefits offered by the Nation will apply to regular employees, whether exempt or nonexempt status, unless otherwise provided in a particular benefit plan or employment agreement/contract.

      (1) Social Security. Social Security benefits are automatically deducted from an employee's payroll check.

      (2) Worker's Compensation. See Chapter VII.

      (3) Unemployment Insurance. Employees may be eligible for unemployment benefits upon termination of service with the Nation.

   b. Discretionary Benefits.

      (1) Benefit Plans.

         (a) Group Health-Care Plans. The Nation makes available health-care plans for eligible employees and their dependents. Benefits consist of routine medical care, hospitalization, medical prescriptions, vision, and dental plans.

         (b) Short-term and long-term disability insurance plans.

         (c) Life insurance plans.

         (d) A 401k Plan for retirement benefits.

      (2) Enrollment.

         (a) Employees shall complete enrollment forms at the time of orientation.

         (b) Enrollment becomes effective at the end of an employee's probationary period.

         (c) Health-care benefit coverage under the plan of the Nation terminates (at midnight on the last day of employment.)

   c. Proration and Cost Sharing of Benefits.

      (1) Leave benefits for part-time employees shall be earned at 50% of the benefits of the full-time employee.

(2) Leave benefits for quarter-time employees shall be earned at 25% of benefits of the full-time employee.

(3) The Nation has a salary reduction plan for payment of health benefits, which are separately described in the health benefits handbook and available from the Department of Personnel.

d. Contract Employee. Benefits for a contract employee shall be as specified in the contract between the employee and the Ho-Chunk Nation.

e. Limited Term Employee (LTE). A LTE is not eligible for annual leave, sick leave, and other benefits paid for or sponsored by the Nation, unless otherwise specified herein.

f. Restitution. If the existence of fraud by any person resulting in benefits to which he/she was not entitled, has been found by any court of competent jurisdiction, such person shall be liable to repay such amount to the Ho-Chunk Nation or to have such sum deducted from any future benefits payable to him or her under said laws.

17. **Ho-Chunk Nation Holidays.**

a. All employees are eligible to observe the following recognized holidays.

Holiday	Date Observed
New Year's Day	January 1
Good Friday (1/2 Day)	Varies each year
Easter	Varies each year
Memorial Day	Last Monday in May
Corporal Mitchell Red Cloud Jr. Day	July 4
Labor Day	First Monday in September
Veteran's Day	November 11
Thanksgiving Day	Fourth Thursday in November
Hocak Day	Day after Thanksgiving
Christmas Eve (1/2 Day)	December 24
Christmas Day	December 25
New Year's Eve (1/2 Day)	December 31

b. Weekend Holidays.

(1) For employees who regularly work Monday-Friday, if a holiday falls on a Saturday, the holiday will be observed on the Friday before the Saturday. If the holiday falls on a Sunday, the holiday will be observed the following Monday. See paragraph b(2), below for Christmas and New Year holidays.

(2) If the Christmas and New Years Holiday fall on a Friday and Saturday, the holiday shall be observed with one-half (½) day on Thursday and a full day on Friday.

Ho-Chunk Nation Legislature
Employment Relations Act

Should the Christmas and New Years Holiday fall on a Sunday and Monday, the holiday shall be observed with one-half (½) day on Friday and a full day on Monday.

    c. Holiday Pay.

    (1) Nonexempt employees will be paid double pay on the holidays worked. If a person does not work, he or she will receive eight (8) hours holiday pay at his or her regular rate.

    (2) Exempt employees will be paid their regular salary on the holidays whether or not they work.

18. **Annual and Sick Leave**.

    a. Annual Leave. Eligible employees accrue annual leave for each full week of service in which the employee is actively employed and in a paid status.

    (1) Full-time employees will accrue paid annual leave credits as follows:

Service Length			Weekly Credit Hours	Annual Leave Hours
New Employee	-	End of 3rd year	1.85	96
Start of 4th year	-	End of 8th year	2.77	144
Start of 9th year	-	End of 14th year	3.69	192
Start of 15th year	-		4.62	240

    (2) Any hours over one hundred sixty (160) will be paid to the employee at the end of the fiscal year provided that the employee has used sixty (60) hours of annual leave during that fiscal year.

    (3) Selection of leave dates is subject to approval of the employee's supervisor. Leave scheduling preference shall be given to employees based on earliest date of a request for leave and/or employee's seniority. Leave requests must be submitted to the supervisor in writing at least ten (10) working days prior to the start date unless otherwise approved by the supervisor.

    (4) Regular employees will retain leave upon transfer or promotion with the exception of staff/programs that are federally or state funded.

    b. Sick Leave.

    (1) Sick leave is a privilege of paid time away from work where such absence is necessary because an employee is incapacitated by sickness, temporary disability, injury, or for medical, dental or optical examination or treatment; or where, by reason of exposure to a contagious disease would jeopardize the health of others.

(a) Full-time employees shall accrue paid sick leave at a rate of .92 hours per week.

(b) No sick leave may be taken in advance of being earned.

(c) Illnesses extending beyond accrued sick leave will be charged as annual leave.

(d) Accrued sick leave time, which has not been used by the employee, will, upon separation in good standing, be applied to continued health insurance coverage.

(e) Sick leave may also be taken for illness in the employee's immediate family. Immediate family is defined as: parent, grandparent, sibling, child, step relations, and spouse or cohabitant.

(f) Regular employees will retain all sick leave upon transfer or promotion with the exception of staff/programs that are federally or state funded.

(g) Eligible employees must promptly notify their supervisors whenever the use of sick leave becomes necessary.

(h) A supervisor may require an employee to produce evidence (attending physician or medical provider's statement, death certificate, employee's affidavit, etc.) to substantiate the reason for or length of sick leave exceeding three (3) days.

(i) Should an employee receive disability insurance payments during a sick leave, the employee may only use that number of sick hours that, together with such insurance payments, would not represent more than normal pay.

(j) Employees will not be allowed to receive pay in excess of 40 total hours per week in which an employee is compensated for any form of leave is taken during that pay period.

(2) Conversion of Sick Leave to Extended Medical Benefits.

(a) Accrued sick leave may be used, upon qualification, to extend health, dental, vision and prescription insurance beyond the date of an employee's separation by using the employee's remaining sick leave hours multiplied by the employee's base rate of pay. When multiplied, this amount is the "dollars" that an employee may use to extend his or her coverage if they qualify.

(b) Qualifications.

1 An employee who resigns qualifies if:

a Covered under insurance on the last day of employment; and b Resigned in good standing (see paragraph 11b); and

    c Has enough "dollars" to pay for a minimum of one (1) full month of COBRA premiums for the plan the employee was covered under (i.e., Single Non-Tribal, Family Non-Tribal, Single Tribal, or Family Tribal) on the last day of employment.

   2 An employee who is permanently laid off qualifies if:

    a Covered under insurance on the last day of employment; and

    b Was permanently laid off; and

    c Has enough "dollars" to pay for a minimum of one (1) full month of COBRA premiums for the plan the employee was covered under (i.e., Single Non-Tribal, Family Non-Tribal, Single Tribal, or Family Tribal) on the last day of employment.

   3 Spouses/Cohabitants and dependents of deceased employees may qualify, providing that the deceased employee on the date of his or her death:

    a Was employed by the Nation; and

    b Had family coverage in effect; and

    c Had enough "dollars" to pay for a minimum of one (1) full month of COBRA premiums for the dependent(s).

  (c) If an employee qualifies for sick leave conversion, the Insurance Department will mail a letter to the employee's last known mailing address stating how many hours of sick leave the employee had remaining and the end date of the extended medical benefits.

  c. <u>Transfer of Leave Time</u>. Employees may transfer leave hours to another employee who is eligible to use accrued leave hours. This policy does not apply to an employee who has given notice of resignation or an employee being separated because of lay-off or termination.

  (1) To be eligible to receive these hours an employee must meet the following criteria:

    (a) Have forty (40) or less hours of accrued leave hours.

    (b) Not receiving any other type of pay (i.e., Short Term Disability, Worker's Compensation, etc).

    (c) Approval of his or her supervisor.

(2) To be eligible to transfer hours, the donating employee must meet the following criteria:

    (a) Execute a voluntary option of consent with signature and a specific amount of hours donated/transferred.

    (b) Maintain a minimum balance of 24 hours in his or her respective donating leave account.

    (c) Approval of his or her supervisor, where applicable.

(3) This policy is strictly voluntary and no employee shall be required to transfer accrued leave time.

(4) In the event that an employee decides to transfer his/her accrued leave time, such leave time shall not be recovered and the employee will be eligible to utilize only hours that he/she has remaining and thereafter accumulates.

(5) Any leave transferred that violates this policy shall result in the transferred leave being revoked from the receiving employee.

19. Funeral Leave.

a. For the funeral of family relations, the following family relations will be recognized under this policy as blood relations (unless defined as step relations): Spouse, cohabitant, children biological, adopted, foster and step parents, grandparents, siblings and grandchildren.

b. All employees, including Initial Probationary employees, are eligible for paid funeral leave.

c. A half (½) day of unpaid leave will be allowed for attendance at funerals of extended family relatives or community members. An employee may use other earned or accrued leave if requested and approved by the employee's immediate supervisor.

d. Funeral leave will be granted to employees for leave with pay for a maximum not to exceed four (4) calendar days (32 hours) following the death in the immediate family spouse, cohabitant, children (biological, adopted, foster and step), parents, siblings and grandchildren, grandparents and in-laws.

e. Funeral leave will be granted to employees for leave with pay for a maximum not to exceed two (2) days (16 hours) following the death of an extended family member, including aunts, uncles, nieces and nephews. Employees may apply to take leave.

f. The employee shall advise his or her supervisor of the duration of his or her absence.

g. The employee shall advise his or her supervisor if he or she intend on using accrued Annual Leave or leave without pay in conjunction with the paid Funeral Leave.

h. <u>Enrolled Tribal Members</u>. See paragraph 21d(1) for funeral leave under the Waksik Wosga Leave Policy.

i. The Ho-Chunk people honor their warriors. Paid funeral leave will be granted to Ho-Chunk legion and auxiliary members who are asked to honor Ho-Chunk veterans with military rites.

20. **Cultural Leave**. Enrolled members of the Ho-Chunk Nation may request time off to attend cultural and traditional events.

a. The time off for Cultural Leave will be leave without pay, unless the employee requests annual leave.

b. The employee must submit a Leave Application Form for time off at least fourteen (14) days in advance.

c. The supervisor shall comply with this policy to accommodate requests for time off in compliance with this policy. Additional staffing and training necessary to support all Cultural Leave requests shall be made available in the event that multiple requests from the same work area may be accommodated "without causing disruption" of the business enterprises.

d. If an employee schedules time off for a cultural event abuses and violates this policy by not attending the cultural event, then the employee shall not be eligible to request time off for a period of ninety (90) days. For a second similar violation of this policy, the employee shall not be eligible to request time off for a period of 180 days.

21. **Waksik Wosga Leave Policy**.

a. <u>General</u>. To promote participation and preserve the Nation's culture, a Waksik Wosga Leave Policy is provided for Ho-Chunk Tribal employees. Due to traditional responsibilities held by the Ho-Chunk People, enrolled Ho-Chunk member employees may occasionally require leave from their place of employment when obligated, because of clan membership to be a "worker" at a Defined Event. The Waksik Wosga Leave Policy provides enrolled Tribal member employees the ability to observe their religion, culture, and tradition, when obligated to, without the threat of losing a job or losing pay. This Policy is only to be used for those families, clans, and individuals who are required by tradition to perform for another clan during employment hours.

b. <u>Eligibility</u>.

(1) All enrolled Ho-Chunk Tribal member employees are eligible for paid Waksik Wosga Leave. The employee must be a participant "worker" in a Defined Event as described in paragraph d, below. Waksik Wosga Leave may be taken by Tribal employees during their Initial Probationary Period.

(2) Spouses. Non-Ho-Chunk spouses of enrolled Ho-Chunk employees granted Waksik Wosga Leave are also eligible for this leave if they are a participant worker.

(3) Nebraska Winnebago. Based on the familial relationships, shared religions and ceremonies between the Ho-Chunk and the Nebraska Winnebago, the Traditional Court has made an exception to allow for a tribally enrolled Nebraska Winnebago employee of the Ho-Chunk Nation to apply for unpaid Religious Leave for the events defined below. Enrolled Nebraska Winnebago applicants shall be required to use annual or unpaid leave.

(4) Leave. An enrolled Ho-Chunk Tribal member employee who has attended a religious ceremony or event defined under paragraph d, below, can claim paid leave only for the days that the event actually occurs. An enrolled Tribal member who has attended a religious ceremony or event can claim unpaid leave for one (1) day following an all night ceremony or event, or has the option to use annual or sick leave. See paragraph d(2), below, for an exception for the Medicine Dance.

c. Process. In order to receive paid Waksik Wosga Leave, eligible employees shall:

(1) Submit to their supervisor a Waksik Wosga written notice when it becomes necessary to participate in a Defined Event. In the event written notice cannot be submitted, the employee shall notify the supervisor verbally or by telephone. The notification will include the reason for taking Waksik Wosga Leave and the duration of the absence.

(2) An employee's name must appear on the official Wosga Sign-in Work Form (daily, if the Defined Event is longer than one day) to verify that the employee was present and did participate in the Defined Event. All employee's using Wosga Leave must sign-in on the Work form to be eligible for paid leave. The Wosga Sign-in Work Form will be provided to the Personnel Department for the calculation of hours when timesheets are due.

(3) The Clan Leaders will be consulted to verify all sign-in participants, if necessary.

(4) Should a participant be signed-in who did not actually participate in the Defined Event, the work pay for that day will be deducted from the employee's pay the following week.

(5) If an employee schedules time off for a cultural event abuses and violates this policy by not attending the culture event, then the employee shall not be eligible to request time off for a period of ninety (90) days. For a second similar violation of this policy, the employee shall not be eligible to request time off for a period of one hundred and eighty (180) days.

d. Defined Events.

(1) Funerals. The traditional and Native American Church Funerals customarily require four (4) days of leave since there are four (4) days and four (4) nights of continuous mourning, ending with an all-night ceremony for the grieving family on the last night. Various clans are involved in a funeral, including a need for warriors, or veterans, throughout the sacred funeral burial process. All enrolled Tribal member employees who are required to work at a funeral, including warriors if needed, pursuant to clan obligations, shall receive Waksik Wosga Leave pay for those days that are regularly scheduled work days only. The leader (officiator) of the funeral and four named helpers shall be allowed forty (40) hours of paid Waksik Wosga leave time, as an exception to paragraph e(1), below.

(2) Medicine Dance. The Ho-Chunk people are divided into five (5) respective groups in the Medicine Lodge. The Medicine Dance consists of eight (8) days at one time respectfully from Sunday to the following Monday. Part of the Medicine Lodge includes a Medicine Feast, which takes an additional two (2) days for a Memorial Meeting. All enrolled employees of the Nation required to work at a Medicine Dance pursuant to their clan obligations shall receive Waksik Wosga Leave for those days that are regularly scheduled workdays only. The only exception being that an eligible employee who has been in attendance the entire weekend may take off the following Monday with paid leave.

(3) Feast Lodge. The customary time is three (3) to five (5) days in accordance with the Ho-Chunk clan way of life. This includes Tribal member employees who are leaving or returning from the Armed Forces. All enrolled employees of the Nation that are required to work at the Feast Lodge pursuant to their clan obligations shall receive Waksik Wosga Leave for those days that are regularly scheduled work days only.

(4) Native American Church. The customary time for Native American Church ceremonies is two (2) days. All enrolled employees of the Nation that are required to work at Native American Church ceremonies pursuant to their obligations shall receive Waksik Wosga Leave for those days that are regularly scheduled work days only.

(5) Scalp Dance. This ceremony is fairly rare and the customary time for a Scalp Dance requires five (5) days. Most often these days are split into two (2) days and two (2) nights, requiring two (2) separate three (3) day leave periods. All enrolled employees of the Nation that are required to work at a Scalp Dance pursuant to their clan obligations shall receive Waksik Wosga Leave for those days that are regularly scheduled work days only.

(6) Doctoring. Most Indian Medicine Men and Medicine Women require four (4) days and nights of continuous doctoring, so the customary time is four (4) days of leave. All enrolled employees of the Nation that are required to work at a Doctoring Ceremony pursuant to their clan obligations shall receive Waksik Wosga Leave for those days that are regularly scheduled work days only.

(7) Ghost Meal. All enrolled employees of the Nation that are required to work at a Ghost Meal pursuant to their clan obligations shall receive Waksik Wosga Leave for those days that are regularly scheduled work days only.

e. Limitations.

(1) The maximum amount of paid Waksik Wosga Leave is ten percent (10%) of the employee's total hours worked for a given year.

(2) Extension of a leave of absence must be secured with a written note from any member of the Traditional Court. For example, when there are consecutive funerals and certain clans must serve as workers for both funerals, the worker must obtain a new leave approval.

(3) Abuse of this Policy may result in denials from the Traditional Court and ultimately, the Director of Personnel.

(4) This Policy shall not include any paid leave for enrolled Tribal member employees to attend pow-wows, including any events held at pow-wows.

f. Authority. If required, the Traditional Court shall make recommendations and provide advice to the Director of Personnel regarding all questionable paid Waksik Wosga Leave. After consideration of advice from the Traditional Court, the Director of Personnel shall have final authority on all matters contained in this Policy.

22. Jury Duty and Witness Leave.

a. Jury Duty. Employees are to notify their supervisors promptly upon receipt of a jury summons and subsequent notice of selection to serve as a juror. An employee selected to provide this community service will receive his or her regular rate of pay for normal hours worked, up to a maximum of 10 workdays, provided the employee submits evidence of the summons and selection notice. Employees will be allowed to retain any mileage and other compensation paid by the court.

b. Witness Duty. Employees will be paid leave for the time required to provide testimony in work related litigation or court proceedings. Employees are to notify their supervisor immediately upon receipt of a job related subpoena.

23. Military Leave.

a. An employee who enters active duty in a branch of the U.S. Armed Forces or is a member of the Reserve Components of the U.S. Armed Forces who attends annual training, active duty for training, or is called to active duty will be granted military leave.

b. To be entitled to military leave an employee must present official orders requiring attendance for a period of training or other active duty as a member of the Armed Forces.

c. An employee may opt not to use military and, instead, use accrued annual leave.

d. Military leave is further classified as paid supplemental military leave, unpaid military leave, or unpaid military leave of absence.

(1) Paid Supplemental Military Leave.

(a) Paid supplemental military leave is defined as that amount of pay necessary, when added to the military pay received for that day, to bring the employee to his or her full wage/salary level for that day.

(b) Fifteen (15) days of paid supplemental military leave will be granted annually to an employee who is member of a Reserve Component or who enlists for active service.

(c) For Reserve Component members this leave may be used for Annual Training, Active Duty for Training and other active duty (called to active duty or mobilized) verified by published military orders. Inactive Duty Training (i.e., weekend training) as a member of the National Guard or Reserve does not qualify for paid supplemental military leave.

(d) A day of paid supplemental military may only be used for a regular scheduled work day. The use of the fifteen (15) days is not limited to a single period, but may be used incrementally as long as the employee presents official military orders.

(2) Unpaid Military Leave. Unpaid military leave applies only to those employees who are eligible for paid supplemental military and decline to take either annual leave or paid supplemental military leave. It may only be used for 15 days or less. (As an example, this leave would apply to an employee who's military pay exceeds his or her wage/salary.)

(3) Unpaid Military Leave of Absence. Unpaid military leave of absence will be granted to an employee for extended periods (beyond 15 days) of active duty supported by published official military orders. The following periods of active duty qualify for unpaid military leave of absence:

(a) An employee who is inducted into or enlists in an Active Component of the Armed Forces of the United States.

(b) An employee who is a member of the Reserve Components attending any of the following duty:

    <u>1</u> Initial Entry Training (i.e., basic training).

    <u>2</u> Active Duty for Training (i.e., military schooling).

    <u>3</u> Called to federal active duty by the President of the United States during a national emergency (i.e., mobilized).

    <u>4</u> Called to state active duty by the Governor during a state emergency.

e. Employees returning to work are entitled to the same seniority, status, and pay they would have received had they not entered military service. Employees returning from military service may not be terminated from re-employment except for cause during their first year of re-employment.

24. Educational Leave.

a. Employees may request leave with pay for no more than 24 hours per month for attending educational courses/classes.

b. Requests for educational leave shall be made at least 30 days before class/course starting date. Tuition reimbursement is permissible and granted at the discretion of the department Executive Director based upon factors including length of service and quality of performance and availability of funds. Reimbursement will be contingent upon successful completion of a class/course with grade point average of 2.0 or better and availability of Tribal/program educational funding. Reimbursement is limited to tuition only and for only the classes/courses approved by employee supervisor. Reimbursement of educational costs will not exceed six (6) credits per semester or quarter of an academic year. All final grade transcripts will be provided before reimbursement is made.

c. <u>Professional Continuing Education Credits</u>. All professional staff are responsible to meet mandated Professional Continuing Education Credits. Reimbursable costs shall be all tuition, registration fees, textbooks, class supplies, time, travel, lodging and meals.

25. Administrative Leave.
Administrative leave status or normal work curtailment may be granted to employees by the Office of the President. Administrative Leave may be used for inclement weather conditions, hazardous working conditions, voting purposes, blood drives and other exceptional circumstances. Administrative Leave is considered unpaid leave unless otherwise specified in the Executive Order, Legislative Order, or Judicial Order.

26. Medical Leave.

a. <u>Maternity/Paternity Leave</u>. The Ho-Chunk Nation will provide maternity/paternity leave for employees when specific conditions are met. Abuse of the maternity/paternity leave may result in the loss of this privilege.

(1) Forty (40) hours of paid Maternity Leave for the maternal birthing parent employee shall be provided if either of the following conditions is met.

(a) Certification by the attending physician or medical provider is presented that shows the birthing parent employee is no longer able to perform her duties safely and efficiently and/or is adversely affected by the pregnancy.

(b) The birthing parent employee delivers the child(ren).

(2) Additional unpaid Maternity Leave for the female/birthing parent employee can be provided when conditions of employment are met. When the pregnancy pre-exists employment with the Nation, the employee can receive up to 30 days leave without pay. Otherwise, Family Medical Leave can apply if the pregnancy occurred during her employment with the Nation subject to qualification under Family Medical Leave.

(3) Eight (8) hours of paid Paternity Leave for the paternal parent employee shall be provided.

(4) Additional unpaid Paternity Leave for the paternal parent employee can be provided when conditions of employment are met. When the pregnancy preexists his employment with the Nation, he can receive up to seven (7) days leave without pay. Otherwise, Family Medical Leave can apply if the pregnancy occurred during his employment with the Nation, subject to qualification under Family Medical Leave.

b. <u>Family Medical Leave</u>. The Ho-Chunk Nation will provide up to twelve (12) weeks of unpaid, job-protected leave referred as Family Medical Leave (FML) for "eligible" employees to attend to certain family medical matters. All FML requests must be approved by the Department of Personnel.

(1) To be eligible for FML, the employee must have worked for the Nation for at least twelve (12) months and have worked at leave 1,250 hours during that twelve (12) month period.

(2) If an employee does not meet the eligibility criteria noted above, the FML pending window can close sooner than the usual 15-day pending period.

(3) If an employee and supervisor fail to notify the Department of Personnel that an employee is past FML pending stage and has not been approved FML use, disciplinary action, including termination, can occur.

(4) <u>Leave Schedule</u>.

(a) FML permits the employee to take either full-time off or intermittent leave. Upon request for FML, schedule of time off must be stated, or otherwise, the employee will be reported as using full-time FML.

(b) An employee may change his or her FML schedule when medical improvements occur; provided that the Department of Personnel is notified prior to the schedule change.

(c) An Intermittent/Reduced Schedule is permitted when such schedule does not unduly disrupt the Nation's operations and when either of the following circumstances occur.

<u>1</u> When medically necessary to care for a seriously ill family member with a foreseeable medical treatment schedule is established for the employee.

<u>2</u> When an employee with a serious medical condition is medically released by the supervising health care provider to work a reduced schedule. In such cases, the Nation may transfer the employee temporarily to an alternative job with equivalent pay and benefits that better accommodate the employee's recurring periods of leave.

<u>3</u> To care for a newborn or newly placed adopted or foster care child, as approved by the employer.

(5) An employee who fails to keep the Department of Personnel and his or her supervisor current on his or her medical status while on FML may be denied possible extensions of any leave time.

(6) An employee who fails to report promptly for work at the expiration of the FML will be considered to have voluntarily resigned with the exception of an employee with a Worker's Compensation claim (see Chapter VII).

(7) The FML can run concurrent with Short Term Disability, annual leave, sick leave, Maternity/Paternity Leave, Worker's Compensation and/or an unpaid Leave of Absence.

(8) <u>Leave Entitlements</u>.

(a) Such leave entitlements shall not include ailments that do not constitute "serious health conditions" as described in paragraph (c), below. This includes, but is not limited to, general work related stress, common colds, earaches, the flu, headaches other than migraines, upset stomach, minor ulcers, routine dental, orthodontic or periodontal problems.

(b) Leave entitlements do include the following reasons: the birth of a child, and to care for the newborn child; placement with the employee of a child for adoption or foster care, and care for the newly placed child; care for an immediate family member (spouse, child, or parent-but not a parent-in-law) with a serious health condition; and when the employee is unable to work because of a serious health condition.

    (c) <u>Serious Health Conditions</u>.

        <u>1</u> Serious health condition means an illness, injury, impairment, or physical or mental condition and involves: any period of incapacity or treatment connected with inpatient care (i.e., overnight stay) in a hospital, hospice, or residential medical care facility; a period of incapacity requiring absence of more than three (3) calendar days from work, school, or other regular daily activities that also involves continuing treatment by (or under the supervision of) a health care provider; any period of incapacity due to pregnancy, or for prenatal care; any period of incapacity (or treatment therefore) due to a chronic serious health condition (e.g., asthma, diabetes, epilepsy); a period of incapacity that is permanent or long-term due to a condition for which treatment may not be effective (e.g., Alzheimer's, stroke, terminal diseases); or any absences to receive multiple treatments (including any period of recovery) by, or on the referral of, a health care provider for a condition that likely would result in incapacity of more than three consecutive days if left untreated (e.g., chemotherapy, physical therapy, dialysis).

        <u>2</u> A regimen of continuing treatment under this provision that includes the taking of over-the-counter medications such as aspirin, antihistamines, or salves; or bed-rest, drinking fluids, exercise, and other similar activities that can be initiated without a visit to a health care provider, is not, by itself, sufficient to constitute a regimen of continuing treatment for the purpose of Family Medical Leave.

    (9) <u>Maintenance of Health Benefits</u>. The Nation shall maintain group health insurance coverage, including family coverage for an employee on Nation's FML. During the leave, the Nation will pay both the employer's and employee's premium during the week(s) the employee does not receive a payment from the Nation. The maintenance of the health benefits stops if and when an employee informs the Nation of intentions not to return to work at the end of the leave period, or if the employee fails to return to work when the leave entitlement is exhausted.

27. **Unpaid Leave of Absence**. An employee with more than twelve (12) months of continuous services full time service may be eligible for an Unpaid Leave of Absence for a period not to exceed three (3) months. All requests must be approved by the Department of Personnel.

    a. An Unpaid Leave of Absence may be granted for the following reasons:

    (1) Continued illness or personal reasons, which extend in time beyond available annual, sick, or FML. During an Unpaid Leave of Absence for medical reasons, health benefits will continue for up to ninety (90) days;

(2) Advanced training, higher education, or research, which will increase employability and job skills that are in the best interests of the Ho-Chunk Nation. Employees will be responsible for maintaining or discontinuing any employment related discretionary insurance benefits with the Nation.

b. Upon expiration of the Unpaid Leave of Absence, the employee shall be reinstated in the position held at the time this leave was granted. An employee who fails to promptly report to work at the expiration of such leave will be considered to have voluntarily resigned.

c. Under no circumstances will Departments be allowed to announce the position and hire a probationary employee; as if there were an official vacancy.

28. **Employee Assistance Program (EAP)**. The Employee Assistance Program is to assist employees with personal problems and supervisors in need of assistance in dealing with employee personal issues. The EAP is available to all employees of the Ho-Chunk Nation and their family members.

CHAPTER V
WORK RULES AND
EMPLOYEE CONDUCT, DISCIPLINE, AND ADMINISTRATIVE REVIEW

29. **General Hours of Work and Attendance.**

   a. Due to the varying nature of Tribal business and service needs, no single work schedule can be established for all employees. Executive Directors, upon consultation with supervisory personnel and with approval of the appropriate Administrator, will determine operational days and hours of work, or the modification thereof. General working times for Administration and Programs are Monday-Friday, 8:00 a.m. to 4:30 p.m., unless altered by Legislative or Executive Order. Working times for Gaming and Non-Gaming Enterprises will be established individually upon operational needs.

   b. Work schedules will be established for each employee by supervisory personnel who may change schedules based on the needs and requirements of work until operations. Supervisory personnel may also require an employee to work an unscheduled day worked shall be treated as modified work schedule and not be subject to overtimes compensation.

   c. <u>Attendance</u>.

   (1) Employees are required to report to their designated work locations at the prescribed time and manner work is to commence. Tardiness, unexcused absence or failure to report as required may result in disciplinary action.

   (2) In the event an employee cannot report to work as scheduled, the employee must notify supervisory personnel at least one hour prior for enterprise employees and within 15 minutes after the scheduled work shift for non-enterprise employees.

   (3) In all cases of an employee's absence or tardiness, the employee shall provide supervisory personnel with a valid reason for the absence and, if applicable, the probable duration of absence.

   d. <u>Excessive Absenteeism</u>. Excessive absenteeism, which renders an employee unavailable for work will be evaluated on a case-by-case basis to determine the merits of disciplinary action or termination.

   e. <u>Abandonment of Employment</u>. An employee who is absent from his or her assigned work location without authorized leave for three (3) consecutive days or five (5) days in a twelve (12) month period shall be considered absent without authorized leave, and as having abandoned his or her employment. The employee shall be automatically terminated, unless the employee can provide the Nation with acceptable and verifiable evidence of extenuating circumstances justifying the absence(s).

30. **Employee Conduct.**

a. Employees are responsible and accountable for adhering to all Tribal laws, policies, rules, directives, and procedures enacted and established by the Nation or appropriate Executive Staff.

b. Employees who engage in, or are associated with illegal, or inimical conduct, the nature which adversely affects the Ho-Chunk Nation, or their ability to carry out their employment responsibilities, will be subject to disciplinary action, including termination

c. Information about the Ho-Chunk Nation, its customers, clients, suppliers, or employees shall not be disclosed or divulged to anyone other than persons who have a right to know, or are authorized to receive such information.

d. The Nation reserves the right to deny services and entry onto the Nation's property to members of the public, visitors, and employees who are physically and/or verbally abusive or disruptive of services and operations. The Nation additionally reserves the right to deny entry onto Tribal properties or access to services to all employees and/or members of the public who may be under the influence of alcohol, controlled substances, and/or illegal drugs.

e. <u>Unacceptable Conduct</u>. The following employee acts, activities, or behavior that are unacceptable conduct.

(1) Improper or unauthorized use of paid or unpaid leave.

(2) Being absent without authorized leave or repeated unauthorized late arrival or early departure from work.

(3) Willful or negligent violation of this Act, Ho-Chunk law, unit operating rules, or related directives.

(4) Refusal to accept reasonable and proper assignments or failure to carry out a direct order from a superior, except where the order is illegal or the employee's safety may reasonably be jeopardized by the order.

(5) Soliciting or accepting gifts or compensation in exchange for influence, contracts, access to information, people or facilities.

(6) Engaging in a conflict of interest activity.

(7) Conduct that discredits the employee or the Nation, or willful misrepresentation of the Nation. An employee may not present himself or herself as a representative of the Nation, or communicate with the news media on behalf of the Ho-Chunk Nation unless authorized or directed in writing by the Ho-Chunk Nation or its delegated representative(s).

(8) Conviction of a crime, including convictions based on a plea of *nolo contendere* or of a misdemeanor involving moral turpitude, the nature of which reflects the possibility of serious consequences related to the continued assignment or employment of the employee.

(9) Knowingly falsifying, removing, or the destruction of information related to employment, payroll, or work-related records or reports.

(10) Soliciting outside work for personal gain during business hours; engaging in off-duty employment for any business under contract with the Ho-Chunk Nation; participating in any off-duty employment that adversely affects the employee's performance of work for the Nation; and engaging in unauthorized off-duty employment.

(11) Conduct that interferes with the management of Tribal operations.

(12) Violation of or neglecting safety rules, or contributing to hazardous conditions.

(13) Unauthorized removal, negligent, or improper use of any Tribal property, equipment, or funds or that of its clients, customers, or agents. This includes the private use, use that creates an unreasonable risk of damage to property, and embezzlement or conversion for personal use of Tribal funds or property.

(14) Physical altercations or creating a disturbance among fellow employees that would result in an adverse effect on morale, productivity, and/or the maintenance of proper discipline, i.e. wrestling, rough housing, and horse play.

(15) Participating in a strike, work stoppage, slowdown, sickout, or other job action.

(16) Making false, malicious, or unfounded statements against co-workers, supervisors, subordinates, government officials, or the Ho-Chunk Nation, which tend to damage the reputation or undermine the authority of the Ho-Chunk Nation

(17) Conducting personal business during work time.

(18) Inefficiency, incompetency, or negligence in the performance of duties, including failure to perform assigned tasks or training, or failure to discharge duties in a prompt, competent, and reasonable manner.

(19) Refusal or inability to improve job performance in accordance with written or verbal direction after a reasonable trial period, not to exceed thirty (30) days, which is specified in writing.

(20) Employees may not engage in coercion, nor be subject to coercive tactics that constitute a deprivation of legally protected rights.

(21) Offering or accepting political rewards as consideration for the political support of any party or candidate for public or Tribal office. Upon proof of such reward, disciplinary action will be taken, which may result in termination or removal.

(22) Driving under the influence of alcohol or drugs while on duty or the suspension of driver's license where job duties require driving.

(23) Bringing infants or other dependants to work for the purposes of providing them care and supervision, except in the following circumstances:

(a) To accommodate a mother's right to breast-feed an infant during her break periods, provided that a minimum amount of disruption in office functions occur.

(b) To accommodate an employee who works at any of the Nation's facilities where day care, recreation, or other supervision is provided for infants or dependent children, provided that the employee's work is not disrupted.

(c) In all cases, an employee must request approval of his or her supervisor in order to bring a child to his or her workplace under the above circumstances.

(24) Use of office telephones for personal purposes. Personal calls shall be kept to a minimum and long distance calls shall be reimbursed.

(25) Participating in, planning, or assisting in any illegal or unlawful activity, which affects the day-to-day operations of the Ho-Chunk Nation.

(26) Unauthorized release of confidential information or official records.

(27) Misuse of authority or position for personal gain.

(28) Any other actions considered inappropriate, or detrimental to employee working environment.

(29) Taking employee personnel matters to any public forum.

31. **Employee Discipline**.

a. Depending on the nature of the circumstances of an incident, discipline will normally be progressive and should bear a reasonable relationship to the violation. Based on the severity of the employee conduct, progressive discipline may not be applicable. Supervisors imposing discipline shall afford Due Process to the employee prior to suspending or terminating any employee. Types of discipline include:

(1) Suspension.

(a) Under no circumstances will a suspension exceed ten (10) working days.

(b) It may be necessary to restrict an employee immediately from performing duties at the work site. These circumstances usually involve potential danger to the employee, co-workers or the public, or the employee's inability to discharge assigned duties satisfactorily. In these situations, the following procedure is to be followed:

<u>1</u> Once the employee is suspended, the supervisor taking the action to suspend an employee will immediately notify the Executive Director and prepare a written statement of action taken and the reasons for such action.

<u>2</u> The Executive Director will prepare, together with the supervisor, the statement of charges and document any supporting evidence.

<u>3</u> As soon as possible after the initial action, the Executive Director will prepare written notification to the affected employee.

(c) In no event will the use of paid time be allowed during a period of suspension without pay. Should a paid holiday occur during a period of suspension without pay, the suspension period shall be extended by the number of holidays occurring during the suspension period.

(d) All suspensions shall be unpaid. No employee may be disciplined by issuance of a suspension with pay.

(e) A suspended employee who has been vindicated of any wrongdoing shall be compensated for lost wages and benefits.

(2) Termination.

b. The supervisor shall notify the Department of Personnel of all disciplinary actions.

32. **Alternative Dispute Resolution.** In an effort to provide employees with a method to resolve conflict within the workplace, the Ho-Chunk Nation has elected to implement alternative dispute resolution prior to and, in some cases, in lieu of the grievance process. It is the policy of the Ho-Chunk Nation to afford all eligible employees who have been subject to discrimination or harassment a means of having the circumstances of such action reviewed by an impartial and objective mediator. The Department of Personnel will take all reasonable steps to investigate all complaints. The Department will conduct mediations by facilitating discussions between parties requesting the assistance of the Department of Personnel in resolving their disputes in accordance with the Personnel Department's rules and procedures for mediation.

33. **Grievances.**

a. Employees may seek administrative and judicial review only for alleged discrimination and harassment.

b. Initial Probationary or Limited Term Employees may not grieve on any matters, save those listed in paragraph a, above.

c. Performance Evaluations may not be grieved, and may not be reviewed under the administrative review process or judicially.

d. Candidates for employment may file a complaint with the Department of Personnel regarding the interview and selection process and may elect to file a complaint directly with the Grievance Review Board.

34. **Administrative Review Process.**

   a. Policy.

   (1) The Department of Personnel will take all reasonable steps to investigate any incident, which has resulted in disciplinary action. It is the policy of the Ho-Chunk Nation to afford all eligible employees who have been subject to suspension or termination a means of having the circumstances of such disciplinary action reviewed by an impartial and objective Grievance Review Board (Board).

   (2) Employees are entitled to grieve suspensions or terminations to the Board. The Board will be selected from a set pool of employees and supervisors with grievance training, who will review a case and determine whether to uphold the discipline.

   (3) Following a Board decision, the employee shall have the right to file an appeal with the Ho-Chunk Nation Trial Court (Court).

   (4) Employees electing to appeal to the Board and to the Court may do so freely and without fear of reprisal. This policy and procedure shall be the exclusive remedy for employment review of a disciplinary action.

   b. Grievance Review Board. There shall be a Grievance Review Board to hear grievances for both non-supervisory and supervisory employees.

   (1) For non-supervisory employee grievances, the Board will consist of five (5) members; two will be non-supervisory employees, two will be supervisory employees, and one designated legal representative of the Department of Personnel will hear the case.

   (2) For supervisory employee grievances, reviews, the Board will consist of three (3) members; one designated legal representative of the Department of Personnel and two supervisory employees at the same supervisory level or above as the grieving employee.

c. Notification of Disciplinary Action. At the time an employee is notified of disciplinary action, the employee shall be advised of his or her right to a hearing before the Grievance Review Board.

d. Request for a Hearing. An employee must request a hearing within five (5) business days of the date the disciplinary action was taken. At the time the employee requests a hearing, he or she must inform the Department of Personnel if he or she is to be represented by an attorney. If so, the attorney must also file for an appearance with Department of Personnel within five (5) days of the date the employee requested a hearing. Failure to request the hearing within this time frame will result in the forfeiture of a hearing by the Board.

e. Witnesses and Evidence.

(1) Ten (10) days prior to the hearing, the employee and supervisor shall each provide the Department of Personnel with a list of all witnesses they intend to call at the hearing. They shall also present copies of any documentary evidence that they would like to submit to the Board.

(2) Both parties may amend or supplement their original witness list and/or submit additional documentary evidence within five (5) days after receiving the other party's list of witnesses and evidence.

(3) Time Limitations. Failure to abide by any of the above time requirements will prohibit the non-compliant party from introducing documentary evidence or presenting witnesses to the Board. For the purposes of this section, "days" shall be calculated using business days. Exceptions to any of the above time frames must be approved by the Executive Director, Department of Personnel.

f. Hearing Procedure.

(1) Review of Record. The Board will convene to review the records submitted to the Board prior to appearance by the grievant and supervisor to present their cases. Staff of the Department of Personnel shall also appear and be available to advise all participants with regard to policy and procedure.

(2) Supervisor's Presentation. The supervisor or his or her representative shall present to the Board the reasons why management believes that the disciplinary action should be upheld. The supervisor or representative may call witnesses at this time. This presentation shall not exceed two hours without the Board's permission.

(3) Employee's Presentation. When the supervisor's presentation has concluded, the employee shall present to the Board the reasons why he or she believes that the disciplinary action should not be upheld. The employee may call witnesses at this time. This presentation shall not exceed two hours without the Board's permission.

(4) Questions.

(a) Both parties shall have the right to ask questions of any witnesses.

(b) The Board members may ask questions of either party and may call for any additional information as they deem necessary in reaching a decision. If it requires information that is not readily available, the Board may accept into the record such additional information or choose to suspend the meeting and reconvene when the information is available.

(5) Final Comments. After both parties have made their presentations, and if the Board has no additional questions, then both parties shall have the opportunity make brief and concise final comments not to exceed fifteen minutes without the Board's permission.

g. Proceedings of the Board. At the commencement of a hearing before the Grievance Board of Review, the Department of Personnel will discuss with the Board their responsibilities and obligations including, but not limited to, the following:

(1) The proceedings are confidential.

(2) The proceedings, except for deliberations, will be tape-recorded.

(3) The Board may ask questions of either party and request additional evidence at any time.

(4) The Board may instruct the parties that it has heard sufficient information to make a recommendation, or that the information being offered is not relevant. Aside from relevancy issues, formal rules of evidence do not apply. The Board has the authority to extend/waive time limitations if it believes that the information offered is relevant and probative of the issues presented as defined below.

(5) The Board shall be responsible to make all relevancy determinations throughout the meeting. In making these determinations, the Board shall consider whether the proposed evidence (either witness testimony or documentary evidence) relates to the disciplinary action and whether it will affect the Board's recommendation. Only witnesses who have had direct involvement in the incident leading to the disciplinary action will be allowed to participate and all questions asked should directly relate to said disciplinary action.

(6) The Board may ask questions of the Department of Personnel relating to employment policies and procedures.

(7) At the conclusion of the presentation of testimony and evidence, the Board will privately deliberate and make a decision within five (5) business days. No record of the Board's deliberation will be made. The decision of the Board shall describe the facts

of the case and determine whether the facts support a violation of the Employment Relations Act or applicable Unit Operating Rules.

h. The Board shall have the authority to direct the Executive Director of Personnel to execute the appropriate remedy consistent with the determination of the Board.

35. Judicial Review.

a. Waiver of Sovereign Immunity. Pursuant to Article XII of the Constitution of the Ho-Chunk Nation, the Ho-Chunk Nation Legislature expressly waives the sovereign immunity of the Ho-Chunk Nation in the limited manner described herein. This waiver shall be strictly construed.

b. There is no judicial review of employee evaluations or disciplinary actions that do not immediately result in suspension or termination.

c. Judicial review of a grievance involving suspension, termination, discrimination, or harassment may proceed to the Ho-Chunk Nation Trial Court only after the Administrative Review Process has been exhausted through the Grievance Review Board. An employee may appeal a Board decision to the Trial Court within thirty (30) calendar days of when the Board decision is served by mail.

d. Relief.

(1) This limited waiver of sovereign immunity allows the Trial Court to award monetary damages for actual wages established by the employee in an amount not to exceed $10,000, subject to applicable taxation.

(2) The Trial Court may grant equitable relief mandating that the Ho-Chunk Nation prospectively follow its own law, and as necessary to directly remedy past violations of the Nation's laws. Other equitable remedies shall only include:

(a) an order of the Court to the Executive Director of the Department of Personnel to reassign or reinstate the employee;

(b) the removal of negative references from the employee's personnel file;

(c) the award of bridged service credit; and

(d) the restoration of the employee's seniority.

(3) Notwithstanding the remedial powers noted above, the Court shall not grant any remedies that are inconsistent with the laws of the Ho-Chunk Nation. Nothing in this limited waiver or within this Act shall be construed to grant a party any legal remedies other than those included in this section.

e. Under this limited waiver of sovereign immunity, the Court shall review the Board's decision based upon the record before the Board. Parties may request an opportunity to supplement the record in the Trial Court, either with evidence or statements of their position. The Trial Court shall not exercise *de novo* review of Board decisions. The Trial Court may only set aside or modify a Board decision if it was arbitrary and capricious.

36. Employee Rights.

a. Employees have the right to be represented by legal counsel or advocate at their own expense, including the right to hear the charges, evidence and witnesses against him or her, and the right to cross-examine.

b. It is a violation of this Act for any employee or member of the Ho-Chunk Nation to interfere with, threaten, coerce, restrain, discharge or otherwise take action against any employee or other person because he or she has filed a complaint, gave or will give testimony, or otherwise appeared before a court of the Ho-Chunk Nation or any of Ho-Chunk committee, agency, or board in connection with a grievance or an appeal.

c. Retaliation or punishment of an employee seeking resolution of an employment grievance by using established or prescribed procedures is strictly prohibited.

Ho-Chunk Nation Legislature
Employment Relations Act

CHAPTER VI
DRUG, ALCOHOL AND CONTROLLED SUBSTANCE POLICY

37. **General.**

   a. The Ho-Chunk Nation has a vital interest in maintaining a safe, healthy, and efficient working environment for its employees, contract service providers, and elected and appointed Officials, and each of these parties has the right to expect such working conditions are maintained. Being under the influence of drugs, controlled substances, or alcohol on the job poses a serious health and safety risk to the user, as well as other employees, contract service providers, and Officials of the Nation. The possession, use, or sale of an illegal drug or controlled substance in the workplace also poses unacceptable risk to a safe, healthy, and efficient work environment.

   b. The Ho-Chunk Nation recognizes that its own well-being and future success as a Nation and an employer are dependent on the physical, mental, and emotional health of its employees. Accordingly, it is the right, obligation and intent of the Nation to maintain a safe and healthy work environment to protect its employees, property, equipment, operations, goodwill, and customers.

38. **Purpose.**

   a. This Chapter promulgates and implements policy to maintain a Drug Free Work Place by establishing procedures for pre-employment screening, employee education and assistance, employee testing, and employee disciplinary action for the use, possession, or sale of illegal drugs, controlled substances, and alcohol, as well as for breach of employee confidentiality.

   b. This Chapter also provides the Nation's Zero Tolerance Policy for drugs, controlled substances, and alcohol for elected and appointed Officials of the Ho-Chunk Nation.

39. **Policy.**

   a. <u>General</u>. As a condition of employment, all employees, supervisors, contract service providers, and elected and appointed Officials must abide by the terms of this policy and the procedures contained herein.

      (1) Employees, contract service providers, and elected or appointed Officials are expected to report for work and remain at work in a condition, which enables them to perform their duties and tasks free from the effects of drugs or alcohol.

      (2) The possession, use, sale, purchase, or distribution of illegal drugs or controlled substances, or being under the influence of alcohol on the Nation's premises or in the conduct of related work off-site is prohibited.

(3) It is the responsibility of all supervisors to enforce this Drug, Alcohol and Controlled Substance Policy. Failure to enforce this Policy may result in disciplinary action up to and including termination. Nothing in this Policy precludes supervisors from establishing work or safety rules, which apply to their particular department and specified functions.

(4) Employees, contract service providers, and elected or appointed Officials suspected of being impaired by being under the influence of drugs or alcohol shall be escorted from the work site by the employee's supervisor or security personnel to a safe and secure area. The supervisor shall immediately document the incident and initiate Reasonable Suspicion Testing (see Section 45).

(5) Employee, contract service providers, and elected and appointed Officials rights shall not be violated. Any breach of confidentiality by an employee or supervisor will result in disciplinary action up to and including termination or removal.

b. Peyote. The use, possession, and/or transportation of peyote by Native American Church members in connection with the practice of the Native American Church (NAC) ceremony will not be considered to violate this Policy. The employee, contract service provider, or elected or appointed Official will not be subject to disciplinary action on the basis of such use, possession, or transportation in connection with the practice of the NAC.

c. Zero Tolerance Policy for Elected and Appointed Officials.

(1) Elected and appointed Officials of the Nation are to be held to the highest standards of compliance with the Nation's drug, alcohol, and controlled substance policies. See paragraph 4lm for a definition of "Official." Conduct of official duties by an elected or appointed Official while under the influence of drugs or when impaired by alcohol, as reasonably established by breath or blood alcohol and/or urinalysis testing shall not be tolerated and shall:

(a) Constitute malfeasance in office for purposes of Article IX, Sections 1 and 2 of the Constitution;

(b) Constitute good cause for removal under Article IX, Section 3 of the Constitution;

(c) Constitute good cause for removal under Section 805 of the *Gaming Ordinance*;

(d) Constitute good cause for removal of Election Board Members under paragraph 4d of the *Election Ordinance* (2 HCC § 6).

(e) Constitute malfeasance for the purposes of paragraph 5n of the *Code of*

Ethics Act (2 HCC § 1); and

  (f) Result in the immediate removal by the President of an Executive Director or other presidential appointed Officials from the position in which they serve if a violation of the Zero Tolerance Policy.

  (2) Alcohol Related Misconduct associated with official duties by an Elected or Appointed Official shall be a violation of this Policy punishable by unpaid suspension for three (3) to ten (10) days or, if involving conduct of sufficient severity, by termination or removal as subject to the supervisor's discretion exercised in accordance with the Nation's Constitution and laws. During the Conduct of Official Duties, the stricter standards of paragraph (1), above, shall apply.

  (3) Should there be a conflict in the application of the Zero Tolerance Policy and the Nation's other drug, alcohol, and controlled substance policies and procedures for elected and appointed Officials; the Zero Tolerance Policy shall prevail.

  d. <u>Legal Drugs</u>.

  (1) The use of, or being under the influence of, physician prescribed ("legal") drugs by an employee, contract service provider, or elected or appointed Official while in the workplace, or while on work related travel, is prohibited to the extent that such use or influence may, in the Nation's opinion, affect the safety of co-workers or members of the public, the employee's, contract service provider's, or elected or appointed official's job performance, or the safe and efficient operation of the Nation's facilities. Failure to report to management the use of prescription or legal drugs, which by their nature may impair the employee's, contract service provider's, or elected or appointed Official's abilities to perform his/her duties, may result in disciplinary action by management up to and including termination or removal.

  (2) If management has determined that the employee, contract service provider, or elected or appointed Official does not pose a threat to her or his own safety, the safety of co-workers, and that the employee's, contract service provider's, or elected or appointed Official's job performance is not significantly affected by the legal drug, the employee, contract service provider, or elected or appointed Official may continue to work, even though they may be under the influence of a legal drug.

  (3) If management has determined that the employee, contract service provider, or elected or appointed Official does pose a threat to her or his own safety, the safety of co-workers, and that the employee's, contract service provider's, or elected or appointed Official's job performance is significantly affected by the legal drug, the employee, contract service provider, or elected or appointed Official may be required to take a leave of absence, or comply with appropriate directive as determined by management.

(4) Any violation of this section will subject the employee, contract service provider, or elected or appointed Official to disciplinary action, up to and including termination or removal.

e. Illegal Drugs.

(1) The manufacture, possession, use, purchase, procurement, dispensation, or distribution of an illegal drug or illegal controlled substance or being under the influence of same, by any employee, contract service provider, or elected or appointed Official while in the workplace, on Nation premises, or in the conduct of related work off-site is prohibited. This will subject the employee, contract service provider, or elected or appointed Officials to disciplinary action up to and including termination or removal, and referral to law enforcement for prosecution.

(2) The use of another person's legally prescribed drugs is a violation of this Policy and shall constitute a positive drug test result due to the illegal procurement and use of controlled substances.

f. Alcohol.

(1) The consumption of alcohol or being under the influence of alcohol during working hours is prohibited and will subject the employee, contract service provider, or elected or appointed Official to disciplinary action, up to and including termination or removal. The purchase of alcohol, even if for later off-duty consumption, while being either an operator or a passenger in any Tribal owned or rented vehicles is likewise prohibited.

(2) The Nation will conduct testing for alcohol utilizing both breath alcohol and blood alcohol testing, especially where circumstances, accidents or other incidents in the workplace justify. A positive alcohol test shall be treated the same as a positive drug test for the purposes of the disciplinary rules stated Section 49.

(3) The Nation shall designate a Certified Technician(s) who shall be responsible for administering breath alcohol testing utilizing an Alco Sensor IV RBT IV unit or another comparable or appropriate breath alcohol testing unit.

(4) A breath alcohol concentration equal to or greater than 0.02 is a positive result and the employee or contract service provider shall be subject to disciplinary action consistent with Section 50. The Supervisor, Compliance Division, or Security shall arrange for transportation of the employee or contract service provider to his/her residence.

(5) The Nation provides an Employee Assistance Program (EAP), which provides help to employees who seek assistance to help with problems. See Section 50.

40. **Definitions.**

a. "Alcohol Concentration" means either of the following:

   (1) The number of grams of alcohol per 100 milliliters of a person's blood.

   (2) The number of grams of alcohol per 210 liters of a person's breath.

b. "Alcohol Related Misconduct" associated with official duties means a conviction for any alcohol related driving offense, physical altercation, or other serious wrongful conduct by an elected or appointed Official in which alcohol consumption is established by substantial and reliable evidence to be a contributing factor during travel, meal, and lodging time associated with meetings or other responsibilities regarding the conduct of official business for which the appointed or elected Official is eligible to receive per diem under this Act. For the purposes of this definition, "substantial and reliable evidence" shall mean a breath or blood alcohol test administered by a certified tester showing an alcohol concentration of over 0.01 or credible eyewitness testimony of two (2) or more persons of the consumption by the subject of four (4) or more alcoholic beverages during a period of not more than three (3) hours.

c. "Conduct of Official Duties" means the normally scheduled work duties of elected and appointed Officials whether during the regular workday or at other official meetings, including Area meetings. Conduct of Official Duties does not include informal occasions such as receptions, diners, and similar events at which no official business is transacted.

d. "Contract Service Provider" means a person who is providing services to the Nation pursuant to a Service Provider Agreement and who is treated for tax withholding purposes as though he or she is an employee of the Nation.

e. "Controlled Substance" means any controlled substance, dangerous drug(s) or intoxicating compound as defined under federal or state law and includes, but not limited to, narcotics, opiates, hallucinogens, stimulants, marijuana and so-called "designer drugs."

f. "EMIT" means Enzyme Multiplied Immuno Technique, which is an initial test that identifies which class of drug(s) is present, but not which specific drug(s).

g. "False Negative/Water Dilution" is a way of a possible false negative result that results when large amounts of fluids are ingested or water is added to the specimen after urination.

h. "GC/MS" means Gas Chromatography Mass Spectrometry, which is the confirmatory test that is done after an initial positive test is detected. It will identify that a drug(s) is present and identify which specific drug(s) was ingested, injected, or inhaled and at what concentration it is still present in the person's system.

i. "Illegal Drug" or "Illegal Controlled Substance" means any drug(s) or controlled substance(s), which is not legally obtainable, or has been legally obtained is being used in a manner inconsistent with the prescribed dosage or by an individual other than the person the medication was originally intended. The so-called "Designer Drugs" are included in this category.

j. "Impaired" means an alcohol concentration established by properly administered breath alcohol and/or blood test to be equal to or in excess of 0.02.

k. "Initial Drug Test" is that test administered to a new employee or contract service provider within the first 30 days (guideline) of employment. The initial drug test on occasion may be given after the first 30 days where the Compliance Department work load and logistics capability do not make it practical to administer the test within the 30 days.

l. "Legal Drug" means any prescribed drug(s), over-the-counter drug(s), or prescribed controlled substance(s), which has been legally obtained and is being used in the dosage prescribed according to the manufacturer's and/or physician's instructions.

m. "Official," for the purposes of the Nation's Zero Tolerance Policy, means any person who:

(1) Holds elective office or is a candidate for elective office; or

(2) Is an appointed professional and includes Judges, Department Executive Directors, Gaming Commissioners, and an appointed member of the President's staff.

n. "Reasonable Suspicion" means that level of suspicion established on the basis of particular facts and/or observation by an agent, fellow employee, or supervisor concerning employee behavior, comments, or significant changes in work product that would cause a reasonable and prudent person under the same or similar circumstances to believe that an employee has violated the Nation's drug policy.

o. "Reasonably Established" means that level of drug, alcohol, or controlled substance detected in a person that is determined by a breath or blood alcohol and/or urinalysis test.

p. "Under the Influence" means:

(1) With respect to any drug or controlled substance, that substance is present in a person in any detectable amount based on the results of medically validated testing.

(2) With respect to alcohol, the alcohol concentration of a person established by a properly administered breath alcohol and/or blood alcohol test is in excess of 0.10.

41. **Pre-Employment Screening.** The Ho-Chunk Nation will use pre-employment screening practices to prevent the hiring of individuals who use illegal drugs or illegal controlled substances, or individuals whose use of legal drugs or legal controlled substances indicates a potential for impaired or unsafe work performance. These provisions apply to contract service providers as well as employees.

    a. All applicants will be advised that the final candidates for any position, full or part-time, will be tested for drugs and controlled substances as a condition of employment.

    b. Any applicant or final candidate who, after being advised that testing is a condition of employment, refuses testing for drugs and/or controlled substances, without a valid reason, will not be hired.

    c. Any applicant admitting to current misuse of drugs and/or controlled substances will not be employed. The applicant will be asked to sign a statement or disclosure stating that they understand the reason for non-employment with the Nation.

    d. All final candidates will be asked to complete a Drug Policy Checklist in which candidates agree to take a drug test as a condition of employment with the Nation. Furthermore, the candidates shall acknowledge that he/she understands the requirement as well as the potential consequences of all violations of the Nation's Drug, Alcohol and Controlled Substance Policy.

42. **Initial Drug Test.** All employees and contract service providers will be tested within 30 days of employment at each facility for an initial drug screen. On occasion the Initial Drug Test may be given after the 30 days where the Compliance Division's workload and logistics do not make it practical to administer the test within 30 days. Therefore, failure to administer the Initial Drug Test within 30 days of hire shall **not** be deemed a waiver of the requirement for an Initial Drug Test for each employee or contract service provider.

    a. Compliance Division personnel shall in most cases arrive unannounced at the employee's or contract service provider's work site to administer the Initial Drug Test.

    b. Any refusal or failure to comply with this test, absent a valid medical reason, will result in termination.

    c. If the test result of the employee's or contract service provider's drug test is positive, the employee or contract service provider will be terminated from employment with the Ho-Chunk Nation.

    d. Should an employee be subject to random or reasonable suspicion testing prior to his/her Initial Drug Test, the random or reasonable suspicion test will be considered an Initial Drug Test and a positive test result will subject the employee to termination.

Ho-Chunk Nation Legislature
Employment Relations Act

43. Random Drug Testing.

a. All employees of the Nation facilities shall be subject to random unannounced drug testing. Employees will be selected using a double blind computerized formula administered by an independent consulting firm. At a minimum, forty (40%) percent of all active employees shall be tested annually. Once notified, the employee will report directly for testing.

b. Compliance Division personnel shall, in most cases, arrive unannounced at the employee's work site to administer random drug and alcohol tests.

c. Any refusal or failure to comply with this testing, absent a valid medical reason, will result in termination of employment.

d. The Nation shall include contract service providers as part of the population randomly tested.

e. Elected or appointed Officials of the Nation that are not employees of the Nation may be subject to initial and random drug testing while serving in their official capacity under the Zero Tolerance Policy. Any refusal by such an appointed or elected Official shall be deemed in violation of paragraph 39c of this Chapter.

f. If the result of the employee's or contract service provider's drug test is positive and the person has not had an initial drug test, that person shall be terminated. See paragraph 39c for elected and appointed Officials subject to the Zero Tolerance Policy.

44. Reasonable Suspicion Testing.

a. The Nation may require testing of employees, contract service providers, or elected or appointed Officials suspected of being in violation of the Nation's drug and alcohol policy or where circumstances (i.e., accidents, workplace incidents, etc.) indicate that drug or alcohol use may be involved based on the Reasonable Suspicion standard. Strict procedures have been established (available through the Department of Justice Compliance Division) for determining under what circumstances such a test shall be requested. The procedure includes a number of review steps. An employee's, contract service provider's, or elected or appointed Official's refusal to consent to testing shall result in termination or removal.

b. Any employee, contract service provider, or elected or appointed Official of the Nation that has direct knowledge or has reason to believe that another employee, contract service provider, or elected or appointed Official may be under the influence of alcohol and/or drugs shall report this to the Compliance Division and complete a Reasonable Suspicion Checklist. All information is confidential and will not be revealed without a Ho-Chunk Nation Trial Court Order.

c. The Director of Compliance or designee shall review the Reasonable Suspicion Checklist and either approve or deny a Reasonable Suspicion Test.

d. If the Reasonable Suspicion Test is approved, Compliance Division personnel shall arrive unannounced at the employee's or contract service provider's work site to administer the random test. Elected or appointed Officials of the Nation that are not employees of the Nation may be tested only when serving in their official capacity.

e. Should the Reasonable Suspicion involve alcohol, the employee, contract service provider, or elected or appointed Official will be administered a breath alcohol test in private by a Certified Technician. If this test is positive, a second confirmatory test shall be conducted as well as urinalysis testing.

f. Any refusal or failure to comply with Reasonable Suspicion Testing, absent a valid medical reason, will result in termination or removal.

g. If the result of the employee's or contract service provider's drug test is positive and the person has not had an initial drug test, that person shall be terminated. See paragraph 39c for elected and appointed Officials subject to the Zero Tolerance Policy.

h. In order to limit accident and liability exposure, managers will not allow employee's, contract service providers, or elected or appointed Officials who are unable to perform their assigned duties due to drug or alcohol related impairment to leave the work premises without an escort.

45. Drug and Alcohol Testing for Employees Required to Possess a Commercial Drivers License (CDL).

a. All employees and contract service providers that are required by job description to possess a commercial drivers license are subject to drug and alcohol testing.

b. If the test result of the employee's or contract service provider's drug test is positive, the employee or contract service provider will be terminated from employment with the Ho-Chunk Nation.

c. Any refusal or failure to comply with this test, absent a valid medical reason, will result in termination or removal.

46. Off-Duty Involvement with Drugs, Alcohol, and Controlled Substances.
The Nation reserves the right to take disciplinary action, including termination or removal, for an employee's, contract service provider's, or elected or appointed Official's off-duty involvement with drugs, alcohol, or controlled substances. Off-duty involvement includes, but is not limited to, incidents where such involvement is, in the Nation's view, damaging to the Nation's reputation or business, and/or is inconsistent with the employee's, contract service provider's, or elected or appointed Official's duties or image, or when the off-duty behavior constitutes criminal behavior. This may include the

review of criminal records for convictions with respect to drugs, alcohol, and controlled substances.

47. **Part-time, Summer, and Contract Personnel.** The provisions of this Policy are applicable to all part-time, summer, and contract personnel.

   a. All part-time and summer personnel who could pose a potential for impaired or unsafe work performance shall be tested for drugs, alcohol, and/or controlled substances.

   b. Contract vendors shall not provide contract employees who use illegal drugs or illegal controlled substances, or individuals who use legal drugs or legal controlled substances that could pose a potential for impaired or unsafe work performance.

   c. All youth employees shall be referred to Traditional Court or Clan Mothers for family intervention for positive results for drug, alcohol, and addiction problems.

48. **Searches.**

   a. The Nation reserves the right to conduct unannounced searches for illegal drugs or illegal controlled substances on the Nation's premises.

   b. For purposes of the Zero Tolerance Policy, elected and appointed Officials who are not employees of the Nation may only be searched while serving in their official capacity.

   c. The Department of Justice Compliance Division shall authorize all searches conducted on the Nation's premises. The Compliance Director or designee will coordinate with Department of Justice personnel and local law enforcement officials as appropriate.

   d. Reasonable search of employees and their personal property, including vehicles, may be conducted at any time in order to maintain a safe, healthy, and efficient working environment. If and when any offices of the Nation are not on the Nation's property, any searches conducted will be in accordance with state and federal law.

   e. Employees, contract service providers, or elected or appointed Officials who refuse to cooperate during an authorized search will be subject to disciplinary action up to and including termination or removal.

   f. Should any quantity of illegal drugs, alcohol, and/or controlled substances be found as a result of a proper search, Compliance Division and/or Department of Justice personnel shall locate and escort the employee, contract service provider, or elected or appointed Official to an area with restricted access to other persons. The individual will then be subject to a drug and/or alcohol test and may be subject to arrest.

49. **Disciplinary Action.**

a. New Employees. New employees or contract service providers that test positive on his or her Initial Drug Test shall be terminated as stated in paragraph 43c.

b. Elected and Appointed Officials. See paragraph 39c for provisions for elected and appointed Officials under the Zero Tolerance Policy.

c. Current Employees and Contract Service Providers. If the result of the employee's or contract service provider's drug or alcohol test is positive, the individual will be placed on probation with the following sanctions:

(1) The length of probation shall be one (1) year and one (1) day from the date the employee or contract service provider is served with the positive test result notification. However, should the employee or contract service provider be terminated for any non-drug policy reason, before he or she has completed probation, he or she shall serve the remaining probationary period.

(2) The employee or contract service provider shall be referred to the Employee Assistance Program (EAP) for an Alcohol and Drug Assessment and will be required to follow through with any recommendations that result from that assessment. **Failure to follow through with the recommendations will be considered a second offense and the employee or contract service provider will be terminated.**

(3) The employee or contract service provider shall sign a wage assignment in the amount of $240.00. Upon successful completion of probation one half ($120.00) shall be returned to the employee or contract service provider.

(4) The employee or contract service provider must sign a Condition of Employment Form allowing follow-up testing for up to six (6) months.

(5) Should the employee or contract service provider test positive again during this six (6) month period, this will be considered a second offense and the employee or contract service provider will be terminated.

(6) Should the employee or the contract service provider test positive on any drug test within one the (1) year and one (1) day timeframe, this will be considered a second offense and the employee or contract service provider will be terminated.

(7) After one (1) year and one (1) day of drug free testing, the employee will be put back on a testing program as if he/she were a new hire.

d. Malicious Intent Reports. When a person habitually reports violations of this Policy by persons to whom they have malicious intent and such reports are false, the penalty for such false reports shall be a recurring fine of $200.

50. **Employee Assistance Program (EAP).** The Nation maintains a Ho-Chunk Employee Assistance Program (EAP) which provides referral resources and assistance help to employees who may be experiencing a drug, alcohol, or controlled substance problem. The purpose and practices of this Drug Policy and the EAP are not in conflict but are distinctively separate in their applications.

    a. It is the responsibility of the each employee to seek assistance from EAP before a drug or alcohol problem leads to disciplinary action. Once a violation of the Nation's Drug Policy occurs, subsequent use of EAP on a voluntary basis will not necessarily lessen disciplinary action.

    b. It is the responsibility of supervisors to counsel an employee suspected of drug or alcohol problems to voluntarily seek assistance of EAP.

    c. The employee's decision to voluntarily seek prior assistance from EAP will not be used as a basis for disciplinary action and will not be used against the employee in any disciplinary proceedings. On the other hand, using EAP will not be a defense to the imposition of disciplinary action where facts proving a violation of this policy are obtained outside of EAP.

51. **Rehiring Procedures for Drug Policy Violations.** Employees or contract service providers who are found to be in violation of this drug and alcohol policy and are terminated may be eligible for employment after the following is completed.

    a. The time period between termination and re-hiring, contingent on rehabilitation, shall be no less than six (6) months.

    b. The employee must furnish a discharge summary indicating successful completion of treatment from a certified AODA counseling facility to the Compliance Division Drug Enforcement Unit.

    c. The Compliance Division Drug Enforcement Unit shall certify to the Nation's Department of Personnel the former employee's eligibility for employment.

52. **Testing Procedures.**

    a. The Initial Drug Test will test for at least the following substances:

        Cannabinoids
        Cocaine
        Benzodiazepines
        Opiates
        Barbiturates
        Amphetamines
        Phencyclidine
        Propoxyphene

Methadone
Methaqualone

b. False negative/water diluted tests will be re-tested only one time. After the second "false negative" test the employee or contract service provider will pay for any subsequent testing until a determinative result can be obtained. There will be no more than a forty-eight (48) hour span between any tests given. After three (3) false negative tests without determinative results, the employee or contract service provider will be placed on suspension without pay for up to two (2) weeks until a determinative test is completed. If no determinative test is completed within the two (2) weeks from date of the first test, the employee or contract service provider will be terminated.

c. If the employee or contract service provider is unable to produce an adequate specimen level in the time allotted, the Compliance Division personnel shall notify the employee or contract service provider that he or she is responsible to obtain and submit a medical report from a Licensed Medical Doctor citing a medical reason for the employee's or contract service provider's inability to produce a specimen. The employee or contract service provider must submit the report to the Drug Enforcement Unit within two (2) business days from the original date of collection.

d. If an invalid or adulterated result is received by the contracted laboratory, the result shall be considered a violation of this Policy and the employee or contract service shall be subject to disciplinary action consistent with Section 49 of this Policy.

e. All initial positive tests will be confirmed with a second testing procedure to eliminate false-positive results. The initial test will be performed by EMIT. The confirmation test will be GC/MS.

f. A chain of custody on all test samples will be utilized at all times.

g. Access to test results must be restricted to authorized personnel only. Test results will be secured in a locked container. Without written consent of the employee, information about the results of his/her tests shall not be released to anyone.

53. **Reporting Procedures for Drug Policy Violations.** When drug test results are received from the laboratory, the Compliance Director or his/her designee will report the drug policy violation to the employee or contract service provider.

a. Employees or contract service providers who have a positive Initial Drug Test will be reported out using the following procedures.

(1) The Compliance Director or designee will coordinate with individual work schedules to report the positive drug test results directly to the employee or contract service provider.

(2) The employee or contract service provider will be given a verbal and written drug test result.

b. Employees or contact service providers who have passed their Initial Drug Test or pre-employment screening, but have subsequently tested positive on a random or reasonable suspicion drug test, will be reported out using the following procedures.

(1) The Compliance Director or designee will coordinate with individual work schedules to report the positive drug test results directly to the employee or contract service provider.

(2) The employee or contract service provider will be given a verbal and written drug test result.

(3) The employee or contract service provider will sign a Condition of Employment Acknowledgement Form, which sets down the conditions the employee or contract service provider must comply with to retain employment.

(4) An explanation will be given to the employee or contract service provider that in order to monitor his or her compliance with the EAP, he or she will need to sign a Consent for Release of Information Form.

(5) The Consent for Release of Information Form allows the Compliance Division to contact the EAP Office and schedule an appointment and to place that appointment on the referral form.

(6) If an employee or contract service provider completed an EAP Alcohol and Other Drug Abuse assessment and does not have a positive drug test for his or her six (6) month condition of employment, but tests positive for a second time within one (1) year and one (1) day, he or she will be terminated.

(7) If the employee or contract service provider tests positive after one (1) year and one (1) day it will be treated as a first positive and referral to the EAP and the signing of the Condition of Employment Acknowledgement Form will be repeated.

(8) Copies of this documentation will be given to the employee or contract service provider, to the appropriate Executive Director and EAP. The Compliance Division will file the originals.

c. If an employee or contract service provider would like a copy of the drug test result, a request must be in written form, notarized, and submitted with self-addressed stamped envelope by mail to: Ho-Chunk Nation, Compliance Division, PO Box 667, Black River Falls, WI 54615.

d. Any breach of confidentiality with respect to reporting drug test results will result in disciplinary action up to including termination.

54. **Enforcement of the Zero Tolerance Policy for Elected and Appointed Officials.**

    a. <u>Presidential Enforcement</u>. The President shall enforce the policies and procedures of the Zero Tolerance Policy for the following persons:

        (1) Department Executive Directors.

        (2) Appointed Presidential Staff Members.

    b. <u>Legislative Enforcement</u>. The Legislature shall enforce the policies and procedures of the Zero Tolerance Policy for the following persons:

        (1) Members of the Legislature.

        (2) <u>President</u>. If the President is alleged to have violated the Zero Tolerance Policy, the Legislature shall afford the President the option to have a hearing to contest the alleged violation and confront witnesses to establish reasonable cause prior to submitting the matter to General Council.

        (3) <u>Chief Justice</u>. If the Chief Justice is alleged to have violated the Zero Tolerance Policy, the Legislature shall afford the Chief Justice the option to have a hearing to contest the alleged violation and confront witnesses to establish reasonable cause prior to submitting the matter to General Council.

        (4) Gaming Commissioners.

    c. <u>Judicial Enforcement</u>.

        (1) The Chief Justice shall enforce the Zero Tolerance Policy for the following persons:

            (a) Members of the Trial Court.

            (b) Members of the Supreme Court.

    d. Termination or removals of elected or appointed Officials shall be effected in accordance with any notice, hearing, and procedural rules that may apply under the Constitution and laws of the Nation. Reasonable hearing rights may be afforded to any other Official at the discretion of the person or body charged with enforcement of this Policy if any issues of fact are presented that are material to the finding of violation of this Policy.

    e. Nothing in the Zero Tolerance Policy precludes a Tribal member or employee from reporting alleged violations directly to the Ethics Review Board.

Legislative History:

Ho-Chunk Nation Legislature
Employment Relations Act

1/4/95	Legislature enacts Drug and Controlled Substance Policy.
10/16/01	Legislature amends Drug and Controlled Substance Policy by enacting the Drug, Alcohol and Controlled Substance Policy as Chapter VI to the draft Employment Relations Act (6 HCC § 5) by Legislative Resolution 10/16/01D.
10/11/02	Corrects the numbering of paragraph 15. Testing Procedures (renumbered from 17 to 15).
10/23/02	Amended and restated by Legislative Resolution 10/23/02B.
10/19/04	Restated with enactment of the Employment Relations Act (6 HCC § 5) by Legislative Resolution 12/9/04A.

Ho-Chunk Nation Legislature
Employment Relations Act

CHAPTER VII
WORKER'S COMPENSATION PLAN

55. Purpose and Scope.

a. The purpose of this Worker's Compensation Plan (Plan) is to provide a system of compensation and medical benefits for the employees of the Nation who suffer Compensable Injuries in the employment of the Nation. Benefits under the Plan are the employee's exclusive remedy against the Nation.

b. All employees, as of the first day of employment with the Nation, are covered for Compensable Bodily Injuries whether the Accident and Bodily Injury occur on or off the Nation's lands. Benefits are limited as indicated in this Plan.

c. This Plan is a self-funded, self-insurance program of the Nation, a sovereign tribal government and is operated for the benefits of its employees.

d. Nothing is this Plan, including any assertion of right of privilege, shall waive, or be construed to work as a constructive waiver of the Nation's sovereign immunity from suit by any party.

56. Definitions. As used in this Plan, the following terms have the meaning indicated:

a. "Accidents" mean a specific occurrence, neither expected nor intended, which causes bodily injury to an employee and arises under circumstances constituting a Compensable Injury.

b. "Administrator" means the company with whom the Nation has contracted to act on behalf of the Nation in the administration of this Plan.

c. "Bodily Injury" or "Injury" means actual physical injury to the body that arises by accident under circumstances that constitute a Compensable Injury. Injuries due to a repetitive or cumulative trauma may be deemed compensable if the condition is established to be solely related to the employment with the Nation and if the employee has no history of a preexisting condition, as established by medical evidence.

d. "Commission" means the Ho-Chunk Nation Insurance Review Commission.

e. "Compensable" or "Compensable Injury" means a bodily injury of an employee caused by an accident when that injury arises out of risk of employment, the injury occurs during a period of employment, and while performing the duties of the employment in or on the premises of the Employer or whenever the Employer requires the employee to perform the employment activities.

f. "Compensation Rates" means 66⅔ percent of the weekly wage as determined under paragraph o, below, subject to the maximum rate adopted by the state's Department of Workforce Development. A reduction of 25 percent of weekly wage will be enforced when safety equipment is required, but not used. Rate of pay determined at the time of injury will be used throughout the term of loss.

g. <u>Dependents</u>.

(1) "Dependent Child" means a natural or legally adopted unmarried child of the employee, including a posthumous child, under eighteen years of age, or under the age of twenty-two (22) if the child is regularly attending a high school, college, university, vocational, or technical school as a full-time employee.

(2) "Dependent Spouse" the lawful wife or husband of the employee, unless voluntary living apart from the employee at the time of the employee's injury or death. A dependant spouse does not include a "common law" spouse.

(3) "Other Dependents" means that stepchildren, grandchildren, nieces, and nephews may be considered dependent but only if actual dependency can be show.

h. "Employee" means any person who performs labor services alone for the Nation for hire at an established wage or salary.

i. "Employer" means the Nation where it has obtained the labor services of a person for hire.

j. "Independent Medical Examination" means the medical examination and/or evaluation of the employee scheduled by the Nation or Administrator at the Nation's expense for the purpose of obtaining medical information or opinion.

k. "Nation" means the Ho-Chunk Nation, also referred to as the Employer, or its designee. Unless otherwise provided herein, the Department of Personnel shall act for the Nation/Employer.

l. "Plan" means the Ho-Chunk Nation Worker's Compensation Plan.

m. "Primary Physician" means a Nation approved health care provider within 75 miles of the employee's home at the time of the injury and from whom the employee receives medical treatment for a Compensable Bodily Injury.

n. "Referral Physician" means a licensed medical doctor or chiropractor to whom the employee is referred by the Primary Physician for further specialized treatment with the approval of the Administrator or the Nation.

o. "Waiting Period" means the first three (3) scheduled days lost, for which no Worker's Compensation benefits will be paid, counted from the first day of disability due to a Compensable Injury. If the disability continues beyond seven (7) calendar days, compensation is payable for scheduled days lost from the first day of disability. No annual or sick leave may be used for the first three (3) scheduled days lost. If the employee chooses to be paid annual or sick leave, it will be deducted from the loss time paid.

    p. "Weekly Wage" means:

    (1) For a full-time employee, it is the weekly salary or wage normally earned in a normal full-time week of employment by the Nation.

    (2) If the hours worked are irregular or difficult to determine, the average daily wage is determined by totaling the earnings from employment by the Nation over the 26 calendar weeks prior to the injury and dividing the sum by the number of calendar weeks within the 26 week period in which the employee had earnings from employment by the Nation to determine the average work week. The average workweek is then multiplied by the average daily wage to arrive at the Weekly Wage.

    (3) In no case are overtime wages considered in determining the Weekly Wage.

    (4) If an employee is employed in more than one capacity by the Nation, the earnings of the employee in each will be considered in determining Weekly Wage.

57. Reporting Obligation.

    a. An employee must report any injury, no matter how slight, to his or her supervisor no later than the end of the employee's workday on the day of the accident causing the Bodily Injury. A Bodily Injury may be reported by another on behalf of the employee. Failure to report a job related injury no later than the end of the employee's workday shall result in the employee not being eligible for compensation and/or medical benefits under this Plan.

    b. A supervisor, upon a report of an injury, shall immediately complete an Injury Report Form and forward the Report to the Department of Personnel within 24 hours of the report of an injury.

    c. A supervisor upon receiving a report or notice of an employee claim for compensation or benefits under this Plan shall immediately report the claim to the Department of Personnel. The Department shall then notify the Insurance Department.

    d. No compensation or medical benefits will be paid if a Bodily Injury is not reported within ten (10) calendar days of the employee first receiving medical treatment for the Injury.

58. **Medical Benefits.** This Plan will pay the cost of all reasonable and necessary first aid, medical, surgical and hospital services incurred by the employee as direct result of a Compensable Bodily Injury subject to the following restrictions.

   a. Once an employee has made a second visit to a physician, that physician is the employee's Primary Physician under the Plan. After this second visit, the employee may not change Primary Physician without the approval of the Administrator or the Nation. The Nation reserves the right to require care to be provided by a provider with whom the Nation has a preferred or discount arrangement.

   b. This Plan will pay hospital and related charges only for services ordered by the Primary or Referral Physician.

   c. This Plan will pay the reasonable and necessary medical costs and the cost of medicines and supplies and equipment of a therapeutic nature to treat the Bodily Injury only if ordered by the Primary or Referral Physician.

   d. This Plan will pay surgical charges only if the surgery is done an emergency basis or if it has been previously approved by the Administrator or the Employer. The Administrator or the Employer may require a second opinion before approving any surgical procedure.

   e. This Plan will reimburse the employee for the reasonable cost of mileage and other related expense necessarily incurred to obtain medical treatment other than the cost of childcare. The mileage reimbursement rate shall be that rate as established by the State of Wisconsin for worker's compensation purposes.

   f. If the employee unreasonably fails to appear for a scheduled Independent Medical Examination, the responsibility of the Employer for payment under this Plan of medical expenses incurred after the scheduled date of that Examination ceases. Likewise, the Employer's responsibility for payment of all other benefits accruing under this Plan ceases immediately upon that failure to appear.

   g. The Administrator or the Nation may contract for the services of a rehabilitation consultant to assist the employee in rehabilitation and return to work efforts. If the employee fails to cooperate in rehabilitation efforts the responsibility of the Employer for payment of all benefits and medical expenses under this Plan will cease.

   h. The employee must provide written authorization for present and past medical records when requested by the Administrator or the Nation. If the employee fails to provide authorization within 20 days of a written request to do so, the responsibility of the Employer for payment of all benefits and medical expenses under this Plan will cease.

   i. When the employee has reached his or her end of healing, payments for medical costs will cease.

59. Return to Work.

a. Positions with a Compensable Injury or illness will be held for up to three (3) months. At that time the position may be filled by a regular employee. An equivalent position with comparable wage/salary will be offered when the employee is released to return to work.

b. Light duty positions will be restricted up to three (3) months. At the completion of the three (3) months a revaluation will be conducted by the Administrator.

60. Disability Benefits.

a. <u>Temporary Total Disability</u>. Temporary Total Disability is that time, after the Waiting Period when, solely as a direct result of the Bodily Injury, the employee is totally disabled from performing for the Employer the employee's normal duties which the employee was engaged in at the time of the Bodily Injury, or of other light, restricted or modified work that the Employer offers.

(1) Total Disability must be evidenced by medical opinion based on examination and treatment rendered at the time of the claimed disability.

(2) The weekly benefits for Temporary Disability are limited to the applicable Compensation Rate under paragraphs 56f and 56p.

b. <u>Temporary Partial Disability</u>. Temporary Partial Disability is the loss of actual earnings suffered by an employee who has returned to light duty, restricted or modified work offered by the Employer solely because of the ongoing effects of the bodily injury and the employee's physical inability to return to employee's normal duties of Employment with the Nation which the employee engaged in at the time of the Bodily Injury.

(1) The weekly benefits for Temporary Partial Disability is $66\frac{2}{3}$ percent of the difference between the Weekly Wage at the time of the Bodily Injury as determined under paragraph 57p and the wage the employee is able to earn in the light duty, restricted or modified work that the Employer offers.

(2) Temporary Partial Disability benefits are limited to the maximum compensation rate under paragraph 56f.

c. <u>Permanent Disability</u>.

(1) This benefit is intended to compensate the injured employee for a permanent loss of or loss of use of a member suffered directly as a result of a Compensable Bodily Injury.

(2) Preexisting disabilities are not to be included when rating a Permanent Partial Disability. A rating of Permanent Partial Disability must represent only that loss resulting solely from the Compensable Bodily Injury.

(3) All ratings of Permanent Partial Disability shall be based on the Permanent Disability Schedule adopted by the Nation and published as Annex A to this Plan.

(4) In cases of Permanent Partial Disability due to injury to a member resulting in less then total loss of the member, not otherwise compensated in this Schedule, compensation shall be paid at the prescribed rate during that part of the time specified in the Schedule for the total loss of the member which the extent of the injury to the member bears its total loss.

(5) Benefits paid for Permanent Partial Disability shall be computed at two-thirds of the average weekly earnings of the employee, up to the maximum weekly benefit established the state's Department of Workforce Development, and multiplied by the calculated proportion of the number of weeks specified in the Schedule.

(6) The amount payable to the employee shall be paid in one lump sum.

(7) Payment will be made as soon as reasonably possible after receipt of the rating by the Administrator, but no later than thirty (30) days after receipt unless the Administrator has scheduled an Independent Medical Examination.

d. Permanent Partial Disability benefits are neither payable concurrently with Temporary Total or Temporary Partial benefits, nor payable to the employee's dependents or heirs, regardless of the cause of death of the employee.

e. The Nation or Administrator will pay Temporary Total or Temporary Partial disability benefits on a weekly basis.

f. If an employee refuses light, restricted or modified work offered by the Employer or becomes voluntary unemployed, or is dismissed for violation of the Employment Relations Act all indemnity benefits will cease.

g. If a Bodily Injury results in disability that is partially due to congenital condition or a prior disease or injury, the benefits payable for the disability will be reduced by the proportion of the disability that is due to the preexisting disability.

h. If the employee unreasonably fails to appear for a scheduled Independent Medical Examination, the liability of the Employer for payment of disability benefits ceases. Likewise, the Employer's responsibility for payment of all other benefits accruing under this Plan ceases immediately upon the failure to appear.

i. Receipt by the employee of Social Security Retirement Benefits will be considered conclusive evidence of retirement and the liability of the Employer for payment of further disability benefits will cease.

j. When an employee has reached his or her end of healing, payment of loss of time will cease.

61. **Dependent Benefits.** In the event of the death of the employee due to a Compensable Injury, payment of all disability and medical benefits shall cease and a maximum of $139,800.00 will be payable to the Dependents of the deceased employee. Dependents will receive weekly payments equal to the indicated percentage of the Weekly Wage as determined under paragraph 56p. Weekly payments are subject to the maximum Compensation Rate under paragraph 56f, and will be paid as described as follows.

a. Dependent Spouse alone: 50 percent of Weekly Wage.

b. Dependent Spouse and one (1) or more Dependent Children: 66⅔ percent of Weekly Wage.

c. One Dependent Child but no Dependent Spouse: 40 percent of Weekly Wage.

d. Two or more Dependent Children but no Dependent Spouse: 60 percent of the Weekly Wage.

e. Other Dependents will receive benefits in the percentage that their provable dependency on the decedent bears to the maximum benefits available and the dependency of the other Dependents. Regardless of the number of Dependents, the maximum benefits will not exceed 66⅔ percent of the Weekly Wage at the time of injury.

f. If a Dependent Spouse remarries, no further benefits shall be payable to that Spouse. If one or more children remain Dependent, benefits will continue to be paid for the benefit of the Child, or Children, pursuant to paragraphs c and d, above, until they cease to be Dependent.

g. Benefits payable to Dependents shall be paid to them or to any guardian or other responsible party as directed by the Nation for the use and benefit of the Dependents.

h. If a Dependent Child, upon reaching the age of which that Child would cease to be Dependent, is totally disabled due to a physical or mental impairment, benefits will continue to be paid under the appropriate provision above until the disability ends or the maximum is paid, whichever comes first.

i. The Nation or the Administrator will pay Dependency benefits on a weekly basis.

j. In cases where an employee's death results from Compensable Injury, the reasonable expense of burial, not to exceed $4,000.00, will be paid in addition to any other benefits payable under this section.

62. **Recurrence**. If, within one (1) year from the date on which an employee has returned to full-time, light, restricted or modified work, the employee, in course of employment by the Nation, suffers a Recurrence of the original Compensable Injury, the Recurrence will be considered a continuation of the earlier claim and injury and subject to the monetary and time limitations of the initial claim. A recurrence occurring in employment other than for present claims is not compensable under this Plan.

63. **Election of Remedies**.

a. If an employee's Compensable Bodily Injury or death is contributed to or caused by a party other than the employee or the Employer and the employee or Dependents could file a claim or lawsuit against the other party, the employee or Dependents may not present claims under this Plan and against the other party.

b. If the employee or Dependents elect to claim benefits under this Plan, the employee or Dependents must assign their cause of action against the other party to the Nation and cooperate with the Nation and the Administrator in pursuit of the action. Once assigned, the Nation shall bear all costs of collections. If the employee or Dependents fail to assign the cause of action or fail to cooperate in the pursuit of that action, all benefits under this Plan will cease and the employee or Dependents will be required to reimburse the Nation for any benefits paid to or on behalf of the employee or the Dependents under the Plan.

c. If the employee or Dependents elect to pursue a cause of action against the other party, no benefits will be payable under this Plan unless, within a 180 days of the injury, the employee or Dependents assign their claim to the Nation and agree to cooperate in the pursuit of the action. In that event, only benefits accruing or medical or collection expenses incurred after the date of the assignment will be paid under this Plan.

d. If an employee or Dependents have assigned a cause of action to the Nation under this section and if the recovery from that cause of action exceeds the amount paid or payable to the employee or Dependents, any excess, after reimbursement to the Nation of the benefits paid or payable under this Plan and deduction of the costs of collection, will be paid over to the employee or Dependents.

64. **Administrator**. The Administrator will act on behalf of the Nation in receiving and processing Worker's Compensation claims under this Plan. The responsibility of the Administrator to make determinations and decisions will include, but not limited to, the following areas.

a. Based upon investigation and available medical information, the Administrator will make a determination of the responsibility of the Nation and will either accept or deny a claim. Within thirty (30) days of receipt of an Injury Report Form, the Administrator will advise the employee and the Nation of its determination.

b. The Administrator will determine the reasonableness and necessity of medical care and charges under Section 58 and will determine amounts payable under the Plan. The Administrator will also approve or disapprove any change of Primary Physician, Referral Physician, or surgical procedure.

c. Based on information supplied by the Employer and/or employee, the Administrator will determine the Compensation Rate payable for Temporary Total, Temporary Partial, Permanent Partial Disability, and for Dependency.

d. The Administrator will determine the length of time during which Temporary Total Disability or Temporary Partial Disability benefits are payable.

e. The Administrator will determine the eligibility of Dependents and the term of any Dependency Benefits payable.

f. In the event of the need to allocate Dependency Benefits between Dependents living in different households, the Administrator will make necessary allocation, based on the obligations, legal or otherwise of the decedent.

g. If an employee claim is subject to the limitations of Section 62, the Administrator will advise the employee and Employer of the effect of this limitation in writing.

h. The Administrator will, on the behalf of the Nation, vigorously pursue any cause of action assigned to the Nation under Section 63.

65. **Appeals.** The Ho-Chunk Nation will establish an Insurance Review Commission to hear any issues and make any necessary final determination relative to Compensability of Bodily Injury, medical care or charges, extent of Disability, Dependency, or other issues that may arise under this Plan.

a. The Commission will consider evidence, hear witnesses and receive exhibits in keeping with its goal of making a just final determination.

b. The Commission shall not consider any information that has not been provided to the Nation's Insurance Department at least 15 days prior to the Commission has scheduled a Hearing.

c. The Commission will weigh the evidence, testimony of witnesses and exhibits and will make its decision on the basis of the preponderance of evidence and credibility of the evidence and witnesses.

d. The burden of proof in any hearing before the Commission will be on the employee or Dependents.

e. The employee or Dependents may have legal representation at any hearing before the Commission. The cost of representation will be borne by the employee or Dependents.

f. Any employee or Dependent who disagrees with the determination made by the Administrator may request in writing a hearing before the Commission. The Appeal of Insurance Denial Form must be signed, witnessed and returned within 30 days of the date on the denial.

g. The matter will be scheduled for a hearing before the full Commission within 90 days of receipt of the request for a hearing from the employee or Dependents. The employee or Dependents may request an extension of up to 90 days, which must be granted by the Commission.

h. Any decision of the Commission must have the concurrence of a majority of the Commission members to have a legal effect. All decisions of the Commission are final.

i. A Commission decision must be issued in writing and copies must be mailed to all interested parties. The decision need not recite nor review the evidence or testimony nor need compare the merits of the evidence or testimony of the opposing parties. The decision need only set out the final determination of the Commission on all issues before it.

j. The Department of Personnel shall maintain a file of all Commission decisions.

ANNEX A – Permanent Disability Schedule

Annex A (Permanent Disability Schedule)

Disability	Benefits
Loss of arm at shoulder	500 weeks
Loss of arm at elbow	450 weeks
Loss of hand	400 weeks
Loss of palm where the thumb remains	325 weeks
Loss of thumb and the metacarpal bone thereof	160 weeks
Loss of thumb at the proximal joint	120 weeks
Loss of thumb at the distal joint	50 weeks
Loss of all fingers on one hand at their proximal joints	225 weeks
Loss of index finger and the metacarpal bone thereof	60 weeks
Loss of index finger at the proximal joint	50 weeks
Loss of index finger at the second joint	30 weeks
Loss of index finger at the distal joint	12 weeks
Loss of middle finger and the metacarpal bone thereof	45 weeks
Loss of middle finger at the proximal joint	35 weeks
Loss of middle finger at the second joint	20 weeks
Loss of middle finger at the distal joint	8 weeks
Loss of ring finger and the metacarpal bone thereof	26 weeks
Loss of ring finger at the proximal joint	20 weeks
Loss of ring finger at the second joint	15 weeks
Loss of ring finger at the distal joint	6 weeks
Loss of little finger and the metacarpal bone thereof	28 weeks
Loss of little finger at the proximal joint	22 weeks
Loss of little finger at the second joint	16 weeks
Loss of little finger at the distal joint	6 weeks
Loss of leg at hip	500 weeks
Loss of leg at the knee	425 weeks
Loss of foot at ankle	250 weeks
Loss of great toe with the metatarsal bone thereof	84 weeks
Loss of great toe at the proximal joint	25 weeks
Loss of great toe at the distal joint	12 weeks
Loss of second toe with the metatarsal bone thereof	25 weeks
Loss of second toe at the proximal joint	8 weeks
Loss of second toe at the second joint	6 weeks
Loss of second toe at the distal joint	4 weeks
Loss of third, fourth or little toe with the metatarsal thereof	20 weeks
Loss of third, fourth or little tow at the proximal joint	6 weeks
Loss of third, fourth or little toe at the second or distal joints	4 weeks
Loss of an eye by enucleation or evisceration	275 weeks
Total impairment of one eye for industrial use	250 weeks
Total deafness from accident or sudden trauma	330 weeks
Total deafness of one ear from accident or sudden trauma	55 weeks

For permanent partial disability not covered by the above schedule, the total number of weeks of indemnity shall be 1,000 weeks and shall be payable at the rate 66⅔ percent of the average weekly earnings of the employee up to a maximum of $158.00, the earnings to be determined under paragraph 57o of the Plan.

Richard G. McGee practices law in Minneapolis, Minnesota. Mr. McGee's practice focuses on tribal employment, gaming regulation, and litigation. Mr. McGee represents parties in numerous tribal, state, and federal courts. As an engaging trainer in the tribal employment arena, Mr. McGee works with tribal governments and enterprises. He is also called upon to serve as hearing officer and investigator of employment-related matters.

Mr. McGee was assistant general counsel for the Prairie Island Indian Community. The Prairie Island Indian Community owns and operates Treasure Island Resort & Casino, which employs more than two thousand workers. Both the Prairie Island Indian Community and Treasure Island Resort & Casino are located in southeast Minnesota.

Before joining the Prairie Island Indian Community, Mr. McGee spent a decade litigating business and employment cases as a lawyer at Arnold, Anderson & Dove in Minneapolis, Minnesota. Mr. McGee is a graduate of the Oklahoma University Law School located in Norman, Oklahoma.

Mr. McGee can be reached at *richardmcgee@comcast.net*.

INDEX

A

ADA (Americans with Disabilities Act) 41, 61-2, 172, 186
ADEA (Age Discrimination Employment Act) 73, 77, 88-9
ADR (Alternative Dispute Resolution) 217
Age Discrimination Employment Act, *see* ADEA
Alaska Native Claims Settlement Act (ANCSA) 118
Allen v. Gold Country Casino 69
Allotment Act 131
Alternative Dispute Resolution (ADR) 217
American Arbitration Association 123
American Indians 16, 60
Americans with Disabilities Act, *see* ADA
ANCSA (Alaska Native Claims Settlement Act) 118
at-will employment 227
Atkinson Trading Company v. Shirley 131

B

BIA 61, 199, 200
Bird v. United States 25
Bryan v. Itasca County 115
Buckingham, M.
 First, Break All the Rules 209
Bureau of Indian Affairs 16, 18, 153, 199, 225, 235

C

California v. Cabazon Band of Mission Indians 52, 115, 160
Cano v. Cocopah Casino 89
canons of construction 57
Chao v. Spokane Tribe of Indians 69, 70
Chayoon v. Sherlock 142
Cherokee Nation 55, 73, 76, 88-9, 108, 111, 113, 137, 144, 185
Chuck and Shirley 154
Civil Rights Act 100
civil rights laws, federal 43

Coffman, C.
First, Break All the Rules 209
Cohen v. Winkleman and Comanche Nation College 141
Commerce Clause 54, 199
comprehensive employment laws 98
Congress 16, 35, 50-2, 54, 63-4, 66-8, 73-7, 82-3, 89, 90, 100, 117, 136-7, 141, 145, 153, 171-2
Connecticut 116
Connecticut Land Claims Settlement Act 116
consensual agreements 128, 132-4
contractor, independent 22
Crime Control Act 103

D

Davidson v. Mohegan Tribal Gaming Authority 137
Dawavendewa v. Salt River Project Agr. Imp. and Power Dist. 18
Dawes Act 131
definition of employee 22
definition of tribe 17
Donovan 67-8, 73-5, 77, 83, 186
Donovan v. Coeur d' Alene Tribal Farm 67 *see also Donovan*
Double Jeopardy Clause 157
Dry Creek Lodge 101

E

EEOC 22-3, 25, 63, 68, 73, 76, 88-9, 201, 203, 217-8
EEOC v. Karuk Tribe Housing 89
EEOC v. Peabody Western Coal Company 200
Elders Committee 226
Elk v. Wilkins 65

employee benefit plans 217
employee-employer relationship 23
employee handbooks 9, 10, 43, 62, 86, 97-8, 120-1, 134, 142, 189, 191-2, 208-9, 211, 213-4, 217-8, 220-1, 223-4
employee-management disputes 76
employee safety 180, 237
employee workplace disputes 135
employees
    Indians 39
    non-Indians 39
employer-assistance 61
employer-decisions 37, 212, 217, 237
employer-employee relationship 20, 23, 27, 71, 84, 164, 189, 213, 216
employment activities 69, 70, 127-8
employment application 182
employment relationship 13, 38
Employment Retirement Income Security Act, *see* ERISA
enterprise boards 169
Equal Employment Opportunity Commission 22
ERISA (Employment Retirement Income Security Act) 74, 91-3, 172

F

Fair Labor Standards Act, *see* FLSA
Family and Medical Leave Act, *see* FMLA
federal antidiscrimination laws 96, 232
federal employment laws 15, 38, 56, 64
federal gaming laws 112, 164, 166, 171, 183
federal government 15-7, 24-5, 27-30, 34-6, 46-55, 57-9, 65-7,

83, 94-101, 103, 114-5, 117-9, 131, 153-5, 164-6, 202-4
federal Indian laws   15, 108
Federal Register   17
Federal Tort Claims Act   26, 153
First, Break All the Rules (Buckingham and Coffman)   209
Florida Paraplegic Association, Inc. v. Miccosukee Tribe of Indians of Florida   61
FLSA (Fair Labor Standards Act)   38, 41, 64, 67, 69-71, 81-4, 140, 211, 218
FMLA (Family and Medical Leave Act)   38, 64, 67, 84-6, 88, 104-5
FTCA (Federal Torts Claim Act)   19, 24, 153-4

G

gaming   20, 35, 50, 52, 59, 70-2, 78-9, 84, 86, 94, 98-9, 112, 115, 137, 160, 164-7
gaming commission   9, 123, 158, 167-8, 175-83
gaming ordinance   9, 163, 167, 175-7, 179, 181, 191
General Allotment Act   131
geography   43
government action   84, 173
government employees   19, 21, 24-5
government employer   210
Grand Ronde tribe   143
grievance procedures   120

H

handbook   9, 10, 86, 189, 208, 210-5, 221, 223, 226-7, 237
Harvard Project on American Indian Economic Development   31, 194

Haudenosaunee *see* Six Nations of the Iroquois Confederacy
hierarchy   195-8, 207, 211-3, 233
Hierarchy of Hiring   234
Ho-Chunk Nation   80, 90, 98, 111, 120-1, 143, 190, 193, 228-30, 232-3, 238
Ho-Chunk Nation Personnel, Employment and Labor Code   120
Housing Committee   226
human resources   20, 65, 86, 120, 130, 168-70, 197, 236
human rights laws   111-2, 171, 232

I

ICRA   100-1, 145
ICRA state court subject matter jurisdiction   138
IGRA (Indian Gaming Regulatory Act)   18, 69, 98-9, 112, 160-1, 163-7, 169-71
Indian Child Protection and Family Violence Prevention Act   102
Indian Civil Rights Act   18
Indian Country   17, 45-7, 100, 115, 118, 122-4, 136-7, 154, 157, 186, 210, 215, 219
Indian Gaming Regulatory Act, *see* IGRA
Indian Reorganization Act   18
Indian Self-Determination Act   97
Indian Self-Determination and Education Assistance Act   102, 153
Internal Revenue Code   27
Internal Revenue Service   27
ISDA   97

J

Johnson v. Harrah's Kansas Casino Corp.   87

Prairie Band Potawatomi 86
jurisdiction 40, 45-6, 48, 93, 98, 100-1, 115, 123-5, 127-8, 130, 132-3, 135-41, 148, 155-7, 189, 215-7

K

Kiowa Tribe of Oklahoma v. Manufacturing Technologies Inc. 45, 95, 145, 153

L

Labor Force Report 18
Las Vegas-style gaming 43, 52, 72, 79, 94, 99, 112, 160-1, 165, 171, 185
Little River Band of Odawa Indians 210
Little Traverse Bay Band of Odawa Indians 224
Little Traverse Bay Bands of Odawa Indians 224
Lurch v. United States 26

M

Major Crimes Act 155, 157
Mashantucket Pequot tribe 113, 117
Merrion v. Jicarilla Apache Tribe 131
Miami Nation of Indians of Indiana v. United States Department of the Interior 17
Michigan Indian Defense Association 225
Michigan Indian Foundation 225
Middletown Rancheria of Pomo Indians 114, 116
Mohegan Nation of Connecticut Land Claims Settlement Act 117
Mohegan tribe 117
Montana v. United States 110, 128
Mundt (senator) 60

N

NAHASDA (Native American Housing and Self-Determination Act) 96, 205
National Congress of American Indians 18
National Farmers Union Insurance Company v. Crow Tribe 143
National Indian Gaming Association 18, 78, 159, 162
National Labor relations Act, *see* NLRA
National Labor Relations Board, *see* NLRB
National Labor Relations Board v. Pueblo of San Juan 72
National Rules for the Resolution of Employment Disputes American Arbitration Association 123
Native American Housing and Self-Determination Act (NAHASDA) 96, 205
Navajo Nation 36, 63-4, 69, 81, 98, 125, 141, 143, 186, 189, 200-3, 205-6
Navajo Preference in Employment Act 98, 143, 202, 206, 234
NIGC (National Indian Gaming Commission) 99, 112, 164-5
NLRA (National Labor relations Act) 67, 69-72, 77-9, 81, 84, 111, 160-1, 172
NLRB (National Labor Relations Board) 50, 63, 69, 72, 76, 78, 80, 83, 133-4, 160-1
NLRB v. Pueblo of San Juan 76, 83

NPEA *see* Navajo Preference in Employment Act, Section

O

Occupational Safety and Health Act, *see* OSHA
Office of Navajo Labor Relations   189, 206, 218
Oklahoma   116
Oklahoma Tax Commission   34, 46, 87, 116, 139, 144, 146
Oklahoma Tax Commission v. Citizen Band Potawatomi Indian Tribe   34
OSHA (Occupational Safety and Health Act)   38, 67, 74, 90-1, 171

P

Peabody   201
Pevar, Stephen L.   16-8, 35, 55, 194
  Rights of Indians and Tribes, The   16, 18, 117, 194
plenary power   67
Prescott v. Little Six   93
Public Law   57, 97, 102-3, 114, 116-7, 153, 155-6, 185

R

RCRA   66-7
Resource Conservation and Recovery Act   66
responsibilities   24, 26, 31, 93, 97, 163, 168, 172, 180, 187, 207, 226, 234-5
resumes   20, 196-7
revenues   69, 70, 84, 87, 133, 149, 161, 169, 173-4

Riggs v. Bishop Paiute Gaming Corporation   138
Rodriguez v. Wong   110

S

Sabiron v. Gregory   151
San Manuel Indian Bingo and Casino v. NLRB (San Manuel)   72
Sanderlin v. Seminole Tribe of Florida   95
Santa Clara Pueblo v. Martinez   34, 101, 145
Seneca Niagara Casino   86, 98-9
Simpson, Homer   214
Six Nations of the Iroquois Confederacy   36
  Cayuga   36
  Mohawk   36
  Oneida   36
  Onondaga   36
  Seneca   36
  Tuscarora   36
sovereign immunity   24, 87, 93, 96, 138, 140-1, 147-8, 151
sovereign nation   63, 223
sovereignty spectrum   33
state jurisdiction   109, 111, 138
State of California   99
Statement on Indian Policy   60
Stroud v. Seminole Tribe of Florida   204
Supreme Court   24, 47, 51, 65, 74-5, 86, 96, 100, 108, 111, 129-31, 137, 145-6, 153, 198-9, 203

T

Taylor v. Alabama Intertribal Council Title IV   204

TERO (Tribal Employment Rights Ordinance) 9, 20, 136, 188-9, 205-7
TGA (Tribal Gaming Agency) 167
Tibbetts v. Leech Lake Reservation Business Committee 111
Treaty of New Echota 73
tribal employee handbok 21
tribal employers 19
tribal employment 17
Tribal Employment Rights Ordinances 20, 136, 188, 205
Tribal Gaming Agency (TGA) 167
tribal government
  business entities 19
  recognized tribe 19
tribal leadership 9, 33, 39, 104, 106, 122, 177, 192, 221, 226
tribal members 21
tribal officials 26-8, 39, 87, 90, 149-51, 159
tribal preference 195
tribal rules 35, 41, 46, 110, 135, 147, 165, 189, 191, 213, 220
tribal sovereignty 13
Tribally Controlled Schools Act of 1988 102
Tuscarora-Donovan analysis 61, 65, 74, 76, 88, 91

U

United States 24
United States Bureau of Indian Affairs *see also* BIA
United States Department of Health and Human Services 18
United States Department of Labor 74, 91 *see also* DOL

V

Van Etten v. Mashantucket Pequot Gaming Enterprise 151

W

Williams v. Lee 109
Willis v. Bashas Inc. 141, 205
Worcester v. Georgia 108-9

Y

Yakima Tribal Court 186
Yankton Sioux Tribe Housing Authority 96

Made in the USA
Coppell, TX
21 September 2021